FOCUS ON THE FAMILY

The Gift of Grandparenting

Building Meaningful Relationships With Your Grandchildren

ERIC WIGGIN

TYNDALE

Tyndale House Publishers, Wheaton, Illinois

THE GIFT OF GRANDPARENTING

Library of Congress Cataloging-in-Publication Data
Wiggin, Eric E.
   The gift of grandparenting : building meaningful relation-
ships with your grandchildren / Eric Wiggin.
         p. cm.
   "A Focus on the Family book"—T.p. verso.
   ISBN: 1-56179-925-4
1. Grandparenting. I Title.
   HQ759.9 .W538 2001
   306.874'5—dc21

                                                    2001002073

A Focus on the Family book published by
Tyndale House Publishers, Wheaton, Illinois.

All Scripture quotations, unless otherwise indicated, are from the
New International Version of the Bible (NIV), published by the
Zondervan Corporation, copyright 1984 by the New York Bible
Society. NIV quotations are used by permission of Zondervan, a
licensee. Those marked KJV are from the King James Version.

Cover design: Amy Kiechlin
Cover photograph: Tim O'Hara

Printed in the United States of America

01 02 03 04 05 06 07 08 09 10 / 10 9 8 7 6 5 4 3 2 1

Advance Acclaim for *The Gift of Grandparenting*

"We may not have been prepared to be parents, but now there's no reason we can't be prepared to be grandparents. Well-researched and well-written and greatly appreciated home-spun advice flows from this book that's much better than anything that flowed down from Walton's Mountain. You sense the heart of a loving grandfather on every page."
—**Dr. Woodrow Kroll**, *President,* Back to the Bible

"Filled with tips, tidbits, and insight for a modern world, *The Gift of Grandparenting* should be on every family's bookshelf. I love Eric Wiggin's practical advice and agree wholeheartedly with one particular suggestion: grandparents should learn how to e-mail!"
—**Angela Hunt**, *Novelist*

"Every parent eventually comes to the day we discover that the job never ends—the Mom/Dad responsibility never goes away. Kids grow up, leave home, are on their own, but our heart is forever bound to love, pray, care, weep, rejoice, etc. . . . and then it starts to multiply all over again: grandchildren! And then that happiness reveals its own requirements, too. So, if you've found yourself (as Anna and I have) even less prepared for the uniqueness of this trip than you were for your 'first round,' you'll feel with us how greatly rewarding it is to have help like Eric Wiggin offers us here."
—**Jack W. Hayford**, *Founding Pastor,* The Church on the Way

"In these days of so much divorce and single parenting, grandparents may be the only touch of love that some children seem to have. This book will give you the tools to be the best grandparent you can be."
—**Florence Littauer**, *Speaker and Author*

"As the grandparents of thirteen very lively grandkids, we know we have much to learn. This comprehensive book will be most helpful to us and to countless others who, like us, are learning grandparenting by the seat of their pants!"
—**Stuart and Jill Briscoe**, *Ministers-at-Large,* Elmbrook Church

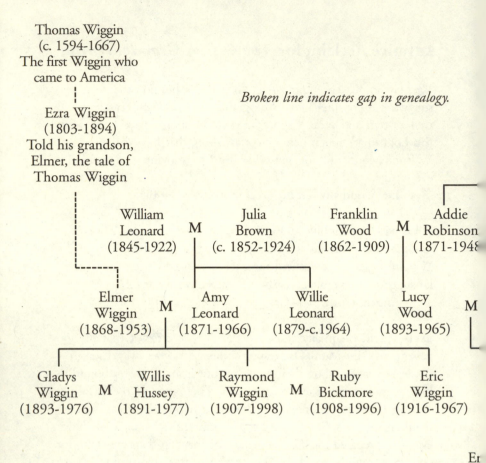

Thomas Wiggin
(c. 1594-1667)
The first Wiggin who
came to America

Ezra Wiggin
(1803-1894)
Told his grandson,
Elmer, the tale of
Thomas Wiggin

Broken line indicates gap in genealogy.

William Leonard (1845-1922) **M** Julia Brown (c. 1852-1924)

Franklin Wood (1862-1909) **M** Addie Robinson (1871-1948

Elmer Wiggin (1868-1953) **M** Amy Leonard (1871-1966)

Willie Leonard (1879-c.1964)

Lucy Wood (1893-1965) **M**

Gladys Wiggin (1893-1976) **M** Willis Hussey (1891-1977)

Raymond Wiggin (1907-1998) **M** Ruby Bickmore (1908-1996)

Eric Wiggin (1916-1967)

Er
Wig
(b. 1

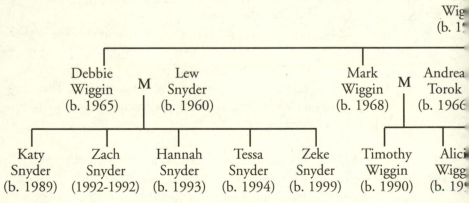

Debbie Wiggin (b. 1965) **M** Lew Snyder (b. 1960)

Mark Wiggin (b. 1968) **M** Andrea Torok (b. 1966

Katy Snyder (b. 1989)

Zach Snyder (1992-1992)

Hannah Snyder (b. 1993)

Tessa Snyder (b. 1994)

Zeke Snyder (b. 1999)

Timothy Wiggin (b. 1990)

Alici Wigg (b. 19

Family Tree of Eric and Dot Wiggin, with names mentioned in the book, *The Gift of Grandparenting*

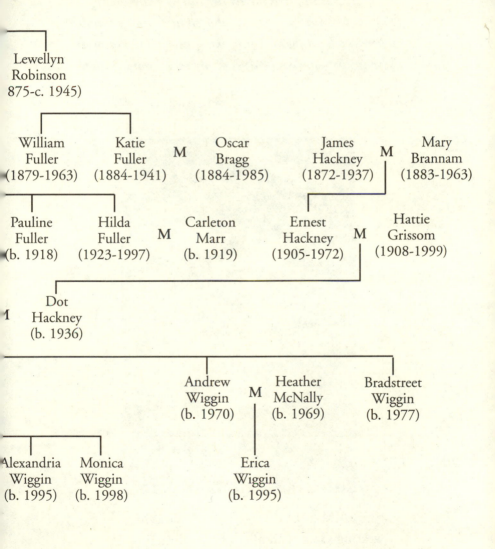

Lewellyn
Robinson
875-c. 1945)

William
Fuller
(1879-1963)

Katie
Fuller
(1884-1941)

M

Oscar
Bragg
(1884-1985)

James
Hackney
(1872-1937)

M

Mary
Brannam
(1883-1963)

Pauline
Fuller
(b. 1918)

Hilda
Fuller
(1923-1997)

M

Carleton
Marr
(b. 1919)

Ernest
Hackney
(1905-1972)

M

Hattie
Grissom
(1908-1999)

1

Dot
Hackney
(b. 1936)

Andrew
Wiggin
(b. 1970)

M

Heather
McNally
(b. 1969)

Bradstreet
Wiggin
(b. 1977)

Alexandria
Wiggin
(b. 1995)

Monica
Wiggin
(b. 1998)

Erica
Wiggin
(b. 1995)

To the grandmother of my children,
Pauline Fuller Wiggin (b. 1918), and to my children's
grandfather, Eric E. Wiggin (1916–1967).

Mother has inspired me by her quiet, godly courage.
Dad's willingness to serve his church and family humbly
where the Lord planted him has given me vision to see
beyond the years in the lives of my own grandchildren.

Author Eric Wiggin (b. May 1939)
wearing Grandpa Fuller's hat, summer of 1940

Contents

Foreword

~

The blood runs thick between grandparents and grandchildren. If you want to see grandparents come alive, ask them about their grandchildren. Then sit back and observe as they "show and tell."

Most grandparents have had little training for their job. Their sincere efforts sometimes put them in conflict with their children, the parents of their grandchildren. Perhaps even more tragic is that sometimes the actions and words of grandparents do harm rather than good to their grandchildren.

Grandparenting is one responsibility where sincerity is not enough. We need insight into the hearts and minds of children and teenagers if we are to genuinely help them mature into responsible and productive adults. In *The Gift of Grandparenting* Eric Wiggin gives grandparents practical help. Weaving together his experiences as a grandchild and a grandparent, the advice of Christian leaders, the findings of research, and the wisdom of Scripture, he gives grandparents the tools needed to do an effective job.

As I read Eric's description of his childhood and the role of his grandparents, I must admit that feelings of nostalgia brought me to tears a few times. In addition to tears, there was laughter as he described his grandfather squirting milk to a kitten during the evening milking. The squirts of milk gave sustenance to the kitten and created memories in the mind of a young grandchild.

However, Eric does not linger in the past. He realistically describes the contemporary world in which grandchildren live today; a world that grandparents must understand and enter if they are to make a significant impact on the lives of their grandchildren.

In my opinion, no generation has needed grandparents more than the present one. I don't find that today's grandparents are reluctant to step up to the plate, but I do find that many are striking out with their grandchildren. Most want to be good grandparents, but many do not know how. For the novice grandparent, this book is a godsend. For the experienced grandparent, this book will give you new and creative ideas on how to continue the important task of loving and guiding your grandchildren. I hope that you will not only read it, but linger with its pages long enough to allow the sound principles of grandparenting presented here to become a lifestyle for years to come.

Remember that you are not only grandparenting your grandchildren; you are teaching them to be good grandparents a few brief years from now. The potential is great and the journey will be easier because Eric Wiggin took the time to pen these words. Your model as a grandparent will influence your grandchildren years after your voice has fallen silent.

—Gary D. Chapman,
Winston-Salem North Carolina

CHAPTER ONE

Grandparenting Is "Absolutely Wonderful"

"We all think you're absolutely wonderful at the two most important kinds of fathering—regular and grand." This was the caption on a Father's Day card from my daughter, Debbie, her husband, Lew, and my granddaughter, Katy. Nearly every Father's Day since Katy's birth has added another grandchild who thinks I'm absolutely wonderful. Three of our four children are married, and Grandma Wiggin and I look on with delight as our grandchildren continue to sprout like "olive shoots" around our table (Psalm 128:3).

 Surprised at becoming a grandparent? I was!

I'll admit I was anything but prepared to become a grandfather when it took me by storm, literally. At the time, a Monday morning in September, I was in the living room of my son's apartment in Charleston, South Carolina, at daybreak. My wife, Dot, and I had landed in Charleston the day after Hugo, one of the twentieth century's worst hurricanes, had come straight up Charleston Harbor on its way inland. Lines were down, and long-distance calls were unthinkable, except for after midnight or very early in the morning.

But the phone rang before dawn. It was my mother in Indiana. Our daughter, Debbie, in Michigan, had just become a mother, and she and Lew had found the lines jammed when they tried to call us. Dot and I were new grandparents, so I dressed and went to the bathroom, where I washed my face and combed my hair in the light of a wax candle. No use to consider the electric razor. Right then I decided to grow a beard!

In only moments, Grandpa and Grandma received another blessing—we learned from Debbie's brother Mark that daughter-in-law Andrea was expecting her first child. Months later, little Timothy became our second grandchild.

Some grandpas have gray beards. Some are bald. Some, like myself, still have enough salt-and-pepper hair to comb. Some grandmas have white hair and sit in rockers and knit. Some have brown, black, red, or blonde hair; they jog, swim, and bike. Some grandparents are 90-something and live in nursing homes. A few are 30-something and busy with the stuff of daily living. Many are 40-something or even 80-something.

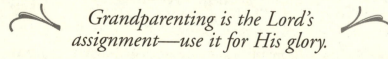

Grandparenting is the Lord's assignment—use it for His glory.

All grandparents have one thing in common: In a quieter, more profound way than when they first became parents, they are brought face-to-face with their importance in the continuity of life. Some quickly look away, trying to avoid their responsibility. Some shrug, frown, and make fools of themselves by seeking their lost youth in the world's sullied fountains. Some—the grandparents to whom this book is written—embrace their newfound responsibility and in God's grace begin to fulfill it.

For the Christian grandparent, God has His special blessings in store. God's mercy and righteous dealings are extended from one generation to another, even to the grandchildren of the godly "who . . . remember to obey his precepts," David writes in Psalm 103:17–18. For instance, my grandparents were Christian believers who honored the Lord. Their grandchildren, myself included, have all been blessed as a result. Over the years as a pastor and teacher, I have had opportunity to observe multiple generations of godly parents—who, far more often than not, came from homes where Christ was honored by grandparents as well as parents.

New parents are captivated with the joy of the tiny, precious life the Lord has entrusted to them. But new grandparents, having the perspective that comes from watching generations roll by, can uniquely view themselves as a vital link between Eden and eternity in a way not understood simply through parenting.

 Grandparenting will change
your perceptions of aging.

Most folks conceive their notions of grandparents early in life. My own notion, which I'm sure is shared by many, was that grandparents were elderly, had gray hair, wore old-fashioned clothes, and, if not feeble in the muscles, were at least stiff in the joints. In my childhood, all grandparents seemed at least 70; some appeared to be past 90. And those that I knew had a musty, slightly Victorian air about them.

I had four grandparents and a great-grandmother, all born in the nineteenth century. When I was small, these grandparents still had fragments of their own families alive—aunts, uncles, cousins, sisters, and brothers. My maternal grandmother's mother was still living, though I couldn't for the life of me figure out why two "old" ladies with steel-gray hair were both called "Grandma" by me, while the one who did the house-work called the other "Mother." It didn't seem right, some-how. My mother's mother was actually a prematurely gray 40-something, but they both seemed the same age—and almost eternal.

My paternal grandparents furnished our family with the basis for a happy Fourth of July reunion each summer, to which my mother's family was also invited. The families would gather on the lawn in front of great-uncle Willie's barn, and the adults would spread planks on sawhorses for tables. Brothers, sisters, and cousins took turns doing loop-the-loops in Uncle Willie's canvas hammock stretched between two spreading maples by the gravel road. The celebration would end with homemade ice cream, frozen in hand-cranked freez-ers with ice from Dad's icehouse—there was no electricity in our corner of rural Maine in those days. Then our family would return home to milk the cows and shoot Roman candles into the starry night.

The wheel of life has turned full circle since those happy celebrations dominated by my elders. In a span of some 20 years, my great-grandmother and four grandparents died. The last leaf fell a third of a century ago at age 95, and I am now a grandparent 10 times over.

 ## *Life's little lessons: Pass them on!*

The good things I learned as a grandchild I wish to pass on to my grandchildren and to grandparents who may find them useful in their grandparenting. Beyond the nostalgia, life has practical, important, valuable lessons.

This book also includes personal conversations with other grandparents, such as Jack Wyrtzen, founder and director of Word of Life, whose influence as a youth leader has reached millions. Jack's strength as a father and grandfather, though he is now with the Lord, continues to touch generations of Christian leaders. It contains talks with Jim Franks, founder of Concern International, who with his wife, Shirley, raised five children of their own, as well as three adopted Korean girls and an adopted son. Christian financial expert and director of Stewardship Services Foundation, Jim Rickard, discusses the topic of a grandparent and his money in this book. Dr. Kevin Leman, Christian psychologist and author, talks about the effect of the midlife crisis on grandparenting. We also chat with several lesser-known grandads and grandmas.

But the next several pages shall be devoted to lessons from the past, from my childhood when my grandparents were living. These vignettes will serve to introduce me and furnish a foundation for what follows in later chapters.

Grandparents are meant to stoop —to a child's level.

This is one of the first impressions a child should receive in early life. Growing up on the farm, I remember that my dad had hired his bean thresher and tractor out to my grandmother's uncle. Dad and Mother worked together on the thresher, and great-great-uncle Lewellyn and his crew hauled the dry yellow-eye beans from the field.

Grandma Fuller took little brother George and me to the bean field in a baby carriage, then we bumped down the graveled country road to a rustic plank bridge where she lifted us out. I knelt at the edge of the bridge to watch a spotted bullfrog hop from a mossy rock and swim off down the brook. We left for the house, Grandma pushing the empty carriage, I happily holding her hand, and George toddling along, clutching her long skirts.

Though that old wooden bridge has long since been replaced by a steel culvert, fun in simple pleasures still builds bridges between the old and the very young. Thoughtful grandparents will exploit these bridges thoroughly. The grandparent who impacts his grandchild's life is the one willing to kneel down to the child's level, to laugh at what he or she laughs at, to cry at what makes him or her tearful. When I was small, I *knew* that Grandma Fuller could feel what I felt.

One winter evening I watched Grandpa Wiggin milk a cow in the light of a kerosene lantern. Out of the shadows came a half-grown kitten, and Grandpa took aim with the teat he was squeezing and squirted the kitty in her mug. One more shot of milk, this time over the kitten's head, and the hungry creature stood on its hind legs to reach, mouth wide open, for the cow squeezings. Three or four squirts, and he had the kitten trained to reach for the milk whenever he called and took aim.

Cats learn fast. Grandpas are slow to forget. A silly trick he'd learned three-quarters of a century earlier as a kid would still entertain a child. Yet in retrospect, my grandfather was not being silly. He had learned that the action-reaction of a stream of milk and a stretching cat would build a bridge into the heart of a grandchild.

In a child's eye, grandparents can be strong, wise, and very smart.

Grandma Wiggin was a tall woman with broad hips and long, strong arms. She moved with Victorian dignity, but she wouldn't hesitate to wrestle her heavy pressure canner off her hot, wood-fired range and carry it loaded across her country kitchen to the sink. Mother, a small woman, couldn't do that, even though she could pitch bean vines into a threshing machine. A child never exposed to the elderly may exaggerate his grandparents' frailties, perhaps perceiving gray hair or an arthritic hobble as serious handicaps. But the child close to his grandparents, on the other hand, may be awed by a grandparent's abilities, which can seem almost superhuman.

My grandfathers knew everything and they had done everything—or at least everything anybody could wish to know or do. Grandpa Fuller had been a Boston streetcar conductor at the turn of the century, and he had once seen Jimmy Durante in a vaudeville show in Boston. He had watched Harry Houdini chained and locked into an iron box and lowered through the ice of the Charles River. In the years after the Civil War, Grandpa Wiggin had helped his father clear stump-filled pastures to make the fields that were later Father's farm. Before mowing machines, he had cut hay with a hand scythe and carted it to the barn with his oxen.

So, when my grandfathers argued politics during the presidential election of 1952—these two men of unfathomable wisdom who knew so much—I sat thrilled on the edge of my chair, taking it all in. One grandfather was a Taft Republican and the other an Eisenhower man.

One of the greatest thrills of my life (I was 13 in 1952) was to sit up late with Grandpa Wiggin and listen to the election returns on his radio. Children admire the wisdom and knowledge of grandparents they love. In later life, such influences often have a profound effect on adult decisions and actions.

 Grandparents are forever.

Like Melchizedek, a small child's grandparents are "without beginning of days or end of life" (Hebrews 7:3). Though I was eight when my great-grandmother died, this did not affect me seriously. We had not been close, for she had sat in the shadows of my grandmother's kitchen, seldom venturing from her platform rocker when children were around.

But I had always been close to my four grandparents, and always would be, it seemed then. They were constant. They were predictable. Grandpa Fuller had always been a storekeeper and a part-time sheriff (though he sometimes told otherworldly tales of his youth in Boston). Grandpa Wiggin had lived much of his 80-some years farming the same farm where he grew up. Only later did I learn that he had also been a mail carrier, a mill hand, a school superintendent for a time, and for many years moderator of our town's annual public business meeting.

I was in my 14th year when Grandpa Wiggin died, and he in his 85th. I remember well the raw January forenoon when he took sick with pneumonia. He was splitting wood and I was tossing it into the shed. Grandpa began to spit blood, and I was scared.

Three weeks later Grandpa died. With a shock, I learned something new: Grandparents are not forever. They are given by God for us to appreciate while we can.

Grandparents give children life perspectives badly needed in the culture of century twenty-one.

The presence of one or more grandparents in a child's life helps him put into mature perspective the importance as well as the brevity of his own existence. This maturing process requires that an individual understand and respect the relationships between the three great phases of life: childhood, adulthood, and old age. Today's youth-centered culture has, sadly, lost even its ability to mature.

Author Neil Postman, writing in his classic study, *The Disappearance of Childhood*, comments that our culture has reached the stage where "American adults want to be . . . children,"[1] yet children have vicarious adult experiences daily thrust upon them through TV and the movies and, since Postman's research, the Internet. After World War II, Postman observes, the "social environment that triggers and nurtures"[2] childhood rapidly regressed toward the unbridled brutality of the Middle Ages that preceded Gutenberg, Luther, and the great era of Bible translation. My grandchildren—and yours—daily associate with children from dysfunctional homes such as Postman describes. These kids feed on violence, coarse language, and raw sex, both from the media and in their homes.

We grandparents are the last generation privileged to have been born during the only era of Western civilization that recognized childhood as a distinct stage in life to be nurtured and protected: 1850 to 1950, according to Postman.[3] We have seen in our own lifetimes (I was born in 1939) a return to the brutalizing of children. Only those fortunate youth, whose parents have managed to intervene and protect them, have escaped this return to barbarism.

Consider a contrast Postman raises between the images of two child movie stars: Shirley Temple in the 1930s and Brooke Shields 40 years later. Temple interacted with adults onstage while maintaining—at least before the moviegoer—her innocence. Shields, from age 12 to about 17, was portrayed nude and engaged in faux sex in films made for . . . older children! Could the millions of American youth who viewed *Pretty Baby* or *Endless Love* have come away with their own innocence intact?

We who are grandparents have been given to our precious grandchildren to aid in their development and Christian maturity for what years we have left. Some of us will see the first of our grandchildren grow to adulthood, have children of their own, and start the cycle over again. Some of us, like my dad, whom the Lord took home at age 51, may not have that privilege. Some of us have grandchildren nearby. Others, in this American culture where families move once every six years—and young families more often than that—[4] must do much of our grandparenting by phone, mail, e-mail, family Web site, tape, or video recording. Or we may become the surrogate grandparents for the grandchildren of others.

Whatever our case, our tasks are alike: to seek the glory of God in the lives of our grandchildren as we live Christ before them, and to see them grow into—"be conformed to the likeness of" —the Master (Romans 8:29).

Around the Corner to Grandma's House

Grandma's kitchen always smelled of baking bread, beans, and molasses cookies fresh from the oven. And Grandma didn't complain if I took a cookie without asking—or more than one!

"There's milk in the fridge to go with the cookies," Grandma would say as she bent to stir the beans. If I spilled my milk on the tablecloth, Grandma didn't scold me, but merely murmured, "Never mind; I'll mop it up"—and she did, without complaining. Grandma never yelled at me. Not once. She treated me like a human being. Grandma was unhurried, so she had time to appreciate me as an individual.

Grandma's House was a haven from the shrill competition of siblings, from the stern corrections of parents, from the sullen cares that crowd into the life of even a child. "Grandma's House"—your grandma's or mine—might have been over the river and through the woods, as in the days of long ago, or just a tricycle ride around the corner of an urban neighborhood.

The Grandma's House of my childhood didn't have the sterile smell of air freshener and new carpeting found in today's homes. Grandma had a wood- or coal-fired range, common in many rural and village homes as recently as about 1950, so her kitchen smelled of oak or pine or occasionally on a winter day of coal smoke. On the back of her range in summer simmered a pan of sweet apples, picked from the gnarled old tree just outside her kitchen door, left open to let fresh breezes waft through the screen.

In winter, spring, or fall, Grandma's kitchen was the coziest place on earth. But in the summer her kitchen was hot, except in early morning. But no mind; we would eat at an old table set up on the back porch.

Grandma kept a box of toys under the stairs that you could have all to yourself without having to share. There were cast-iron enameled autos to push on the floor, an Erector set, and a battered old bisque doll. I spotted one of those dolls in an antique shop recently, and I'm not sure whether I was moved more by memories of Grandma's House or by the price: nearly $1,000!

When the evening supper dishes were cleared away, Grandma brought out a box of board games. There were backgammon, checkers, and Parcheesi. Chinese checkers and maybe even a Monopoly game with no missing pieces were in Grandma's old wooden soapbox. And at Grandma's I always stayed up to finish the game, no matter how late. At Grandma's House bedtime was whenever I couldn't keep my eyes open any longer.

Breakfast came at Grandma's House later than at home, for Grandma was never in a hurry to go anywhere. I got up to the smell of hot biscuits, and when I came downstairs I discovered that Grandma had already been to the garden to pick fresh raspberries for breakfast.

I have combined my memories of several Grandmas' Houses in the paragraphs above. You can add your own memories of Grandma's House to those mentioned here. Like me, you are a grandmother or a grandfather now. And these memories furnish us a starting point for preparing our own houses to receive grandchildren.

Children need the solace of Grandma's House or Grandfather's Mountain to develop into fully rounded adults (see chapter 5). Grandparents can do many things to make their homes special for grandchildren. As a grandparent, new or experienced, you honor Christ by seeking ways to make your home a place your grandchildren will remember in the latter years of their lives.

Make physical preparations for these special guests, your grandchildren.

This may mean a high chair, a crib in the guest room, and perhaps such items as a potty chair, a stroller, and a child's car seat. Sooner or later you will probably need a playpen—or a Ping-Pong table in the basement or garage. But last year you gave that family heirloom crib in the attic to your niece? And you've shot your wad of pin money on baby clothes, a shower, and perhaps a plane ticket to see your daughter or daughter-in-law with her precious bundle? How can you now afford to supply your own nursery?

It's time you discovered yard/garage sales! For openers, nobody expects you to have *new* equipment on hand for occasional use by young guests. With the aid of a newspaper you can discover half a dozen pieces of serviceable baby furniture or play equipment for older children. Parents whose kids are grown often sell such items for a fraction of their new cost. Pass up the broken, dilapidated stuff and look for the best. It might be unwise to buy old items for a new mother, but for use at Grandma's House, used equipment may be exactly what you need.

 ## *Younger children need to be kept busy.*

Look for toys and books appropriate to the needs of your grand-children. These should be chosen with an eye to keeping the child occupied with a minimum of supervision, and the simple ones are best. A book of one hundred or so dot-to-dot puzzles, for example, will fascinate most children with the dexterity to trace a line with a crayon or pencil. Push toys, such as trucks, tractors, and autos for backyard or sandbox play will entertain for hours. A doll and a stuffed animal or two will please the under-10 set, and the animals are all the more appreciated if you give them names!

If you wish to branch out, tricycles and bicycles of all description are to be found in yard sales. These will keep your older grandchildren from feeling stranded at their home away from home. Swing sets and sandboxes are sometimes found in yard sales, as well.

 ## *Prepare for your preteens and teens.*

There are toys appropriate only for Dennis the Menace or Bart Simpson, however. Though slingshots, bows and arrows, or air rifles (BB guns) sometimes have their place with developing children under parental supervision, you are not depriving your grandchild by refusing to let him or her bring hazardous toys on a weekend visit. A pocketknife would be okay, if the child is used to carrying one, but a bow can send arrows into your neighbor's yard! One young teen, reared in a suburban subdivision, visited his grandparents who lived on a rural road. Here he set up his pup tent and with a .22-caliber rifle terrorized the neighbors for some days until he wounded his grandfather's dog. Children, placed in an unaccustomed environment, often behave in inappropriate ways.

Sports equipment should be purchased with caution. You may wish, for example, to restrict the child to soft balls (for example, soccer balls, rubber balls); no hard balls, such as baseballs or golf balls, since these often break windows, unless used under closer supervision than you may be ready to supply.

Your choice of toys will vary with your circumstances and the ages of the children, of course. The grandparent who owns a five-hundred-acre Nebraska ranch can be more liberal than one who lives in a New York apartment. If grandparents own a farm, it might be okay to let a 14-year-old grandson fire Grandpa's 12-gauge (under adult supervision, of course).

   Make your home safe.

If Grandpa owns hunting guns, they must never, ever be left loaded. They should have trigger locks, and preferably they should be kept in a locked cabinet. And many adults, grown accustomed to living in a home without small children, fail to realize the serious potential of even the common, seemingly harmless habit of leaving one's keys in the car or riding mower for a few minutes. Toddlers have turned keys on, slipped the car into neutral, and coasted it into the street or over another child—or frightened, have jumped out and fallen under the moving vehicle themselves. Recent news reports have shown how tragically common it is for five- to eight-year-olds to use car keys to open the trunk—then hide inside until they suffocate.

Toddlers can fall down stairs, so stairs need gates. Sandboxes need a sturdy fiberglass tarp, but not just to keep out rainwater: Neighborhood cats may use yours to deposit feces, often full of worms easily passed on to small children.

A locked medicine cabinet, or at the least one out of reach of toddlers, is mandatory. Keyed locks to secure cleaning chemicals can be fitted onto wooden kitchen cupboards by anyone handy with tools. Childproof temporary locks are available in stores like Wal-Mart, Kmart, or Target, and easily slip onto kitchen cupboard door handles. A garage cabinet can easily be supplied with a hasp and a padlock.

Speaking of garages, did you know that antifreeze tastes sweet, like a delicious punch? It comes in child-resistant containers, true enough. But a lot of folks, like myself, mix it 50/50 with water, then put the extra gallon in a plastic milk jug! Be sure that jug is clearly labeled and kept in a locked car trunk or an inaccessible garage cabinet.

A lot of grandparents, especially granddads, own tempting adult toys. A grandfather friend of mine lost a grandson, a child of about six, when he fell into a mowing machine while riding behind Grandpa on the tractor seat. Another grandfather took his 15-year-old grandson, who could drive a car, for a ride in his single-engine pontoon plane at their lakeside cottage. He showed the boy how the controls worked and even let him try flying. The teen had access to the plane's keys and later tried to fly alone. He got the airplane airborne, then landed—nosedown in the water.

 ## *Make your home comfortable for children.*

This will require some compromise, to be sure. If your living room is supplied with a white carpet, Chippendale furniture, fine porcelain lamps, and cut glass vases, it may be best to make the living room off-limits to all but adults who remove their shoes. This *may* work *if* your living room can be shut off from the rest of the house without seriously disrupting the household traffic flow. Otherwise, put the breakables out of reach, temporarily install a plastic runner across the carpet, and resort to frequent washings to keep your grandchildren's hands as pure as you imagine their hearts to be.

 ## *Provide suitable overnight accommodations.*

Creative planning can result in some delightfully unusual arrangements. One farm family has a rustic cottage tucked away in the woods on a stream half a mile back where the grandchildren and married children can vacation. Others, with smaller spreads, can let the grandkids set up a tent in the backyard. Many communities permit householders with large lots to park camping trailers in the back or side yard for a few weeks. Such privileges should be taken advantage of only where the neighbors don't mind, of course.

Usually, however, most grandparents find a simple solution in redecorating what was once a child's bedroom as a guest room, then furnishing it with a double bed, a dresser, and perhaps a crib. When the married children come to call, they get the guest room and the kids sleep on a fold-out bed in the family room or in sleeping bags on foam pads, or even on the back porch, weather permitting. When your grandchild visits alone, he gets the luxury of "the big bed" all to himself.

How well I remember my own childhood experiences with my grandparents, whose nineteenth-century home, formerly a country inn, had never been wired for electricity above the ground floor. Grandma would accompany me upstairs where the double bed in the back bedroom was cozy with flannel sheets and a soapstone heated in the oven of her wood-fired kitchen range. Grandma carried matches and I a flashlight. She lit the lamp on the dresser, and after prayers were said and I was tucked in—feet firmly planted on the towel-swaddled hot soapstone—she then blew out the lamp and left me with a flashlight under my pillow. I felt princely grand yet terribly alone during those nights upstairs in that old inn.

An advantage grandparents have over parents is that they can decide how many grandchildren can stay at once and for how long without being accused of cruelty. My own grandmother, though she occasionally would baby-sit my siblings and me, never permitted more than one grandchild to visit overnight at a time. Such an arrangement has the obvious advantage of enabling Grandma to keep her sanity. Some grandparents revel in a houseful of kids. Grandma and

Grandpa Hackney, my wife's parents, often entertained a merry crowd of youngsters. But the one-child-at-a-time approach offers the advantage of a child having the one-on-one attention of a loving adult. This is an experience not realized by many children.

 Lay in a supply of kid food.

You may subsist on minute steaks. Your active grandson may prefer macaroni and cheese—lots of it! It's certainly futile to try to change a child's (wretched?!) eating habits in the week he's your houseguest. You'll only make yourself and the child miserable if you don't cater to *some* of his eating habits, at least.

Crackers and peanut butter will keep most kids happy for between-meal snacks, and peanut butter is nutritious. (Despite what the TV ads say, few children can tell the difference between the cheap stuff and the high-priced spread.) Homemade cookies, cakes, and pies will make them happier still, along with giving you a sense of satisfaction in creative cooking. A really resourceful grandma will be long remembered for cooking her grandchildren's favorite dishes.

 Use visits to let cousins enjoy each other.

This must be done with concern for compatibility, however. One purpose of grandparenting is to help a child develop as an individual, rather than as a member of the herd, as happens in school and day-care settings and far too commonly in the home. So it is my feeling that cousins or siblings should not be invited to share the grandparents' time if they are going to compete for attention. This may sometimes be avoided by inviting cousins with no competing interests. For example, a teen girl who helps Grandma with the housework may also entertain an eight-year-old cousin, and each enjoys the companionship of the grandparents on his or her own level.

This approach—an older child and a younger one—to pairing grandkids when they visit may help solve the problem of not enough weekends or summer vacation days to go around. Some grandparents may have only two or three grandchildren. But we knew one lady, past 90, who had a descendant for every year of her life—children, grandchildren, great-grandchildren, and great-great-grandchildren. Most of them lived nearby and treated her home as their second home. "Mom, come get me; I stopped at Grandma's after going fishing," was a phone request her daughters and married granddaughters heard often—I know; I'm the grandfather of 10 of her great-grandchildren!

Holidays are exceptions to the "one grandchild" rule. And this requires special attention to the needs of the children *and* the needs of grandparents. Some grandmothers past 80 will still insist on cooking Thanksgiving dinner for the entire brood. Finally the daughters and daughters-in-law protest that they are themselves now grandmothers, and will Mother (now a great-grandmother!) please allow them to have their own family celebrations, to which she is of course invited.

This aged matriarch eventually found a creative solution to this dilemma that enabled her to continue to express her mothering instincts, enjoy her extended family, yet give her descendants memorable Christmases until she passed away. She gave up on cooking Christmas dinner years earlier when her brood was no longer able to crowd around her table, even in successive seatings. But each year this granddame started Christmas breakfast at six o'clock with the aid of a daughter. A merry, constantly changing crowd of children and adults climbed over each other for the next four hours, feasting on bacon, sausage, eggs, and biscuits. Then the paper plates were whisked away, daughters did the dishes, and great-great-grandma was bundled off to spend the rest of the day (which included a long nap!) with one of her many families.

 Find special ways to entertain your grandchildren.

Entertaining guests need not require the grandparents' full-time attention, however, and it will necessarily be limited by whether either or both grandparents are employed, and by the length of the stay.

The simplest is an overnight stay. My own stays with my grandparents usually began on Saturday afternoon, and I had entertainment enough for several hours watching my grandparents wait on customers in the small grocery store in the wing of their house. Grandpa was a part-time sheriff on call Saturday nights. My encounter with him on such evenings was the thrill of seeing him, dressed in his business suit, his silver badge discreetly pinned inside his coat, stride off to keep order at the local dance hall. If I returned with my parents after Sunday school for dinner the next day, I often heard

Grandpa regale us with tales of troublemakers he'd tossed out or even hauled off to jail.

Alone with Grandma for the evening, I'd listen to radio programs such as *Amos 'n' Andy* or *Inner Sanctum* while she did the supper dishes. Then we'd play checkers or backgammon until bedtime. It was my thrill to occasionally beat Grandma at checkers!

Today, the TV set and solitary computer games are the handiest forms of entertainment ever invented—and probably among the worst. Solitary games and sitcom watching can be deadly to your grandchildren's social maturity. If you are going to offer your grandchild worthwhile experiences, it will often be necessary to forgo your favorite show and pay attention to *him*. This is not an objection to TV or computer technology *per se*. Rather, grandparents need to consider that one of God's great purposes in placing people in families is to develop social skills.

It's up to you, Grandma and Grandpa, to take the initiative in interactive play with that precious grandchild. Besides those old-fashioned board games—still great fun for kids willing to learn them—you might buy a Nintendo or Sega game system to connect to your TV set (about $100), then rent a few games from a video store. Such games operate with up to four players. Your grandchild will love to teach you!

Did you know that many of the old, favorite Parker Brothers and Milton Bradley games are now available on CD for you to play with your grandchild on your computer? Log on to <www.familygamenight.com> for ordering details.

Special seasonal events, such as fairs and plays, offer occasions your grandchild will long remember. Dot and I made it a practice when our four kids were growing up to take them to watch the *Nutcracker* ballet every couple of years. We do this now for our grandchildren. And boys and girls from stroller size through early teens enjoy zoos and picnic lunches.

I recently crawled beneath my old pickup truck to learn why the motor tipped crazily whenever I put it in gear. "What's wrong with it, Grandpa?" Nine-year-old Timothy had squirreled in next to me, and he lay on the grass staring with mechanically minded concern at the oily parts and grimy pipes above.

"Broken motor mount, I think, Tim."

"There it is, Grandpa!" Tim pointed a small finger at a torn, oily neoprene pad sandwiched in steel between the truck's frame and its V-8 motor.

Surprised, I had just learned how easy entertaining a fourth-grade boy can be. That old red truck is important to Tim's imagination because it's important to Grandpa, whom he loves dearly.

Try to think of unique events not available to your grandchild in his hometown, and plan to enjoy these together. A grandmother in Fort Wayne, Indiana, used to invite her grandchildren for a weekend in November or December. She would then take them for a tour of the reconstruction of the colonial Old Fort Wayne. Room after room was filled with folks in period costume celebrating Christmas in the traditions of European settlers in early wilderness America. City-dwelling grandparents have access to museums, theaters, and interesting stores and malls. You might take a grandchild downtown on the bus or subway, then thrill her with lunch in a restaurant atop your city's tallest building—and be sure to insist on a window seat! Country grandparents have simpler yet interesting entertainments to create memories for their grandchildren. A visit to an agricultural fair can coincide with a grandchild's week with his farm-dwelling grandparents, for example.

 Entertaining teens and young adults can be trying— or a pleasure.

This experience can be even more interesting if you raised only girls or only boys, and the grandchild is of the other sex. To prepare yourself for when you entertain a grandchild of a different gender, remember that a teenager is essentially an immature adult. He or she has the desires, ambitions, and appetites of an adult, and many of the abilities. Your teen grandchild can probably drive a car, and your grandson may be fairly competent at repairing one. Your teen granddaughters can tend babies—and give birth to babies! Teens can discuss politics, spiritual matters, or sex with adultlike perception. Teens can take care of their own physical needs: They can dress themselves, shave, curl their hair, and take showers that would challenge Niagara. They can cook and do laundry. They may also leave the dishes undone and the bed unmade, unless you gently remind them that you could use some help. A weekend with a teen can be a pleasure or a pain, and you, Grandma and Grandpa, the mature members of the group, can be the catalysts to make the difference.

Young people who visit their grandparents, with few exceptions, do so because they want—often very badly—the companionship of their elders. The same grandmother who beat me at checkers when I was nine became a friend in whom I could confide when I was 19. She wrote me letters, long and full of family news. When I came home from college, we talked. And you know what? Grandma wanted to listen to me! I soon found that she was fascinated with what I had to say, and she had more time to listen than did my parents.

It's taken me a few years to sort out the reasons why Grandma had such an interest in me, but now a grandfather myself, I think I know. First, Grandma was an only child raised by a widowed mother, so boys and men were not a large part of her early life. She married my grandfather at 22, he being 37. He was not a Christian until shortly before his death, so there was little spiritual communication between them. Their children were both girls. I think both my mother's parents saw me as a substitute for the son they would have liked to have had.

I was a college student, and having attended a year of college herself, a high privilege for girls in the days before World War I, she admired me for that. My grandfather's education had ended with the seventh grade, and neither of my parents had been to college, nor had my aunt, Grandma's younger daughter.

I write these things to point out a universal yet little understood phenomenon: God puts people in complementary relationships to meet one another's needs. I met Grandma's need to have a young college man she could admire. She met my need for a female who would listen with interest when I spoke. Such need meeting is important, especially in relationships with teen or single young-adult grandchildren. For your teen or young-adult grandchildren, perhaps the most important "entertainment" you can give them is to listen when they talk!

 Guests are like fish—they both stink after three days, Benjamin Franklin once said.

While there's no magic in the three-day limit—a happy visit may last three weeks or only three hours—there comes a time when the grandchildren need to say good-bye to Grandma's House. Consult the parents to determine the length of stay as you consider both the child's needs and your resources. A three-hour afternoon visit with your three-year-old personification of mischief may be all you can manage, but it may be all his mother needs to get her shopping done. Three days, and a five-year-old may tearfully beg to go home. A child of 8 to 12 who lives half a continent away may be a joy for three weeks and beg to stay the entire three months of summer.

Some grandchildren and grandparents are temperamentally suited for each other. Others are not suited to spending long periods in each other's company. In such cases, a grandparent needs to ask the Lord for grace while also thanking Him if the child has other grandparents he can bounce his ball off.

Ready or not, Grandma, you are now the lady of Grandma's House. It's up to you to make visits a pleasure your grandchildren will long remember. But more than a pleasure, a properly managed Grandma's House can add immeasurably to your grandchildren's sense of security and to their maturing experience.

CHAPTER THREE

Seeing Through Your Grandchild's Eyes

A sage once remarked that the elderly slow down and stoop over so that they can see things as children once again, so that they can hold the hands of children who toddle along on inexperienced feet. That bug on the sidewalk, the snail under the cabbage leaf, the robin pulling the worm from rain-moistened earth—these are the things small children and their grandparents notice.

When Christ wished to illustrate greatness, He chose a child from the crowd milling about the Master Teacher and His disciples. Sitting himself among them, Jesus took that small boy on his lap. I imagine Jesus may have wiped a runny nose or tied up an errant sandal thong as He spoke (see Mark 9:35–37). Jesus got down to child level, to the level of little things.

"Come see" is the cry heard again and again by the parent, teacher, or grandparent of the very young. If you've taught the small ones, or if you're a grandparent, you've experienced being called aside to view a crayon drawing, a stack of blocks just one higher than yesterday—a world record for that child—or the discovery of an exotic bug on the back side of a leaf.

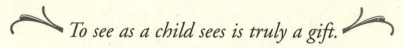

To see as a child sees is truly a gift.

Children, whether toddlers or young teens, see little things in ways adults have forgotten how to comprehend them. Adults may carelessly fail to appreciate those little things, and thus miss the opportunity to build into that grandchild much-needed concepts of competence and self-worth. Children view their world as a series of small things because they lack the ability to appreciate the whole. Grandparents, on the other hand, may have to struggle to get down to a child's level.

Joshua, at 13, has just discovered Corvettes. "Oh, wow, Grandpa! Sweet!" he suddenly explodes in ecstasy as they slide past a used car lot in Grandpa's big sedan one Saturday morning. "Stingrays—eight of 'em!"

Grandpa, a man of affairs in his late 50s, is unimpressed. He's owned cars ranging from Volkswagens to Cadillacs for over 40 years. An automobile is to him a convenient means of getting from point A to point B on his business rounds. *So what's the big deal?* he's thinking.

Then it occurs to Grandpa that here's a chance to develop a relationship with Josh, and at the same time let his grandson learn a bit about the relative importance of Corvettes in the big picture of the world of transportation. So casually remarking, "Let's have a better look," he circles the block and stops under the sign reading, "'Vette World." Moments later, Grandpa and

Josh are peering under the hood of a reconditioned Corvette as Grandpa patiently explains that this particular jewel, the gee whiz of General Motors's Chevrolet line, actually has the same motor as the four-year-old car they are riding in. And Joshua chatters to Grandpa about acceleration rates and top speeds and streamlining—facts he dug from a borrowed auto magazine during a seventh-grade study hall.

Automobiles and insects are both "little things" in the great scheme of life. As we mature and see the larger world, both cars and bugs shrink in significance. For a grown-up, looking at the little things is an art requiring cultivation. And the sooner a busy adult of middle years learns to develop this art, the sooner he or she will be able to relate meaningfully to his or her grandchildren. "A grandparent is for awe," says author Charlie Shedd.[1] Can you enjoy with and *as* a small child such small things as the buzz of a bee on a clover blossom, the murmur of a woodland stream, or the nap of the wool on a freshly shorn lamb at a county fair or petting zoo?

Shortly before I became a grandparent, I took a job as a part-time substitute teacher to bridge the gap between a career as an instructor in a college that closed its doors and a new career as a writer. My experience had been as a secondary teacher, so I signed up for that department. I had kids of my own, but the thought of my taking charge of two dozen elf-sized humanoids, each with his peculiar needs, unnerved me.

Then early one morning the phone rang. It was the sub caller for an elementary school, and she was desperate. A fourth-grade teacher had suddenly taken ill. Ruefully I agreed to take her place.

I soon learned that fourth graders—nine-year-olds—are

peaches and cream. So are third, second, and first graders. Kindergartners, too, I discovered that school year. Few things lift my day more than half a dozen small ones (usually girls!) jumping up and down outside the classroom window at a quarter to eight screaming, "Hey, we've got a *man* for a teacher today!"

But then comes the small stuff—a day filled with the little things of life. An uncoordinated child who has to have his boots pulled on and his coat zipped every recess. Chairs so low that if you join the reading circle you must park your legs off to the side. There are endless crayon pictures of houses with chimneys perpendicular to the pitch of the roof—you admire the artwork, patiently showing second graders that chimneys go straight up and down. A gerbil needs to be fed and, yes, petted by the children and admired by you—and all the while you're wishing the cage had a padlock and only you had a key!

> *Children are little, and their concerns and complaints are little in adult eyes, and you and I must become little in order to truly appreciate them.*

In my second-grade classroom, an adopted Chinese girl with a Polish name, Ashley Shozenski, was hurt because the boy behind her (also Polish!) made an unkind racial remark about her. I mended her spirits by telling her that "God must love Chinese, because He made more of them than any other people." Two years later Ashley showed up in a fourth-grade class where I was the substitute, and she remembered me and told me, "Mother says you're right; there *are* more Chinese than any other people." I've got a friend for life!

Philippians 2:5–8 best expresses the attitude that Christian grandparents must assume if they are to meet the needs of their grandchildren. Christ "made himself nothing." This is a translation of a single Greek verb *kenoô,* "to empty." He "emptied himself" is a marginal reference in many Bibles. J. B. Phillips translates this "stripped himself of all privilege." This is precisely what Jesus was illustrating when He picked up the child in Mark 9:36–37. Our willingness to empty ourselves of adult privilege, to become nothing, that we may experience the little things with our grandchildren, is the measure of our ability to communicate with our grandchildren.

It grieves me to see an adult caricature a child. I recall an elderly woman with no children of her own who was a guest in our home for a while when I was a teenager. She had little use for children (my parents then had five). When she wanted to speak to a small child, she'd talk baby talk, demeaning the child's attempts to express himself. But mere imitation is mockery, and this is sensed by the child for the fraud that it is. To know a child, you must become like a child.

On a practical level, the little things are bridges to our rapport with our grandchildren. Grasping life a piece at a time is the way each of us had to learn life's great lessons so long ago, and this is how our Joshuas and Ashleys are even now learning them.

Our grandchildren live in imperfect homes, reared by imperfect parents—our sons or daughters who are married to our sons-in-law or daughters-in-law, all of them imperfect. Although we all made mistakes raising our children, the good news is that as godly grandparents, walking with the Lord, we can expect the Lord to use us. Because of our own immaturity when our children—now parents—were growing up, we may have disappointed them. But by keeping us alive to enjoy our grandchildren, the Lord is giving us a ministry to help fill in these gaps in our imperfect child rearing.

In the rush of the young or middle-aged adult world, little things tend to get pushed aside. That's partly because adults are so busy assembling the little things to make a complete picture that we lose sight of the pieces. While daddies are working for a promotion, building a business, or repairing the house, grandfathers are needed to fix Josh's bicycle, wipe little Amy's nose, or even help an older grandson change a fuel pump.

Let's suppose eight-year-old Hunter shows up at dinnertime with an assortment of aquatic denizens he's pulled on baited hook from the muddy creek under the highway bridge behind your subdivision. He proudly brings that day's catch into the house: three shiners, a sunfish, two perch, and a catfish.

"Leave the fish in the shed and wash up," Mother calls, her irritation betraying her dread of helping Hunter clean them. "I don't know what you brought those fish home for, anyway. Your grandmother's freezer is full of them, and she gives us all we want. Besides, I'm sure that stream is polluted."

Dinner over, Hunter turns to the TV, and Dad goes out to wax the car. He sets the bucket of fish on the shady side of the garage, and while he's at work, Bowser has *his* supper— Hunter's catch of the day!

But a week later, Hunter's parents, having been remorseful at being so careless with Hunter's fish, leave him with Grandma overnight. Her village home is near a lake with a lagoon that runs behind her street. As the sun sets over the lake, Hunter and

Grandma are casting their lines where the bluegills and perch are the hungriest.

From this experience, young Hunter learns an important lesson about the food chain (fish eat worms; people eat fish). More importantly, he learns that his fish, so important to him because he's caught them himself, are important to a person very special in his life—Grandma. She helps Hunter bait his hook and shows him how to disengage a barb from a fish's mouth. She makes an assembly line process of cleaning the fish they have caught together. She spreads cutting boards and newspapers on her back-porch table, where heads, fins, scales, and innards are removed by Grandma, who has learned not to be squeamish, and by Hunter, who has not yet learned squeamishness.

The next day, when Mother picks Hunter up at Grandma's house, Hunter proudly presents her a frozen package labeled "Hunter's fish"—to which Grandma has added several she caught herself. Hunter's shining eyes tell the story: He is a very important person to Grandma, for she accepted his fish as valuable and even helped him clean them as he helped with hers, bolstering his self-esteem even more. And his parents, who had been planning on broiled salmon (at $9.89 a pound!) for dinner, gamely help Hunter eat them and call them delicious.

"Little things mean a lot" is a lyric from a song on the radio nearly 50 years ago. Little things mean a lot to the little people in our lives, for to them, these are the stuff life is made of—a young teen's interest in an auto, a small boy's fish. I wonder what were the memories of the boy who saw his little lunch of five biscuit-sized loaves and two tiny fish used to feed the throng by the Sea of Galilee. Isn't it possible that this unnamed lad was later one of the great men of the book of Acts who tramped across Europe to plant churches with the apostle Paul, motivated by the multiplication of his work at the word of the Master?

A nickel is a little piece of change, but how well I remember greedily clutching one! Grandma had placed it in my greasy palm and pointed me toward Grandpa, who was already selecting blue and red helium-filled balloons from a vendor at the county fairgrounds. How I gripped that coin, sure that if I dropped it in the milling throng my opportunity for this new (to me!) marvel, a lighter-than-air balloon, would be gone forever! Had not Grandpa, an important sheriff who got free admission by simply flashing his silver badge, warned me that pickpockets lurked behind every tent?

We jounced across the hills toward home, brother George and I, in the back of Grandpa's old panel truck, our balloons secured by their strings to our wrists. That night Mother untied the strings, and our balloons soared wonderfully to the ceiling. I don't recall another thing about that trip to the fair. Yet I do recall the generosity of my grandparents who drove with us to what seemed to me then like the outer edge of the world to return with a treasure more delightful than Marco Polo could have discovered in old Cathay—a helium-filled balloon.

How deep my disappointment to find our balloons on the floor next morning, their buoyancy gone, lifeless, half limp—dead things that had surely cheated Grandma out of two nickels!

It is Grandma's thoughtfulness that lives on in my memory, though. Creatures of appetite that my brother and I were, we'd have readily spent as many nickels as we could bribe out of our grandparents on cotton candy, ice cream, strawberry sodas, or deep-fried elephant ears. But Grandma knew that a five-cent helium balloon, a little thing to her, would delight us long after the ice cream had dripped all over our homemade overalls and the spun sugar had been smeared all across our cheeks.

> *If you would lift your grandchild as Christ lifted a child, you must see small things as they are seen through small eyes.*

Even as the life of those gas-filled balloons was brief, so childhood too is brief. Think back to when you passed a minor milestone in your life, say seven or eight years ago. Perhaps you bought the car you're now driving, or purchased a piece of furniture or a nice pair of leather-lined dress shoes (mine last 20 years!). Think of your grandchild who was born about then, or since. You are 50, or perhaps 70 or 80. But that grandchild, like yourself, is exactly one lifetime old. You must fit yourself into that tiny life, a span of time so short it seems just the other day, while that grandchild is still little enough for you to make meaningful, important marks on him or her.

CHAPTER FOUR

The Extended Family: Yesterday and Today

My sister traced our family tree back to its varied roots. She discovered a tangle of extended families, including several intermarriages, most of which sprang since the Revolutionary War from a plot of rural central Maine soil with a radius of not more than a dozen miles from our family home.

Our farmstead, where five generations of Wiggins lived for a century, was typical of our community. Uncle Oscar (or Cousin Oscar, depending on which side of our family you figured the relationship), for instance, spent most of his nearly 102 years (1884–1985) in the house where he was born, less than a mile from our place. His house, in fact, had been built three-quarters of a century before his birth by Oscar's great-grandfather when our country lane was still a packhorse trail and the land was covered with virgin pine.

The extended family I knew as a child included paternal grandparents, who lived in the house with us—the house built by my grandfather, where my father spent his entire life, and where both his parents died in the bedroom they shared for half a century. It also included my maternal grandparents, just two miles away in a home shared with my great-grandmother and an unmarried aunt. A mile away lived my grandmother's brother and wife in a house built by Grandma's father. Three miles farther on dwelt another aunt and uncle and a house full of cousins.

My wife's family came from the rural South, and after a few years in suburban St. Louis, they moved during the Great Depression of the 1930s to the upper Midwest's industrial belt to find employment. Their move was a family affair: The grandparents came along, as did brothers, sisters, and cousins, like the Okies' exodus to California in *The Grapes of Wrath*. Just before our marriage, I became the last recipient of my wife's grandmother's lecture on how to treat a wife, a family tradition that I have since learned began before I was born. So many relatives from nearby communities were on our wedding guest list that we had to rent a church building in a neighboring village—her family's church would not hold the crowd!

Months after we were married, my wife and I attended a Polish wedding on Detroit's north side, where we learned of another type of extended family. Both bride and groom were descended from immigrants who came from war-torn Eastern Europe in the 1940s, and tables were spread in a church basement for a Polish feast for perhaps two hundred guests, many of them family members from the same city neighborhood.

Whittier's autobiographical poem *Snowbound* paints a picture of a pre-Civil War extended family of several generations, sheltered under one roof. "Shut in from all the world without, We sat the clean-winged hearth about," he wrote of his childhood nearly two centuries ago. Grandparents, parents, and unmarried aunts, along with the children, filled that family circle in the firelight in that New England homestead.

The extended family, as Whittier pictured it, has dispersed across America in several stages.

Several factors have led to this breakup. The industrialization of America in the three-quarters of a century between the Civil War and World War II took Americans from the farm. This usually meant that grandparents no longer lived in the same house with children and grandchildren, or even in proximity.

Money from industrial jobs, as well as massive federal subsidies of housing since World War II, has made it possible for millions of young American couples to live in their own houses. There were the bungalows and duplexes of the 1940s and 1950s, the split-levels built in the 1960s and 1970s, and presently homes of four bedrooms and two or three baths with two-car garages in burgeoning subdivisions. These are almost palatial by standards of the mid-twentieth century, prevalent when today's grandparents were children.

As high-tech industries have migrated to beltways circling American cities, satellite clusters of houses have sprung up outside cities beyond the suburbs along these expressway systems built since the war. This has given our language a new word: *exurbia.* Many families that once enjoyed the support of their extended families in ethnic neighborhoods, such as the Polish districts of Detroit and Chicago or Irish neighborhoods in Boston, have been scattered to the cities' perimeters and beyond.

The average American family now moves once every six years—down from once in five years in the mid-1980s. Young Americans under 30 move about every third year, often to pursue an education, a new job, or a larger home for an expanding family. After age 45, the typical American householder at the beginning of this century moves once in 13 to 20 years. Many this age stay put for life.[1]

The practice of mothers working outside the home dates largely from World War II, when women were badly needed in munitions factories for the war effort, and industrial wages were good. This first wave of mothers to take outside jobs are now great-grandmothers. Like their daughters and granddaughters, many do not even understand the concept of an extended family circle.

Automatic appliances, though available to the well-to-do since about 1920, became cheaply available in quantities following the war. These, along with such amenities as easy-care fabrics and inexpensive, ready-to-wear clothes, have freed both rural and city housewives from household drudgery, and packaged foods and fast-food restaurants have released many women from the daily responsibility of what their grandmothers called "fixin' a meal." Yet household technology and the proliferation of restaurants during the past half century have proven a mixed blessing. Added to the desire to purchase these things, real wages for men supporting families dropped during the recession of the 1980s and have never rebounded.

Many mothers now work outside the home to pay for these recently discovered needs, which their homebound grandmothers lived—often happily—without.

A little-noticed 20-year lull in the trend of mothers in the workplace, 1945–65, coincided with the birth of baby boomers, 1946–64. Sociologist Allan Carlson calls this period "an extraordinary . . . time" during which "Americans did manage to put family life back together in a limited way."[2] Carlson is president of the Howard Center for Family, Religion, and Society, located in Rockford, Illinois.

Interestingly, this 20-year lull also coincided with a slump in the divorce rate. In spite of the much-touted 50 percent rate of marriage failure, this divorce downturn offers hope for today's extended families. Contrary to the popular opinions of the evangelical Christian community, today's youth, the children of the 1980s and 1990s, may be more positively motivated than any for several generations. (See chapter 15, "Are Today's Teens Different?" for further perspective on this phenomenon.)

A U.S. Department of Health and Human Services chart tracks marriage and divorce from 1920 to 1998. Both marriage and divorce spiked sharply upward in 1946, the year following World War II. Both rates declined significantly over the next two decades, rising again after 1965. The raw divorce rate from 1978 to 1981, the highest in history, was about 50 percent of all marriages, though the rate has declined slightly over the past 20 years.[3]

Now here's more good news for the extended family. Barna Research Group, a California firm that tracks statistical trends in churches and families, reported that just 25 percent of couples have experienced divorce[4], *half* what the U.S.

government's raw statistics, reported uncritically by the liberal media, seem to show. Pollster Louis Harris, in fact, said the notion that half of Americans divorce is "specious . . . statistical nonsense."[5] *Statistical Abstract of the U.S.* figures, laid against Barna's and Harris's data, seem to reflect that divorce is largely a repetitive phenomena in which one-fourth to one-third of the population have multiple divorces. The rest, about three-quarters of all married adults, stay with their spouses for life.

Yet there's more: Barna found that baby boomers—today's older parents—have a divorce rate of 34 percent. This rate is high, but it is below that of their parents, whom Barna dubs "builders." These builders—today's grandparents—have suffered a whopping 37 percent divorce casualty. Of the builders' parents (Barna's "seniors," born before 1927, whom newsman Tom Brokaw calls "the greatest generation"), just 18 percent have ever been divorced. Currently, only 7 percent of young couples born since 1964 have divorced.[6]

The fragmentation of the extended family has for many been made complete by the move of older couples into retirement communities, often hundreds of miles from the kids and grandkids.

Florida, Arizona, and parts of California have seen droves of elderly seeking to escape the city for the sun. Upper New England, many pockets in the rural South, and, recently, mid-sized cities such as Madison, Wisconsin, have large settlements of retirees. Michigan's Office of Retirement Services, one of the nation's largest retirement systems, reported in June 2000 that thousands of its retirees eschew the chilly Michigan climate to retire in Texas, Tennessee, North Carolina, or the states mentioned above.

Government grants underwriting nursing home construction, along with Medicaid and Social Security, have, since the late 1960s, made it possible for millions of elderly—the older grandparents and great-grandparents—to spend their final years in nursing homes. Even the poorest elderly person can now get nursing home care by selling off his or her assets, spending the money, then declaring himself indigent in order to qualify for Medicaid funding. Many younger grandmothers, entering the workforce as soon as their children leave the nest, will not later forgo a weekly paycheck to nurse Great-grandma at home. Instead of the daily companionship of family, these elderly often see family members only once or twice a week, nursing home workers attest. And it is usually just the adults who come to visit; children are thus robbed of experiencing life as a rich continuum from birth to old age.

Realistically, American families are not going to return to living on farms and in small villages in great numbers. The back-to-the-land movement, 1970–90, leveled off with the recession of the 1980s. Indeed, many back-to-the-landers were themselves grandparents buying worked-out small farms for retirement homes. But grain-belt states such as Iowa and North and South Dakota have lost young families who moved to the cities for jobs, leaving grandparents far from the grandchildren. These three mostly rural states, in fact, have the highest percentage of elderly over 85 in America, the U.S. Census Bureau reports.[7]

Many grandparents are now more able to afford living in their own homes.

Increased savings and investments, coupled with Medicaid-funded in-home care services, have made this possible. More grandparents now live alone longer than in the past, keeping them from moving in with their children and grandchildren. On the other hand, this gives enough financial security so that most never need to live in a nursing home, a positive effect, since grandparents living in their own homes are much more accessible to grandchildren.

Since about 1990, older grandparents have increasingly stayed at home, or have moved in with family members. Only 15 percent of grandparents over 85 and under 3 percent of those ages 65 to 74 now live in care facilities. This is about half the percentage of grandparents in nursing homes in the 1980s.[8]

It is possible, in most cases, to keep even an invalid elderly grandparent at home without major financial or physical burdens on other family members. Millions of American households currently have grandparents living with an adult son or daughter because the elderly need aid in doing household chores, or because they are no longer able to attend to all of their personal bodily needs. This is beneficial to holding a family together, certainly. But how unlike the pattern typical of yesteryear, when on the farm grandparents were often living with—or next door to—adult children when they were still able to take an active part in household duties and grandchildren were still at home.

I can still envision my paternal grandmother, a tall, rugged woman, though nearly half a century older than my pixie-sized mother, as the two of them canned beans or tomatoes for the winter larder. Mother eventually became Grandma's caregiver in the home where both women spent their married lives, after Grandma, past 90, was confined to a wheelchair.

In a move to cut Medicare costs, Michigan and several other states have started a Home Health Services program, which, according to the Michigan Family Independence Agency, is "much less expensive" for the taxpayer than nursing home confinement. Medicaid caseworker Ed Schertenlieb reported that elderly institutional care in Michigan costs about $52,000 a year per patient at the beginning of the twenty-first century. The Home Health Services program, however, provides a daughter or daughter-in-law with needed cash for extra expenses, such as hiring a part-time caregiver. This program has spun off a new industry—professional caregivers who will help tend an aged or infirm parent for a fee, said Cheryl Thomas of Michigan's Family Independence Agency. Schertenlieb noted that this program has markedly slowed Michigan nursing home construction, as more grandparents opt to keep great-grandma home, using outside help.

> *Many existing extended families can be preserved, and still others be reunited, if the members will consider each other's needs before their own.*

God's will for most of us is to live in families (Psalm 68:6). Families are for loving and sharing and burden bearing. Jesus advised

His followers that others would see that they belong to Him if they actively "love one another" (John 13:34-35). Despite the forces that tear families apart, the twenty-first century is filled with opportunities for family unity as never before.

The idea of taking positive action to keep or draw an extended family together is so opposite the habitual thinking of many American Christians that these concepts may seem strange. Part of the problem, I believe, is that as creatures of extremes, we have placed an overemphasis on Bible passages telling us, like the old Sherwin-Williams paint advertisement, to spread out across the earth. For example, the Bible teaches that a man should "leave his father and mother" as he is "united to his wife" (Genesis 2:24; Ephesians 5:31). The Lord called Abraham to leave his father's house in Chaldea and journey to Canaan where his family would be made a great nation. Abraham, however, passed several years in Syria along the way, and his delay is often used (correctly) to illustrate how Christians may get sidetracked (see Genesis 11:31; Luke 9:57–60). There is, however, no doctrine in the Word of God requiring that one abandon his family.

Two principles here require brief consideration:

First, when the children are growing up, parents and grandparents should not live in the same household, ordinarily. A man is to "leave his father and mother"; not abandon them, but leave the house. Marriage "establishes a new household, with a new center of gravity, which should lead to an alteration in . . . primary allegiances," notes *World* writer Douglas Wilson.[9] No wife should be required to live in her mother-in-law's shadow, and adult disagreements and bickering on matters such as child discipline can leave children confused.

Some families, but by no means all, are indeed called of God to move to other states or even foreign lands for the purpose of the ministry of the gospel. In the case of my own family, after I spent three years in a pastorate, the Lord opened the door to a teaching position and further education in Indiana, a thousand miles from my parents' home in Maine. The tie breaking was difficult, in part because my father had passed away a year earlier at age 51. But my wife, two children, and I made the move to a city where one of my brothers already lived. A year later, Mother and her three children still at home followed. Now my kids had Grandma living just around the block, and their Michigan grandparents were able to visit often.

We have moved several times since to follow the Lord in varied Christian ministries: to Michigan, North Carolina, back to Maine, and finally to settle again in Michigan, near the children's maternal grandmother until her death, and a four-hour drive from their other grandmother in Indiana.

The cycle for our family has gone full circle, and Dot and I now have four grandchildren just blocks from our home. Though my daughter's family is four hours away in Indiana, where her husband teaches in a Christian school, our Indiana grandchildren have Great-Grandma Wiggin nearby, along with my two unmarried sisters who love playing "grandma." Parents must always weigh their own circumstances, trusting the Lord to provide surrogate grandparents if, for instance, He calls them to serve Him in Africa.

The Lord leads, and He sometimes intervenes in our "best-laid plans." But as we build our homes—whether a retirement home or a home for still-at-home children—plan with keeping the extended family together in mind. And when great-grandma and great-grandpa can no longer care for themselves, we who are younger grandparents, whose own children have left, married, and left us with empty rooms, should give serious thought to taking them in.

> *Opportunities often exist for surrogate grandparenting, if we would only open our eyes and hearts to them.*

During our five years living in coastal New England, with our four children ages 2 through 14—ages 7 through 19 when we left—I owned a rototiller, but I had no garden plot. An elderly widow from our church lived nearby, and she had a large backyard of rich soil, but only a small garden and no tiller. I arranged with her to allow me to till up her yard, where we both could garden with the help of my youngsters.

This lady soon became "Grammy Jackson" to my kids, though she had some two dozen grandchildren of her own. Adding my four to her multitude of grandkids did not crowd her schedule, and my children learned to appreciate and love a person of age and wisdom, though both their grandmothers were then a thousand miles away in the Midwest.

My five-year-old rural Texas granddaughter's maternal grandparents live an hour's drive away in the big city of Dallas. We see our second son's girl only once or twice a year, since our home in Michigan is a two-day auto drive away. But a dear, godly Southern grandmother who lives in a small vine-covered home just around the corner on a graveled country road has become Grandma Granger to our precious Erica.

Offering yourself as a surrogate grandparent must be done

quietly, with tact, but with an open heart and home. It may begin with giving a neighbor's kids a ride to Sunday school, offering them milk and cookies, or by Grandpa fixing a swing set for the family next door.

All too easily we fret, "I don't mind spending money or time on my *own* grandkids." We may forget that when we selflessly give of our resources to build spiritual values into the lives of other's children, we lay up treasures in heaven—real jewels—and make the world a better place for our own grandchildren's generation to boot (see Matthew 6:19–21; Malachi 3:17; Matthew 19:13–15).

Young families with children in your church, if they are isolated from their children's grandparents, may appreciate being included in a holiday backyard cookout. Or you might relieve the harried mother of a newborn by taking the older children to the zoo, accepting no pay. Churches near Christian colleges, for instance, often have married students in their congregations with children in need of grandparenting.

Competition from homeschools, Christian day schools, and alternative schools has caused many public schools to become more family friendly. Many now open their doors to volunteer helpers—usually mothers or grandmothers—who quietly slip into the classroom to help with seat work or extracurricular activities. Foster Grandparents, a federal program, works through private social service agencies, as well as both Catholic and evangelical churches, to put grandparents in schools as teachers' aides. Grandparents are paid a small salary for giving loving attention—sometimes to their own grandchildren, I learned while working as a fourth-grade substitute teacher.

And Kids' Hope, sponsored by International Aid, in Spring Lake, Michigan, works through evangelical churches to place Christian workers—many of them grandmothers—into public schools. Kids' Hope volunteers are given training, then assigned a child with emotional, social, or academic problems to tutor. Though no proselytizing is permitted on school grounds, Kids' Hope workers usually invite the child, with his parents, to their homes and to church, as well as to attend special Kids' Hope programs put on by the sponsoring congregation.

The opportunities to grandparent the children of families in your church or nearby school, often isolated by miles or other circumstances from their own senior members, are abundant—as big as your heart!

CHAPTER FIVE

Grandfather's Mountain: The Homestead Model

Walton's Mountain is where all the good things happen, where the family always sticks together, where everything always turns out right, according to the old TV serial. "Give me this mountain" as a reward for my service to God's people, said old Caleb (Joshua 14:12, KJV). Caleb's Mount Hebron became the possession of his heirs in perpetuity.

Many grandfathers can and should establish a family homestead, a "Mountain," where their children can bring the grandchildren. Yet many of today's youngsters are robbed of the privilege of going to Grandma's House or Grandfather's Mountain because their grandparents have retired to Florida or Arizona, leaving the grandchildren with no Mountain as a refuge.

In readying Grandfather's Mountain (or Grandmother's Mountain, if Grandpa is no longer living) for the enjoyment and nurture of grandchildren, an accessible location is much more important than spacious accommodations. I have visited many such Mountains over the years, for grandparents who are hospitable toward their grandchildren tend to be big-hearted men and women who open their homes to others. One such Mountain was a small house at the dead end of an older residential street in the midst of a bustling city. A small, undeveloped field, the property of an industrial plant the next street over, lay just outside the grandfather's back door. So, with the permission of the plant's manager, this grandpa tended a large garden there for many years, and he kept much of the area mowed so that his grandchildren, who visited from their homes on the city's outskirts, could romp and play.

Some grandfathers, because of their lifestyles, have built up these family Mountains during their younger years so they could be used to build family relationships later on in their life. Others, when they reach their mid-to-late 40s, must plan carefully, lest this greatest blessing of their golden years, the fellowship of their grandchildren, slip from them. In the case of the grandfather on the dead-end street, he had reared four children in this home. As he reached retirement, with time on his hands, he took up gardening. The empty lot was available, and the other circumstances of life, such as having grand-children nearby, just seemed to fall into place naturally.

Jim and Shirley Franks raised 10 children, four of them adopted Korean orphans, in a house at a busy in-town intersec-tion. We had "all the noise and everything, and I really craved to get away from it," remembers Grandpa Franks. So the Franks bought a home on 10 wooded acres running back to a muddy lake, just outside the small Midwest city where they'd raised their own children. "I did this specifically for my grandkids," says Jim (there are 25 of them now, newborn to young adult).

"The grandkids can row a boat, swim, help in the garden, run— do whatever they want out here," Jim says, and you can certainly tell this gives him pleasure as you hear him say it.

Over the years, Jim and Shirley have added several wings to what was once a modest ranch-style lakeside house, all aimed at accommodating grandchildren who've come from as far as Japan and Africa, or who live only minutes away. Jim is an expert horticulturist who's served with several missionary relief organizations over the years, and his garden and small orchard give small hands the opportunity for satisfying hands-on experiences under Grandpa's supervision.

Not all retirement homes turn out as happily as the Franks's, however. Christian grandparents Joe and Alice Hayden (names and certain details have been changed for privacy) responded to the old adage that "you can take a boy out of the country, but you can't take the country out of the boy." Joe took early retirement from his city job, and he bought a farm in Minnesota, near where he'd grown up, and where Joe and Alice and their three boys had vacationed on occasion. Their retirement home, however, was hundreds of miles from the children and eight grandchildren, all of whom had settled near the city where they'd been raised.

Joe reasoned that he'd get to see his grandchildren on the occasions when their parents vacationed in Minnesota. Perhaps he could augment this by sending the grandkids an occasional bus ticket to their backwoods community. But the children and grandchildren usually preferred vacations at Disney World or the beach to the Minnesota forest. Even on holidays, it was Grandpa and Grandma who were forced to make an all-day drive to see their family.

But Joe Hayden poured his savings and energy into building up a run-down farm. The sheep and beef cattle he herded on woodland pastures barely paid for themselves, but Joe was enjoying fixing fences, repairing the barn and house, and tending his livestock. A collie, which became his daily companion, rode beside him in the Jeep as Joe checked on cattle in the back pastures.

But in a dozen years, Joe's health failed. He was forced to sell the farm. Oh, he might merely have auctioned off the cattle and machinery and stayed put. But Alice missed the grandchildren. To tell the truth, now that health constraints had forced him to slow down, Joe longed for his family also.

They moved back to their old neighborhood. The Lord was gracious, and He enabled them to find a house with a spacious lot, and Joe, still a farmer at heart, planted fruit trees and a large garden. The Haydens tried to take up where they'd left off. But they couldn't. The grandchildren, all toddlers and preschoolers when their grandparents had moved to Minnesota, were now teens.

Joe and Alice entertained their three families from time to time. Sometimes they would have all-adult parties. But on occasion, one or more of the grandchildren would accompany their parents to Grandpa and Grandma's house, only to slip away to their cars as soon as they were done eating in order to spend time with their teen friends.

"In his heart a man plans his course, but the Lord determines his steps" is the advice of Solomon, who had a very large family indeed (Proverbs 16:9). As we grow older, many of us see retirement as a chance to work out unfulfilled longings: for some, life under Florida palms, fishing, golfing, touring—or for others, a

return to childhood roots, perhaps to farm. Any of these retirement pursuits are fine in themselves, but as we "plan our course"
it's all too easy to take self-directed "steps," rather than heeding
the Lord's direction. If farming, for example, is what you desire,
can you find a farm near enough so that you can enjoy both your
Herefords *and* your grandchildren? Might it not be possible to
satisfy your craving for Florida sunshine by spending a few weeks
there in a camping trailer in the dead of winter, then returning
to Grandfather's Mountain for the rest of the year?

Children and grandchildren are spoken of in the Bible as
a "reward" of the righteous, and as the "crown" of the elderly
(Psalm 127:3–5; Proverbs 17:6). We too easily blame the
young for their wayward ways, yet often we're so far away we
can't nurture them, encouraging our grandchildren to hold the
values we cherish.

Christian grandfathers who would help turn the tide of
rootless youth can build a Mountain where their grandchildren
can retreat for shelter. But don't expect every one of your
grandchildren to realize they *need* this shelter from the storms
of life. *You* provide it; invite them often while they're still
small, and they'll find their way there when they're in their
teens, or are young marrieds with children of their own, bringing blessing to the fourth generation.

Here are some suggestions for building your own Mountain:

 ### *Don't tie up a lot of money in a large or expensive house.*

Pay off your mortgage in 15 years or so. Then, if in late middle age you have an urge to relocate, you can do so with

grandchildren in mind, and with the ability to pay cash for the new home. This will leave you with resources to renovate with an eye to entertaining the family.

 Consider staying put.

Most grandpas today don't own country homes, of course, and perhaps only a few can hope to own such a place when they retire. But a small house on a large lot in a quiet, older neighborhood may be exactly what you need. Add a deck where you can have a barbecue. Enclose a porch, then add a studio couch where a grandchild can sleep. Install a swing set and a sandbox in the backyard. A basketball hoop next to a paved drive will keep preteen and teen boys busy for hours. Lay in a supply of lawn games, such as badminton, volleyball, croquet, and horseshoes.

Most any home in an urban or suburban neighborhood can be adjusted, at modest expense, to accommodate grandkids. If you don't have room to expand or can't afford to add a wing, consider turning your attached garage into a family room or extra bedroom. The garage door framing can be left in place, in case a subsequent owner wishes to return it to garage use. Though making an unattached garage into living quarters may violate zoning codes, such buildings nevertheless make great places to set up Ping-Pong or pool tables, and insulation and a gas heater can make them usable even in cold weather. If codes permit, a hutch of rabbits or even a small coop of chickens will give the small ones endless fascination. And perhaps you might run an underground electrical cable and cold water line to the back fence so that family members with camping trailers can park there on occasion.

Purchase a large, newer mobile home.

Many well-kept, modern trailer parks for seniors have recreation and banquet halls to rent for a modest fee. If a swimming pool and game courts are adjacent, all the better. Two grandparents, the parents of seven married children living in the Midwest, found such accommodations on the edge of a Michigan city when their home proved inadequate to entertain their more than two dozen grandkids. Their mobile home's extra bedroom and bath will accommodate one of their out-of-town families for a short stay, or two or more grandchildren for as long as the grandparents care to keep them. But the rec hall, rented for a holiday, birthday, or a grandchild's graduation party, rings with the merry laughter of the grandchildren several times a year, and in summer the small ones splash in the adjacent pool.

Purchase a country home, if that is your urge ("desire," Psalm 37:4).

A diligent search may turn up a livable old farmhouse with a few acres just outside the city where you now live. Such arrangements are far more versatile than a house in a subdivision, though it's easy to spend a bundle on fixing up such a place if you are the kind of person who must have everything flawlessly decorated. Here's where a grandfather handy with tools can double his family's benefits. Financially, the family gains as he does his own repairs and remodeling. And he establishes bonds with grandchildren as he teaches them self-sufficient skills while they work with him in building a rabbit hutch or painting the porch.

 ## Grandfather's Mountain need not be a principal residence.

A retired couple in Maine, both of whom worked at a Christian summer children's camp near their married children, parked their camping trailer on a lakefront cottage lot next to the camp. Soon they built a cottage shell around the camper, thus adding a living room, bedrooms, and a screened porch—all of which are filled with grandchildren much of the summer. These grandparents, giving of themselves in their retirement years to help the children of others, found themselves, in turn, helping and enjoying their own grandchildren. As with the Franks, they set an example of selfless service their children and grandchildren could follow.

 ## Grandfather's Mountain should include a workshop, if possible.

Preteen and teen boys are attracted to productive, creative adult activity. The visits I remember best to my grandfather's house, or to the homes of friends' grandfathers, involved creative male activity (though girls often love it, too!).

I remember standing sneaker-top deep in the pine shavings of Grandpa Fuller's woodworking shop, or watching Uncle Raymond (himself a grandfather) roll a pine log into the blade of his sawmill, a "toy" he'd bought at retirement. At family reunions my brothers, cousins, and I would explore Great-Uncle Willie's marvelous wood- and mechanical shop until rebuked by fearful parents. A grandfather of my acquaintance has turned his two-car garage into an auto service shop popular with his grandsons. Still another grandfather has set up a fish-fly-tying bench in a small toolshed behind his house, where grandsons and grand-nephews sometimes congregate to learn his art.

One of my earliest memories is going with my father to visit what was possibly the last blacksmith shop in our state. Elderly John Harding, soot-covered, in leather apron, took Daddy's iron bolts and heated them cherry red in his forge. He pounded them into angles on his anvil, then quenched them in a barrel of water.

A child has little appreciation for nostalgia. So I can say assuredly that my appreciation then of the old blacksmith's work was in having the creativity born in me from God drawn out by this unusual (to me) creative activity. As magnetic iron attracts iron, so the soul of a child, created in God's image to be creative, is attracted by creativity (see Genesis 1:27).

The possibilities for workshops are endless, from hobbies to serious adult employment. It strengthens a growing youth's grasp on reality and fires his creativity to see a grandfather at productive activity as well as at play.

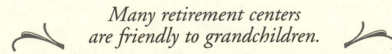

Many retirement centers are friendly to grandchildren.

Thousands of grandparents who have moved into townhouses or condominiums in retirement centers have found them accommodating to visiting grandchildren. Bill and Joyce Gerig are resident managers at the Glencroft Retirement Community, a Mennonite ministry for folks over 62, near Phoenix. Glencroft's parent organization also operates a retirement center near Fort

Wayne, Indiana, just miles from where Bill and Joyce once lived with their family. Similar retirement apartment complexes are now found near population centers nationwide.

Bill's parents, both past 90, now occupy an assisted living apartment at Glencroft, after living 20 years there in a condominium. So when Bill and Joyce's four grandchildren—ages 1 to 10—visit Grandpa and Grandma Gerig, Great-Grandpa and Great-Grandma Gerig are nearby to visit also.

Most Glencroft condominiums have two bedrooms, besides a pullout sofa, so grandkids "can come and stay as long as they want," Bill said. For larger visiting families, Glencroft has rooms to rent and even several efficiency apartments available for guests. Glencroft, like the trailer complex in Michigan, has a swimming pool as well as a large activity room, which the residents can rent for large, multigenerational parties.

Another manager couple, Bruce and Becky Lemmen, take their family to Glencroft's dining hall whenever they visit, where guest meals are half restaurant prices. Many Glencroft residents—average age 85—have grandchildren in and about the city of Phoenix who visit them weekly. One resident, a great-grandmother, baby-sits almost daily. "I don't see any limitations" to interaction with grandchildren as long as you choose a retirement center near your family, Bill Gerig remarked.

Some grandfathers cannot build a Mountain for their grandchildren.

Perhaps you are limited by financial constraints, or a divorce may have disjointed your family, leaving the family's resources limited and ties with children's families badly strained. Partial solutions in these cases can be found by renting facilities at public parks for weekend outings. Many communities have municipally owned banquet rooms or halls; or the local VFW or other civic organization may have rooms available for a modest fee. Churches can help by permitting families of limited means to use the church's fellowship hall and kitchen, following the example of early Christians (see Acts 2:44–47).

My own experience with Grandfather's Mountain takes a chapter right out of *The Waltons*. In fact, there were several Mountains in my childhood that served as refuges and places where I could enjoy adult companionship and mature words of wisdom. My mother's parents' New England country inn, already more than a century old at my birth, pops up in several places in this book, so I'll not describe it here. I'll say only that I would sometimes purposely miss the school bus, then enjoy a long talk with my grandmother as an interlude in a three-mile walk home. Mother's uncle, an elderly widower who was a trapper, lived a mile farther along our graveled road. Since his eyes were weak and he could not drive, I could usually find Uncle Oscar reading with a magnifying glass beside his wood-fired parlor stove, ready to regale my young imagination with tales of shooting a bobcat or trapping a bear.

My dad's elder sister, a schoolteacher not blessed with children of her own, lived with her husband in a Cape Cod house with its long ell attached to a barn in the style of upper New England. Aunt Gladys, who was also a pastry cook at a summer resort, made the best raspberry pie a boy ever tasted from berries that grew half wild behind their horse stable. Her pies more than once enticed me to fill a lard pail with berries without pay, braving the briars and the hornets that lurked among them to gather my reward.

The mountain I remember best is the rambling, Victorian farmhouse built by Grandpa Wiggin in 1899–1900. He came with his parents in 1869 to what for a century was our family's homestead, where they lived in a Cape Cod farmhouse built some 30 years earlier. Shortly after Grandpa built the house where my father and I were both born and grew up, the old Cape Cod burned, though its circa-1840 barn stood until I grew into adulthood.

Grandpa built his house rather large for the family of three he raised there, and the upstairs was not completely finished until his children were adults. His two sons later found room there for upstairs apartments, where several of their children were born; and a fourth generation—my first two—lived there, also, for a time.

Over the years, I explored every nook and cranny of this quarter-section, Maine-hillside farm of about 160 acres. I learned every square inch of the house, barn, and horse stable —bereft of horses and converted into a machine shop by my father and uncle. Probably to a greater extent than my dad, who as the youngest son of older parents grew up without grandparents, I learned on that Mountain to appreciate the continuity of life, coupled with the practicality of small things. I learned, for example, to treasure the hours of sultry August afternoons, when on the screened back porch next to a grove of towering white pines hand-planted by Grandpa Wiggin I would snap beans by the bushel for Mother's canner, or pare apples for pies and sauce. And, after winter hours on Saturday helping Grandpa split and stack stove wood, I learned to listen, or would ply him with questions, as he talked beside our wood-burning kitchen range of events and people long ago. He used terms a small boy could relate to, sometimes punctuating his discourse with words of wisdom from experience or proverbs from the Bible.

Grandfathers should take the lead in preparing a homestead where the grandkids can visit, a Mountain of shelter from the storms of growing up. Too often, the initiative is left to Grandma, who must work around Grandpa's TV ball games, his golf outings, his hunting and fishing trips, or his just not wanting to be bothered by children. But grandfathers have a responsibility not only to make provision for grandchildren, but also to encourage grandmas to invite them over, and to make themselves available for loving interaction with the grandkids. Instead of going fishing alone, take a grandchild with you. Encourage grandchildren to help in your garden. Fix their bikes; then let them learn and gain confidence as they help you change the oil or spark plugs in your car.

One teen girl, deeply hurt by her parents' divorce, had determined never to date or marry boys. But after spending a few days with her loving, Christian grandparents, not only seeing them interact with love toward each other, but observing that they kept romance alive—even to smooching on the back porch swing in the moonlight—she had a complete reversal in her attitude.

God gives grandparents to grandkids largely, I believe, because parents are imperfect. We grandparents can be there to fill the gaps in our children's attention toward their own children. We can furnish our grandchildren with mature role models as we lend them our sympathetic adult ears to listen when their parents are preoccupied with other pursuits. This attention shows them they are important to adults who love them, and it gives them confidence to step forward into maturity. Each grandfather should seek to erect his own Mountain where these ends may be carried out—a Mountain that, if possible, Grandma or Grandpa can continue in a scaled-down version after the other is gone.

CHAPTER SIX

When Grandmas and Grandpas Were Old

One day I passed an old man on a bicycle. It was a battered, fat-tired velocipede of the kind popular when I was a kid. The fellow wore a crumpled felt hat and ragged pants tied at the cuffs with rubber bands that made his unshined brown dress shoes all the more conspicuous, the uppers cracked, soles peeling off. A battered lunch box was wired to his handlebars.

One day I passed an old man on a bicycle. His shock of snow-white hair was sharply accented by a cranberry jogging suit. Lime-green tennis shoes adorned the feet that spun the pedals of his new, 15-speed touring bike as he breezed along with a red Irish setter loping behind.

Time was, grandparents on bikes looked as odd as the poor fellow in the first paragraph. Though my grandfather once said he could ride a bicycle, I'd never seen him on one, and I'm sure I'd have laughed had he tried mine. Grandparents in the 1940s were supposed to be staid, dignified, sensible.

I asked Shirley Franks, a grandmother from the era described in newsman Tom Brokaw's book as "the greatest generation," if she recalled when grandmas were old. "Grandmas wore navy blue, then," she laughed, patting her white polyester slacks, "navy blue and polka dots for variety. At least they had more choices than the men!"

This matriarch of more than two dozen grandchildren ranging from newborn to young adult told of sitting on her own grandmother's lap. "I pulled the skin on the back of Grandma's hand. It was loose," she said, "like mine today." She tugged a loose fold on the back of her own hand. " 'Grandma, you're *old*,' I said," she merrily recalled. "Grandmas today look for the misses' department when we buy our clothes!"

This observation points up some very subtle changes in our culture that we've adjusted to pretty much without understanding what's happened. Some of these changes have been for the good, and others are a part of a dangerous social subculture. If as grandparents we are to affect following generations for the good, we need to understand the influences that have changed—not just our choices in clothing, but our total lifestyles—and adjust our thinking to embrace the good and resist the bad.

 The cult of youth culture is a mark of our age.

A rush toward modernization has been a part of the industrialized Western world since well back in the nineteenth century, but it accelerated after World War II. For example, synthetic fabrics and colorfast dyes led to a rampage of avant-garde clothing experiments in the 1950s and 1960s. A backlash against industry brought a move toward natural and organic products in the late 1960s and 1970s. But the 1980s and 1990s brought a mellowing and blending of these trends, and now in the twenty-first century clothing is usually a blend of synthetic and natural fabrics. It is neither a reflection of the slick 1950s nor the saggy 1970s, but a happy mixture of the best of both.

The millennia-old beliefs that the old should advise the young and that the elderly should let their bodies age, concentrating sensibly on improving their souls and minds, has been reversed in a generation. Physical culture is the fad of our age. Breast implants, liposuction operations, and surgical wrinkle removal are openly advertised on TV. Daily regimens of weight lifting, biking, and jogging have become the rage. Many grandfathers while away their evenings watching well-muscled youths chase an inflated pigskin across a field of Astroturf. Not to be outdone, the grannies spend hours imitating the antics of acrobatic aerobics instructors.

Is there a balance? I think so.

 Grandparents should lead.

We grandparents must first firmly retake the lead, if not of society as a whole, at least of our own families. This is not as drastic a step as it may seem, for the pendulum has begun to swing the other way, and maturity is coming into fashion again. Andy Griffith has been reworked as sagacious, silver-locked Ben Matlock. In Christian circles, Billy Graham, past 80, is still the most admired man in America, and Jack Wyrtzen, until his recent death well past 80, was beloved as a leader of youth and older folks alike. Congress, in early 2000 responded to the ambitions of millions of older folks to continue working past age 65 without reduction in Social Security benefits.

For most of us, however, the point where the tire touches the asphalt is facing our personal crisis with aging. Midlife crisis, Christian psychologist and author Dr. Kevin Leman told me, affects women, "not just men. Particularly, women who have been in the corporate side of life are bailing out." Menopause is a crisis of its own for many women, for which Leman suggests medical help. But Leman sees the circumstances many workers of both sexes past 40 find themselves in, coupled with frustrated feelings that one's job is merely "beating my head against the wall," as the real issues.

Say you're 50-something, you have spent a quarter of a century climbing your company's promotion ladder, then your department is reorganized and you're out looking for work. In the next few days you face several dozen receptionists who you swear could be schoolmates of your teen granddaughter. The several personnel managers whom you do get interviews with impress you as having as much maturity as Jerry Lewis in an old Martin and Lewis comedy. It's not long before you've begun to view yourself as on the way to imitating that old man in the cracked shoes on the fat-tired bicycle.

Or take a more mundane scenario: Your job is secure, but that's all that can be said for it. No more promotions await you, and years earlier you reached a plateau of efficiency past which it seems you have little to learn in this company.

 So, what is money for?

Subtle, but also deadly to becoming a godly grandparent, is yielding to the temptation to flaunt one's financial success. We may buy a larger auto or a fancy motor home—with a bumper sticker boasting, "I'm spending my grandchildren's inheritance!"—or even a new set of golf clubs; not because we need the extra room to entertain our families, the big vehicle to take them picnicking, or the set of clubs so that we can fellowship with our teen grandkids on the golf course. Too often, it's our way of showing the neighbors how successful we are. And it's a means to prove to ourselves that we're not getting older, just better. After all, the ads tell us, we've worked hard—we "deserve" a $40,000 luxury car.

The agrarian society that most of America left behind by the middle of the twentieth century had built-in cushions so that old folks could just be old without feeling cheated out of life's rewards. My dad, who was born in 1916, recalled that when he was a child a man was expected to grow a beard and walk with a cane when he reached 50—whether he needed one or not. There was a dignity then that came with age in an era when you could still find a hoary-headed Civil War veteran among the codgers on the park bench in the town square. A man of mature years can achieve significance in an agricultural setting, where the success of his farming operation is apparent, and where his children are about him, offering support and encouragement in a more tangible way than in today's urban, mobile culture.

My paternal grandfather, for example, at age 69 turned the reins of the farm operation over to my dad. From then on, until his death at 84, Grandpa could view with pride his son's success in managing the farm his father had built, as they lived together, surrounded by children and grandchildren in the house Grandpa had built before Dad's birth—and where both lived until they died.

My grandmothers, too, though both had worked for a time outside the home as schoolteachers, were comfortable in their acceptance of maturity and in becoming grandmothers. Their lives centered on their homes, their kitchens, their husbands, their children, their families. When the constraints of age made it impossible for them to do heavy housework or to help in their husbands' farming or storekeeping, they could knit and sew in their rockers without any basic change in occupations. They were *still* housewives. For them, with their extended family nearby, there *was* no crisis.

 ## Retire? Really?

There's a lesson here. Men or women in middle age, just beginning to become grandparents, should take stock of how they can honestly expect to spend the next 30 or 40 years. This is not presuming on God. Rather, it's making plans subject to God's right to change our direction, saying, "If it is the Lord's will" (James 4:15). With the life expectancy of most Christians of either sex who've lived to become grandparents now past 80, the prudent grandparent considers that the future may hold 30 or 40 years for him yet.

For some facing midlife crisis, one solution may be in starting a business, suggests Leman, speaking to the readers of this book. Such a person "shows the grandchildren that in America you can go out on your own and do something entrepreneurial," he says, noting that control over one's schedule and the satisfaction of building a business is "a good trade-off" for making less money than at a salaried job.

Special training to develop latent skills will make your

services valuable through middle age, on into old age. One lady I know developed her talents as a seamstress, and eventually she was making custom-tailored suits out of her home. When her fingers became too stiff to operate a sewing machine, she ran a small business supplying coffee and doughnuts at break time to industrial plants nearby.

A farmer, past retirement age, sold his herd of milk cows. He continued to raise market crops, but his winter months were idle, so he took up an avocation he'd abandoned half a century earlier—repairing radios. After a home-study course in TV repair, he easily landed a job repairing stereos and TVs with a repair service. Free from having to milk his herd seven days a week, he and his wife now often traveled to visit grandchildren, yet he had a paycheck to carry him through lean times. Former President Jimmy Carter, 76, builds houses for others under the Habitat for Humanity program, writes books, and teaches a Sunday school class.

With worldwide Internet connections available to most Americans, home-based sales opportunities exist that our grandparents could not have dreamed of. Maureen Newell, a Maine grandmother of three, purchased a computerized electronic knitting machine as well as a computer with Internet connections to research sweater patterns. Several pricey boutiques are her customers, and she has all the seasonal work she can handle. The key to a rewarding mature-life career is often in filling a niche with your experience and unique talents—the list for the enterprising entrepreneur is endless.

"Why do we work, and under what circumstances should we stop?" queries Timothy Lamer, writing in *World*. Lamer believes it is often good to "retire" as a means to change careers, but "skills are gifts from God . . . to be used for the good of others," he affirms. "Productivity," Lamer writes, "is our calling."[1] Experience and increased competence often put the older person, like the fabled tortoise, well ahead of youth in the workplace. It's up to each of us to discover where we can best use these heightened abilities to the glory of our Creator.

 Sexual temptation is no stranger to grandparents.

Several temptations await the grandparent caught in midlife crisis, some of which, once yielded to, can have lifelong reverberations. King David, when he ought to have been finding his significance in leading his troops into battle, found himself spying on a young woman taking a bath, with whom he subsequently committed adultery (see 2 Samuel 11:1–4). Elijah the prophet, victorious over the priests of Baal, so mighty in prayer that God withheld or sent rain at his request, found himself in the midst of depression, alone under a juniper tree, wanting to die. The euphoria of success was gone. Elijah took his eyes off the Lord and focused on his circumstances—a woman, Queen Jezebel, wanted his life—and he drew into himself in self-pity.

"Women need to know that men need a lot of reaffirming," says Dr. Kevin Leman. "The physical area of life during those midlife years" needs attention. "Women need it, as well," he affirms. Older women "should accept the fact that they want . . . and enjoy" sex, says Phoebe Jane Osborne, 85, a family life educator in Greenwich, Connecticut.[2] The whole tenor of the Bible regarding sex is that its main purpose is intimacy, as opposed to pleasure or procreation. Older men who find themselves longing for pretty young women (however dressed or undressed) may actually be vainly seeking to rediscover their own youth. The woman with the most sex appeal to an older man will be the wife God gave him 30, 40, or 50 years ago, if he has taken the lead in developing intimacy in marriage and has modeled his marriage after Christ's relationship to the church (see Ephesians 5:31–32).

It's all too easy for couples to grow apart as they age, especially if they move in different circles due to job circumstances. Bitterness and habitual crankiness may ensue. Loving, joyful sexual relations become seldom. Adultery may follow, as one or the other spouse seeks to reaffirm his or her youth and personal worth in an exciting, attentive bed partner. Divorce is the final step, after which little is left that we can give the grandchildren, for we seem to have proven ourselves unable to be "more than conquerors" in Christ (Romans 8:37).

This is not to say that those grandparents who have been divorced in the past must accept defeat. God will renew opportunities to minister to our grandchildren as we follow Him.

We too easily blame teens for sexual promiscuity, forgetting that our culture has placed its satanic lust traps where Christians of all ages, grandparents included, can fall into them. Occasionally, in walking through the fields of life, I trip over a stone, and while nursing a bruised toe, I observe the vermin that crawl out from underneath the stone. One such "stone" caught my attention as I picked up a magazine in a library intending to read an article featured on the cover. An ad for men's trousers portrayed a lean, gray-haired, craggy-faced, 60-something male model on a chaise lounge. Seated at his feet was a girl of perhaps 19. Pouting, voluptuous, and spilling out of her chemise, she awaited his attention.

Feeling sorry for yourself, Grandpa? Buy yourself a new pair of slacks. Fantasize while you wear them. The message was too obvious to miss.

Nor do grandmas escape sexual traps. As a substitute teacher, I found a girl of 14 reading a book from the public library, "with my mother's permission," she said. If the pornographic, explicit sex in that book is typical of today's popular fiction (and it is), grandmas who read such books—or watch soap operas—must kick over quite a few stones.

Not that out-and-out adultery is the only consequence of feeding one's mind on this stuff. How many millions of couples have their relationship harmed by sins of the heart and mind that are an offense to the Lord! The sexual references in the Song of Solomon, by contrast, are designed to lead couples closer together.

Walk close to the Lord if you would walk close with your spouse.

After Jack Wyrtzen was widowed he married a widow, Joan. Together, the Wyrtzens found themselves with 21 grandchildren spread across two continents. In an interview for the grandparents who read this book, Jack said that the secret of spouses maintaining harmonious relationships and victory over temptation is a regular, daily quiet time where God speaks to us through His Word and we speak to God in prayer.

Half a century ago a smiling, handsome young evangelist turned from eating supper in a Maine farmhouse to sign his name and jot down a Scripture reference in the autograph book of a teen boy, temporarily crippled by a hit-and-run driver. "Three chapters a day," he wrote with a flourish of a fountain pen after noting, "Phil. 2:16."

That evangelist signed his name "Jack Wyrtzen." I was that boy. I confess there have been lapses in that regimen. But two decades ago at 40, when I found myself, an English teacher and former preacher, out of work because of the closing of the college where I taught, it was the Word, particularly the books of Job and Psalms, that sustained me in my personal crisis.

Avoid focusing on the constraints of your aging process if you wish to be a positive role model for your grandchildren. It's not enough merely to avoid complaining about your aches and pains to others. Instead, focus on the opportunities maturity has brought you. Here are some examples:

Retirement brings greater opportunity to do good to others.

"I spent the first 65 years of my life working for myself and my family. Now I'm trying to do things for others," Marion Lahr told me. When I met him, Lahr, widowed two years earlier and retired from many years as a mechanical engineer, was rejoicing in the Lord as he served as construction engineer for the Dandya Leprosarium near Maradi, a remote town in Niger, in sub-Saharan Africa. His full life since his year as a short-term missionary with SIM International has included supervising housing construction for Habitat for Humanity and singing with Twelve Men of Praise. In recent years, many evangelical missions have refocused their ministries to make wider use of mature workers on temporary assignment.

Helping those in genuine need helps you avoid becoming a doting grandparent, spoiling grandchildren with unappreciated gifts. Not a few grandparents have been disappointed when a grandson or granddaughter abused a car the grandparents gave them, wasted a gift of money, or wrecked an expensive garment intended for special occasions. The grandparent who seeks to meet genuine needs will not be thought indulgent and will learn to lovingly tailor his giving to real needs, as the Lord lays them on his heart.

I recall that one of the last letters I ever received from my grandmother contained a check for $10. I was a senior in college, and my grandfather, her husband of 45 years, had died months earlier. The money was the tithe of Grandpa's $100 life insurance policy. The only other gift I can specifically recall receiving from her was a modestly expensive flannel shirt when I was in the seventh grade. I had never owned a "store-boughten" shirt, except hand-me-downs, and I had requested this for my birthday. Grandma was not an indulgent woman, but she was giving. The life insurance money from my newly widowed grandmother was received like an alabaster box of precious ointment, I assure you.

 Romance is another hedge against growing old.

If your spouse is living, keep your love romantic by doing special things for him or her daily. Read the Song of Solomon together. Go for walks together. Plan times away from home when just the two of you can be together. We too easily wish to include other family members in affairs that ought to be private, forgetting that it's out of times together that the ability to confidently relate to our grandchildren arises.

When we become too busy to go off for a weekend in a motel, to rent a boat for a leisurely Saturday ride, or to stop at that special ice cream parlor—just the two of us—for an unhurried cone, relationships tend to unravel. As a young pastor in rural Maine I was called to visit in the home of an elderly couple, where the wife's mother had just died. The aged matriarch was laid out in her coffin in a small bedroom off the parlor. After the gray-haired wife, herself past 70, had ushered me by her mother's casket, I inquired politely, "How old was your mother?"

"Ninety-three."

"I'm sorry you lost her," I answered.

"'Bout time!" growled the son-in-law from his seat in the corner. This gentleman, nearly 80, had suffered for years under not having his wife to himself. Not given to creative ways of finding time alone with his wife, he was relieved, for what then seemed to me selfish reasons, that she could now give him some attention.

Neither husband nor wife in this case had learned to cultivate the other's attention, I'm afraid. Saddled by circumstances, she had become a care-worn old woman, and he an old grouch.

"At 85 I feel like a young man in my 30s or 40s," said Ivan Green. Ivan and his bride, Eva, 80, married after being widowed following marriages totaling more than one hundred years. They had had happy first marriages, and after their spouses had passed on, they had both kept busy making others happy. Eva was visiting friends in a nursing home when Ivan, a retired minister, came by to conduct a chapel service. After the service, Eva and Ivan were introduced. "He kissed me and swept me off my feet," recalls Eva.

Today the Greens are "like two teenagers in love," says one of Eva's daughters. Adds Eva, "We have a wonderful life together. We're still honeymooning."

Not all can remarry, certainly; nor should all remarry who can. But whether you have been with your mate 50 years or you're newlyweds of 50 weeks, keeping romance alive will help you live a positive, uplifting life before your grandchildren.

 Exercise is another hedge against growing old.

Fourteen million Americans past age 55 have discovered that walking will "produce a happier frame of mind," writes syndicated columnist Evelyn Sullivan. A brisk walk, says Sullivan, can release tension and stress, elevate moods, and help alleviate depression. Many grandparents who walk 30 minutes a day "insist that walking just makes them feel good," she says.

I took one of my granddaughters, then two, for a walk one day after her persistence dragged me from my easy chair. It was Sunday, and I'd spent the morning sitting in a pew, then sitting for dinner, then sitting to read. Her small legs moved at a trot while my long ones ambled at a leisurely pace. Soon, though, she spied the backyard swing and "Grandpa, push me!" was all her delight.

I returned refreshed from that stroll with little Katy. I'm

not sure if it was the exercise or the social interaction with my granddaughter that lifted my spirits. But I know I was six feet tall when I left for that walk. In Katy's estimation, I was seven feet tall when we returned.

Intellectual stimulation is another hedge against growing old.

The old adage "You can't teach an old dog new tricks" is true only when the dog refuses to learn.

Remko Slagter, 101, graduated from Fruitport (Michigan) High School 30 years after he retired from a career laying bricks. Slagter, whose native tongue is Dutch, immigrated to the U.S. from the Netherlands in 1910. He was 97 when he enrolled in high school, and he continued to take high school classes as a postgraduate student.

More than 1,600 colleges and universities and schools nationwide offer special courses for folks past 50, many of them free. For instance, the University of Delaware's Academy of Life-long Learning, in Wilmington, Delaware, has 2,000 students studying courses ranging from Beethoven to Understanding the Legal System. The school's former assistant coordinator, Robert Robinson, says that "instead of going to a nursing home, these people have decided to pursue learning and cultural aggrandizement." Student Roxana Arsht, 76, a retired judge, agrees. "We want to learn," says Arsht. "We're alive, and we don't want to get stale." Old minds not only don't get "stale" when they're regularly nourished by intellectual fodder; well-fed minds avoid the all-too-common condition of being left behind by the grandchildren when they become teens.

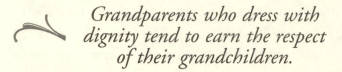 *Grandparents who dress with dignity tend to earn the respect of their grandchildren.*

In my mother's photo album, a palimpsest of family pictures stretching back more than a century, is a snapshot of my grandparents. Grandpa wears a three-piece suit of summer flannel in the photo, complete with high-laced dress shoes, his outfit topped with a straw boater. Grandma is wearing a rather fancy flowing dress, beads, and gloves; like Grandpa, she sports a straw hat, tied down with a silk scarf. They are seated on a blanket, a wicker picnic basket opened before them. This is no studio portrait. The picture, from about 1920, was taken on the beach!

The revolution in clothing styles since that photo was taken has more to do with the propriety of certain clothes to certain occasions than with actual style changes. Grandpa's suit of three-quarters of a century back would hardly turn a head in a business office or a church even today. But as beachwear?

As mature grandparents, though, we must consider more than style and propriety. We recognize that aging, often portly bodies require more subtle disguising with carefully arranged drapery than our grandchildren's lithe figures need. One advantage, though—we can spend more for our clothes and make them last longer!

Today's grandfathers *do* wear jogging suits when they exercise. Grandmas wear jeans and sneakers to picnics. They wear bathing suits on beaches. But the wise grandparent is perceptive enough to realize that certain clothes designed for the young are not suited for 50-somethings in public. A polo shirt can grotesquely accentuate a less-than-flat male belly, for instance.

A lady friend, who once ran a successful ladies' clothing

store in Manhattan, told me that the woman who wants to be thought a lady wears calf-length skirts in public. It was her opinion that pantsuits are for secretaries; business ladies of any age who wish to be taken seriously wear skirted suits. The same goes for a white or pinstriped shirt and tie for men in business.

A healthy sense of humor can insulate you from many illnesses.

Humor will not only open the hearts of your grandchildren, but it may enable you to live longer. "A merry heart doeth good like a medicine" (Proverbs 17:22, KJV) is advice Jack Wyrtzen, founder and, until past 80, director of Word of Life, a youth ministry, was fond of repeating.

Can you chuckle when 10-month-old Tessa dumps her Cheerios on your just-washed kitchen floor, as her mother, unperturbed, remarks dryly, "Your new wet 'n' dry vac'll take it up, Mom"? Do you maintain your ability to smile and smooth things over when your out-of-state families—with seven kids under age seven among them—have camped in your family room, living room, and master bedroom for three days over the Fourth of July? (You and Grandpa are bunking in your son-in-law's pop-up camper!) And can you keep your humor as you work with two recipes of pancake batter because the family from Ohio wants buckwheat in their flapjacks but the ones from Georgia abhor buckwheat and insist on corn-meal? Thankfully, the family from New Jersey eats them either way.

Is it true that folks who laugh a lot live longer, as Wyrtzen asserted? I know of no conclusive study, so I jotted down the names of a dozen comedians, past and present, in the order they occurred to me, with their current ages, or age at death. These are Milton Berle, 93; Red Skelton, 84; Jackie Gleason, 71; Bob Hope, 98; Jimmy Durante, 87; Art Carney, 82; Groucho Marx, 87; George Burns, 100; Lawrence Welk, 89 (Welk was a musician, but his joking manner is known to millions of grandparents); Minnie Pearl, 84; Arthur Godfrey, 80; Jack Benny, 80. Of those in this list who died youngest, three—Jackie Gleason, Jack Benny, and Minnie Pearl—had diabetes.

A grandfather of my acquaintance, a man who, like some in the list above, had several bad habits harmful to his health, spent many years as a Maine rural mail carrier. When he died, the entire community mourned him, for his habit of wisecracking with his patrons at their mailboxes had captured the hearts of his townsfolk. Past 80 at his death because of a stroke, Carl "Happy" Drake is likely his town's best-loved citizen a third of a century after he died. Importantly, Carl Drake, as well as the comedians mentioned, made *others* happy. A significant role of a grandparent is to give the grandchildren—and their parents—practical lessons in happiness.

I think I know now why I was so fond of my maternal grandmother, an affection that lasted from my childhood until her death, shortly after the birth of my eldest child, her first great-granddaughter. She was a quiet, unassuming woman, known for her kindness and generosity. And Grandma Fuller had a sense of humor. When she opened her mouth it was often in mirth, sometimes to tell a funny story like the one about the time her mother-in-law found a skunk robbing her henhouse and caught it by the tail. The poor woman bathed in tomato juice to remove the odor. But burying her clothes didn't kill the stink!

CHAPTER SEVEN

Things Not Found in Books

I can remember being warned as a child not to peek in Grandma's knitting bag during the weeks before Christmas. After the supper dishes were cleared away and we children were tucked in bed by Mother, Grandma would knit in her rocker. She made thick woolen socks and mittens—not the cheap, store-bought kind with loops inside to snag your fingers, but substantial stuff that would keep a fellow's hands warm even after an hour of throwing snowballs.

Grandma alone knew what was in her bag, and she kept it secret. And she knew how many knits and purls were needed to make a boy's mittens, though I never knew her to use a pattern. Like all good grandparents, mine knew a myriad of things, from practical skills such as knitting, to family tales passed down through generations, to spiritual truths learned in a life of maturing and growing in Christ.

Acceptance is an important secret grandparents can share with grandkids.

My wife tells how her grandmother taught her by example and precept to accept and love those with physical deformities. She learned not to laugh at an old man's stoop, nor shun a person with a missing limb, nor tease a child who stutters.

Uncle Willis, though not himself a grandparent, was of my maternal grandmother's generation. He hired me, a teen, to help fix his fences, and we took his pickup truck to the back side of his farm, where a sheep-wire fence bordered his pasture next to the woods. I soon found him aggravating to work with, for he was slow. Not slow and meticulous—*that* I could have appreciated; Uncle Willis was just plain slow, and I wanted to get on to more interesting tasks.

"You know how old this fence is?" he chuckled eventually.

"Twenty years," I ventured, careful to predate my own time.

"I helped my father build it before I went to war."

I visualized then an old photo of him in his American Expeditionary Force uniform before he followed General Pershing to France. His war was the First World War. His fence was new in 1917. I learned to see time in a broader perspective from Uncle Willis that day.

 Grandparents make time for what is important.

They know that many of the things youth hurries for are not worth the bother. "What are those?" I asked Mother's Uncle

Oscar one spring afternoon. He had been for a tramp in the woods. A trapper, Uncle Oscar knew every acre of the forest for miles around, so I wasn't surprised to see his hand-woven, Indian-style wicker knapsack full of woodland herbs.

"Fiddleheads," he explained. "Young ferns."

Here were hundreds of these pale-green, fuzzy plants. And I knew that Uncle Oscar was not a gourmet who gathered these succulents to please a jaded palate. Rather, I learned frugality from Uncle Oscar in the same session that I learned that the springtime woods holds hidden food for the one who will venture forth. He was a widower, a lean, healthy man, whose appetites and needs were as sparse as his stature. William Byrd, a colonial Virginia planter, once observed that he could carry a shilling in his pocket for a month without need to spend it. I'm sure Uncle Oscar could have done the same with a quarter!

Grandparents know family history and stories that are part of the family's heritage.

Such history, related in proper detail, can help give direction and maturity as an older child or teen learns to appreciate who he is in a context of where he came from. Until my manhood, my family's history, except for photo albums and Grandpa's terse diary entries, was entirely oral. Then an aunt, herself a grandmother, began writing a history of our community. In the process she collected bits and pieces of family lore, as well as a family tree researched back over four hundred years.

Aunt Ruby copied some of her material and shared it with

other family members. She published other information as a paperback book, *As I Remember*.

Meanwhile, my mother put together a typewritten collection of her memories over three-quarters of a century. And my sister expanded Aunt Ruby's genealogical records through library research of her own.

I think the most fascinating story of all was told to me and brother George by Grandpa Wiggin when we both were small: the story of "The First Wiggin Who Came to America." When Grandpa was a child, his grandfather, Ezra Wiggin—whose 92 years spanned most of the nineteenth century—was still living. Grandpa evidently heard this tale (which spans more than ten generations) from my great-great-grandfather Ezra.

Tom Wiggin, born in England about 1592, was kidnapped at age 14 (possibly in 1606) and brought to Maine, to the mouth of the Penobscot River, where the ship anchored by the riverbank for the night. Next morning, young Tom was given an axe and sent up the rigging to cut a mast free from overhanging pine limbs. Instead, he swung himself ashore and escaped into the forest. The Lord preserved him, and he managed to get back to England, possibly with fishermen who had wintered on the New England coast to dry codfish. Aunt Ruby later learned that he returned to America as captain of his own vessel to settle in New Hampshire about 1628.

Perhaps your grandchildren would be thrilled to hear of their ancestors' trip on a steamship and their stop at Ellis Island, as thrilled as I was when I listened as a friend told of her father's journey to America from Germany as a young man. Or perhaps, like my wife's family, your family's history disappears into the mists of the Great Smoky Mountains of

North Carolina and Tennessee, where Catherine Marshall's *Christy* is set. Whatever you may know of your family's past, especially its Christian heritage, can help give your grandchildren a sense of who they are and a sense of direction for coming years.

Christian psychologist Kevin Leman recommends that grandparents do a "'*This Is Your Life*,' minus Ralph Edwards." Set up a video camera and "talk to your grandchildren and describe your life, your parents, your grandparents, where they came from, what was important to them, and how you got to where you are in life," Leman suggests. He recommends that the tape be put with your will and other important papers, not to be played back until you have died. Or, you can use a video camcorder with your computer and store your life story on a CD. Be sure to use a *recordable* CD, not the "rewritable" kind, since the latter kind will corrupt and erase themselves with age.

Grandparents have a maturity that can't be found by reading books.

The truly mature grandparent is also the wise man or woman who realizes that maturity doesn't come automatically with age, though when we were children we no doubt thought so. Job observed that "advanced years should teach wisdom" (Job 32:7). Yet he had to admit that "the aged [do not always] understand judgment" (Job 32:9, KJV). Many of life's little lessons—practical, moral, spiritual—take years to appreciate.

When I think of maturity, my mind goes to J. O. Sanders, an elder statesman of Christian missions and well-known author of some 40 devotional books, whom I interviewed on the subject of Christian maturity at Gull Lake Bible Conference in Michigan. But years earlier, James Oswald Sanders was general director of China Inland Mission and I a high school student when I heard him speak at a missionary conference at New Brunswick Bible Institute, in Canada. His speaking delivery was direct and forceful—the kind of message at which one either squirmed in conviction or mocked in rebellion. I squirmed.

Sanders's text then was Romans 10:9: "That if thou shalt confess with thy mouth *Jesus as Lord* [Scofield marginal rendering], and shalt believe in thine heart that God hath raised him from the dead, thou shalt be saved" (KJV). He preached that if "Christ is not Lord of all, He is not Lord at all." As a child of nine I had surrendered my heart to Christ. He had been Lord of my life, but as a teen I had toyed with the notion that one could believe and be saved and bound for heaven, living above moral sin but pretty much leading a self-directed life otherwise. God opened my heart with Sanders's preaching. Christ had to be Lord of my life without reservation. I had lingered between two opinions long enough. I had begun the long march (not without its backward steps) toward Christian maturity.

I was a grandfather past 50 and Sanders, now with the Lord, was nearly 90 when next I heard him! This time I sat down front in a crowd that numbered only a few dozen, compared with packed auditoriums when he was in his heyday. Maturity in Christ does not demand that one's ego be massaged by an ever-larger audience.

The man who had seemed stern and severe when he had been my age, now was a gentle great-grandfather in a cardigan.

"Let us go on unto perfection [maturity]," he read from his text, Hebrews 6:1 (KJV). *Would my own maturity require as many years again since I last heard him preach?* I wondered. Then he said something that startled me: "If He is not Lord of all, He is not Lord at all," his mellow voice intoned, emphasizing his familiar refrain as the starting point in a search for Christian maturity. Truth, which does not change with God, will not change in the hands of God's man!

As a young lawyer in New Zealand, J. O. Sanders was also beginning to be known for his ability to teach the Bible, he told me later as we sat facing each other in his room. Those were the years of the Great Depression, and his audience one day was a prayer group of ladies whose husbands were out of work.

"Mr. Sanders will be all right as a speaker when he's suffered a little," remarked a lady afterward. But as a lawyer, and the son of a well-to-do attorney, Sanders had always been pretty much insulated from the harshness of the workaday world, and he knew this.

Maturity requires time and experience, J. O. Sanders was to learn. Not all folks, however, mature at the same rate, nor do all profit equally from the same kinds of experiences, Sanders told me. "It takes God only three months to grow a squash, but a hundred years to grow an oak," he chuckled. "Which would you rather be?"

J. O. Sanders enumerated for me several steps to Christian maturity that grandparents can apply to their own lives to lead their grandchildren into maturity. "The most potent hindrance to spiritual maturity," he said, echoing the advice of Jack Wyrtzen, is "a failure to maintain a consistent devotional life." In the morning, if you can do it, "feed on the Word of God. Fellowship with Him through prayer and worship," he added.

My godly paternal grandfather had to begin milking his cows at five o'clock, so morning devotions were not feasible. But I can still see him in the evening by his library table in the light of a kerosene lamp, fountain pen in hand, his Bible and diary on the wide maple arm of his chair. Though family devotions were irregular at our house, seeing Grandpa—and since then both of my children's grandfathers—read his Bible in the lamplight has impressed me with the importance of being consistent in the Word.

I have Grandpa's Bible now. It is a 1917 Thompson, rebound shortly before his death. Hardly a page is without one of his markings, and often there are outlines or notes scribbled in the margins.

I had not seen that old book for some 30 years, and it had passed through several family members before it came to me. Tucked inside as a bookmark was the answer to an old enigma. I had once seen a strip of old photo-booth snapshots of my grandfather, cut in half lengthwise. What was on the other half? I found it in his Bible: Grandma Wiggin's photos, four of them, were that bookmark! On the reverse in his handwriting was this note: "October 1, 1925. Always love, I will remember you."

The Grandma Wiggin who is my wife is today about the same age as Grandpa's wife, the Grandma Wiggin of my childhood. Like me, he had two loves—the Word of God and the woman God had given him. And he'd cut the strip photo apart, given Grandma the half with his photos, then kept hers with his dearest possession!

Grandparents know what things to hold dear in life.

As the years pass, we learn to narrow these to a very short list indeed! Suffering, loss, and sorrow were to become a part of J. O. Sanders's experience. Twice, in fact, between hearing him preach the first time and the last, he lost a wife—in 1966 and again in 1972—leaving him to walk alone a road that has taken him throughout the world to minister to others. "Death is a part of life," Sanders affirmed. But the death of one close to you may bring either bitterness or maturity, depending on how you handle it, he said.

"Some people are so swallowed up in grief" over the loss of a loved one that they become "like the psalmist, who said, 'My soul refused to be comforted'" (Psalm 77:2, KJV), reflected Sanders. He told of a lifelong friend who lost a wife of 50 years. "He practically threw in the towel when she died, and he was absolutely lost. This man died (in anguish) five or six years later. He went out on a minor key," Sanders observed.

Yet grief is a "necessary and important response" to death, Sanders said. "Tears often have a therapeutic effect." He spoke of a woman who had been recently bereaved. Told by a friend that "sorrow does color life, doesn't it?" the woman replied, "Yes, but I intend to choose the colors." Sanders mused that "she didn't choose black and she didn't choose purple. She chose gold."

During her last three months of life, J. O. Sanders's first wife was in considerable pain from cancer. "The Lord lifted us above sorrow, buoying up the both of us in a very wonderful way so that we were both carried through it, and she died triumphantly," he exulted.

As J. O. Sanders illustrates so well, grandparents who have lived through loss and grief and come through buoyantly are often in a better position to help grandchildren—kids, teens, young adults—than are the parents. Parents all too often are still wrestling with their own sorrows, or as is frequently the case, they have not reconciled personal differences with their children, which can antagonize their kids, especially the teens.

Sometimes it is the parents' divorce that has brought the child or teen to grief. In such a case, usually the best thing a grandparent can do is gently urge the child to forgive his or her erring parent for wrongs—real and imagined—against the child and the other parent. It is my observation that unresolved anger toward the parent of the opposite sex, often from a divorce, may catapult a child into sexual involvement with another teen, sometimes as a subconscious means to punish the offending parent. Further complicating the matter, teens of either sex have an intense longing for the approval of the parent of the opposite sex. Boys raised by angry mothers are especially prone to such destructive premarital sexual experimentation, and they present a special challenge to grandmothers who wish to love them. If Jason, at 16, finds you, Grandma, to be an understanding mother substitute, you may deflect his bitterness so that he no longer feels compelled to misuse girls.

Grandparents can often draw fire away from parents, whether that child is 6 or 16. Let your grandchild verbalize his hurts and point him to the One who bore his sorrows. Loving grandfathers may give a hurting preteen or teen granddaughter positive male support, as he listens to her fears and frustrations, perhaps preventing the tragedy of premarital sex. Girls who feel estranged from their fathers often begin to experiment with sex as young as age 11.

Your precious Samantha, at 17, is vivacious, pretty, and popular. But she has become blue, moody, and sullen all of a sudden. She finally confides to you that her boyfriend has dumped her for another girl, and her parents—perhaps glad for the breakup of a bad relationship—don't seem to understand her feelings of abandonment. To complicate matters, Sammy has given her boyfriend her virginity, and she concludes that her life is now "ruined."

Grandparents in such cases can often view these catastrophes at arm's length and with greater objectivity and compassion than a parent, who may share the hurt so personally that his or her anger seems (to Sammy) to be directed at her, rather than at the sin. Perhaps you could confide to that granddaughter that you too have had your own sorrows and losses. Your experience doesn't necessarily need to match Sam's situation. What is important is that you triumphed (spare her the irrelevant details!), and in God's grace you came through victorious.

Godly Hagar, torn from the arms of Abraham—whom she must have loved, despite his adultery—was sent to the wilderness with the son whom she expected would become her master-husband's heir. She found comfort in the Lord who delivered and blessed her by making her son, Ishmael, head of a great nation (see Genesis 16:1–15; 21:9–20). I believe this cameo of human agony was put in God's Word to lift erring, wounded youth above their circumstances. Grandparents can wisely use this story, along with the experiences of other victorious teens, such as Joseph, David, and Esther, to challenge their grandchildren to live above the baseness of this world.

What things did Grandpa Elmer Wiggin (1868–1953) know that are not found in books? I have had access to his diaries, and read the stuff he wrote down. Most of it is mundane, maddeningly terse. For example, the entry for January 30, 1916, the date of my father's birth, remarks briefly on the weather, then says, "Baby born at 12:30 P.M." No hint of who the doctor was, how the mother was doing, or the baby's name —no sex given, even. I am glad to report that my Victorian grandmother "sat up for the first time" eleven days later, and that my father (still no name!) had his "first laugh" at one month old, March 1, 1916!

Grandpa told me a bit about his past in some detail. There was one story into which I'd always feared to pry, a story of sorrow, the story of Grandpa's little sister. She is commemorated in a white marble headstone: "Little Clara, how we miss you, / Your gentle voice no more we'll hear; / For you've left and gone to heaven, / Where there is no pain nor care." After Grandpa died I learned that he carried this sorrow with him for many years. In my own maturity I now think I understand why.

Six-year-old Clara had just gotten over a bout with scarlet fever when brother Elmer, age eight, decided to tease her. He followed the long ell from the house to the barn, where he buried himself under the hay that raw early spring day. Clara called and called until she was hoarse, but Elmer refused to answer. Clara had a relapse from the episode. Days later, she died.

I'll never know for sure if Grandpa Wiggin ever reconciled himself to fully accept Clara's death, receiving a sense of

Christ's forgiveness for his childish meanness. But though he reportedly brooded over the incident for years, I've reason to believe that he did come to accept it. Years after Grandpa died a report came to me that does not seem consistent with a man who's heart lay troubled and aching all his adult life.

I was pumping gas at a country store the summer of 1957, right after I graduated from high school. A late-model luxury car with out-of-state license plates pulled up. The dignified, well-dressed, elderly driver said, "Fill 'er up," then asked, "What is your name, son?"

"Eric Wiggin."

"Elmer Wiggin your grandfather?"

"Yes, sir."

"When I was a small boy, your grandfather was our mail carrier. He was the kindest man I ever knew."

Grandpa Wiggin had once driven a horse-drawn RFD wagon. Sometime in the years since Clara's untimely death he had matured, learned the meaning of grief, and had accepted Christ's forgiveness. Half a century later an old man remembered my grandfather for such fruits of the Spirit as gentleness and goodness shown toward a child about the age of Grandpa's sister when she died.

In a message I heard him preach in his sunset years, J. O. Sanders pointed out that the Christian grows, becoming like Jesus, as "the Holy Spirit produces a cameo of the life of Christ" in his life. By producing in our lives the nine fruits of the Spirit, as listed in Galatians 5:22–23, God leads us into maturity. These are enumerated here, with summaries of Sanders's comments, for Christian grandparents:

1. "Love is not self-centered," he said; "it's always giving.

'The love of God is shed abroad in our hearts by the Holy Ghost'" (Romans 5:5, KJV).

2. "Joy," said Sanders, "can exist in the deepest sorrow. True love is joyous. Are you fun to live with?"

3. "Peace" comes from "inner surrender to the will of God," he affirmed. It is shown through tranquility in the midst of turmoil. "Peace is not the absence of trouble; it is the presence of God" in trouble. "Do you borrow tomorrow's trouble today so that you can get double value out of it?" he asked.

4. "Patience—it was just as much the 'now generation' when I was young as it is today. The most difficult thing is to be patient with people," and the spiritually mature person develops this trait, he said.

5. "Gentleness" is "being able to project yourself into the feelings of other people," Sanders said.

6. "Goodness" is the imitation of Christ who "went about doing good" (Acts 10:38, KJV). This is not merely being morally good, but doing good things. "How many times this week have you gone out of your way to do something kind, something good for others?" he asked.

7. "Faith" is here "faithfulness," he explained. "Jesus will not say, 'Well done, *successful* servant,' but *faithful* servant'" (see Matthew 25:23, KJV).

8. "Meekness is not an invertebrate quality. Neither Jesus nor Moses was weak, though they were meek. It's the opposite of self-assertion. There is no retaliation in meekness."

9. "Temperance" is shown in "discipline in one's devotional life," Sanders affirmed.

Elisabeth Elliot, in *The Liberty of Obedience,* observes that as believers walk with the Lord, grandparents included, there is "that marvelous hope—that we *shall* yet reach that ultimate end of all creation—maturity in Christ."[1] For our maturation—that we might "attain . . . to the whole measure of the fullness of Christ" (Ephesians 4:12–13)—God works in our lives. For this purpose we have been left on earth to be grandparents—for our own maturing and to aid in the maturing in Christ of the grandchildren God has given us.

This is a precious secret held by believing grandparents. Can we share it with our grandchildren?

CHAPTER EIGHT

Busy Moms, Baby-Sitting Grandmoms

Fascinated, I watched Bobbi McCaughey and her mother bundle Bobbi's septuplets into the family's van after church. As a news writer, I had driven to Carlisle, Iowa, that spring to interview the grandparents of these seven babies, then the world's most famous kids. During Sunday school I watched, delighted, as Grandpa Bob Hepworth—later my host at dinner—jostled aggressive little Brandon, who refused to sleep. Later, big sis Mikayla fascinated me with her cautious glances from the next pew during morning worship.

Though I spent my time that weekend in Iowa with three sets of the septuplets' grandparents, my brief glimpse of the babies as they were rushed off to home was my heart's real reason for being there that day. Each child, I discovered, is an individual, with a unique personality separate from the others. Other than the oddity of having all been born on the same day of the same parents, these youngsters mirror my own grandkids.

And they reflect yours. Parents Bobbi and Kenny McCaughey need extra help from grandparents, particularly because their gifts from heaven all arrived at once. But I have found that my married daughter and daughters-in-law face the same struggles with contrary or compliant tiny personalities, the same need for time alone or with their husbands, the same emergencies needing a fix from Grandma or Grandpa as the parents of these celebrated septuplets.

Many mothers with school-age children have joined the workforce in the 50 years since American manufacturers geared up to produce armaments at the outset of World War II, in 1941. This process of industrialization has also pushed parents and grandparents into separate housing, often many miles apart. One consequence is that now only 15.1 percent of children whose mothers work are cared for by grandparents. Many grandmothers themselves work in factories, at sales, or in clerical positions, so the shortage of baby-sitters has become acute. Working mothers with means to do so have often resorted to day-care centers. Not to be outdone by secular competition, many churches have gone into the day-care business. The spin-offs of this new industry have not always been pleasant.

 Day care, even at a church, may be a poor choice.

One large church in the South that started a Christian school as a ministry to its own families added a day-care center as a missionary outreach to divorced and single mothers. Within a few years, school directors were dismayed to find that the children of divorcées, admitted to the school as graduates of the pre-K program, had become a disruptive element in the classroom. Secular day-care centers in one survey, however, had fewer than 20 percent of enrollees from single-parent homes. One director stated frankly that her fees were too high for single working moms to afford.

Sexual abuse in day-care centers, while relatively rare, is a hobgoblin that parents who pass their kids to somebody else's care must contend with. Though several famous abuse cases have been shown to be trumped up with false charges by state officials, abuse does certainly occur. The author knows of one Midwestern evangelical church where 64 children were molested over three years by a young nursery worker who was exposed to pornography, and probably abuse, at home. As the presence of porn and the consequences of divorce pervade our society, the danger of your grandchild becoming exposed to sexual abuse increases proportionately.

But consideration of exposing a child to profane company, while a real concern, misses the basic issue of day care as an alternative for a Christian home. Grandparents and parents might well ask themselves if day care of *any* kind—except in very limited circumstances where the mothers are present through much of the day—is at all a viable choice for their kids or grandkids.

The factor of working mothers actually harks back to the massive influx of immigrants into America during the late nineteenth century.

Parochial schools and public kindergartens were established largely to get the kids of working mothers off the streets in those days (their grandmothers had frequently been left behind in Europe). But these families, usually through religious values and strict family discipline, eventually rose above the chaos. The working mothers of the late nineteenth century became the grandmothers of the early twentieth century, as the pattern for mothers to stay home, or for grandmothers to baby-sit when mothers must work, was reestablished.

By the end of the Great Depression most mothers were back in their homes. The Depression actually helped effect this, since jobs were scarce and even men with families could hardly find work. Then came Pearl Harbor, December 7, 1941. By early 1942 the Depression had ended as munitions plants hired women as well as men for the war effort.

My own family has seen at least four generations of parents raising their children with only minimal help from baby-sitting grandmoms; today, our daughter and daughters-in-law are stay-at-home moms. Mother—my grandkids' great-grandma—seldom left her children in the care of either grandmother, except when she was recuperating from another childbirth. But my Grandmother Wiggin's turn to tend grandchildren came 15 years into my parents' marriage when Dad's farming operation folded and he and Mother took employment in a bakery.

There were five of us then, and we were all in school. I remember Grandma's reaction to after-school differences of opinion between me and my brothers: She would retreat to her room and shut the door. She had raised three children of her own, whose births were spread over 23 years, and five at once were a bit more than Grandma could take. Dad would settle with us when he and Mother got home!

Times with Grandma Fuller, our maternal grandmother, were much more pleasant, for she would agree to care for only one of us at a time, usually; two at most.

Mother quit her bakery job after a year, but she continued to raise extra cash as an Avon Lady. The Lord blessed her with two more children right after Dad found a better job as a carpenter. But Grandma's baby-sitting was still infrequent; Mother simply trundled her latest baby along with her on her Avon route while we older kids were at school.

Dot and I began our family upstairs above my parents, and Mother was occasionally the baby-sitter for our two oldest. A grandma by now, Mother was still an Avon Lady. I recall that we sometimes had to arrange times to be alone around Grandma's schedule as a saleslady. A move to Indiana put us across the street from a sister-in-law, and Dot sometimes traded baby-sitting with her. A year later, Mother followed us, and again we had Grandma Wiggin as a baby-sitter, this time just around the block.

We now live in Michigan, four hours from our oldest granddaughter, in Indiana, so our daughter, a mother of five, now sometimes calls on Great-grandma Wiggin to baby-sit. On occasions when the family visits us, you can bet that Grandma Wiggin (my wife, Dot) jealously guards her time so she can spend it with the grandkids, who range from toddler to middle school.

Grandmothers who offer their services as baby-sitters so that married daughters or daughters-in-law with small children can work out of the home full time may be contributing to the instability of the next generation, while contributing little, if any, to the family budget. The dictum "Give me a child until he is seven, and he will always be a Catholic" (Ignatius Loyola) has universal application, I believe. Mothers need to be with their children during their first seven years of life, for it is in these years that basic values and attitudes are formed. Hannah, the mother of the great prophet Samuel, reared him until he was seven before placing him in the priest's hands for training in temple service (see 1 Samuel 1:24–28). Jesus continued to be "obedient to" his mother, Mary, and stepfather, Joseph, even after age 12 (see Luke 2:42–52). Such added costs as the need for an extra car, work clothes, prepared foods, and more frequent restaurant meals can easily add up to it being cheaper for the frugal mother to stay home and enjoy her children and let them enjoy her.

Mothers at home can often do much to help the family budget, however. And grandmothers can gently nudge them in this direction when the mother is receptive to advice. Better attention to budgeting and such traditional household arts as meal preparation from scratch, sewing, and gardening, should be encouraged. Grandma can (and should!) stop by with a casserole or kettle of soup now and then. Both grandparents can help with the gardening, perhaps planting enough for themselves, also. Sometimes Grandpa can help by using his mechanical skills to repair an auto or a furnace, saving a young family from budget-busting emergencies that might push a mother of young children into taking a job.

Some mothers have found work-at-home projects, ranging from copy editing books on a computer to creating bridesmaids' dresses. One mother encouraged her preteens to take on extensive paper routes with her aid to help pay their tuition in a Christian school.

Mothers should be cautious of work-at-home projects widely advertised in newspapers, however, since many of these are out-and-out frauds. Instead, investigate what books and pamphlets your library has on starting home-based small businesses.

Homemade Business, by Donna Partow, has ideas for two hundred home-based businesses, worksheets, and testimonies by mothers who've stayed home and helped their family's cash flow. Mother and Grandma may even find themselves partners in a well-paying venture! Refer to the appendix for ordering information.

Grandmothers can point their daughters or daughters-in-law to one of several family-friendly organizations that help moms with kids to stay at home. You might buy your grand-children's mother a subscription to a magazine such as *At-Home Mother* or *Welcome Home*. Perhaps you might tactfully offer her a book. Titles such as *What's a Smart Woman Like You Doing at Home?*, by Linda Burton and others, or *Sequencing*, by Arlene Cardoza, have become extremely popular with moms who have chosen to stay home with their kids; many of these mothers have college degrees and have held professional jobs. These books and magazines are packed with practical ideas for family management, budgeting, and earning income without leaving home. I have included reviews of these great resources in an appendix to this book, along with contact information to reach the mothers' organizations that sponsor them.

Notably, the decline in the divorce rate, and a more positive attitude among Christian teens, coincide with the rise of these mother-led organizations, as well as the considerable influence on homes and youth of organizations such as Focus on the Family, Youth With A Mission, Word of Life, and Promise Keepers.

How much a grandmother should sit
with a grandchild depends largely
on your circumstances, and those
of the married children.

If Grandma herself is employed, then her times of baby-sitting will necessarily be limited by her work hours. If a daughter is divorced or widowed and needs to work to support herself and her child(ren), then Grandma will probably be the natural resort to give home care.

Grandmothers can add much to a young family's happiness by sharing the load on an endless assortment of occasions. These can range from taking care of an infant or toddler while Mom goes to the Laundromat, to keeping several grandchildren while Mom and Dad take a second honeymoon—perhaps even paying for the honeymoon and loaning the couple your car for the trip!

But if Mom (daughter or daughter-in-law) wants you to help them out so she can take a job—to buy new furniture, a nicer or a second car, adult recreational toys (boats, snowmobiles, etc.), it's probably wisest to resist firmly. Instead, you may wish to urge her and her husband to seek Christian financial counseling before such a decision is made. One young Christian father went to his pastor after his wife had taken their two kids home to Grandma and sued for divorce. About a year earlier, after he'd gotten a raise, at his insistence they had traded their cozy, older, three-bedroom house for a new, four-bedroom house with two baths and a two-car garage. The old furniture looked shabby in new surroundings, so new furniture was bought on credit. Then the wife went to work to meet the furniture payments, putting the kids in day care.

"I didn't want this house and furniture in the first place," she wrote in a note she left behind. "I wanted a family!"

Christian financial counselors Ron Blue and Larry Burkett have both written several books, available in Christian bookstores or your church's library, to help young parents through such money squeezes. As a starter, Burkett's office recommends *The Complete Financial Guide for Young Couples.* See appendix for ordering information.

But wait! Why have things gotten to the point that a young mother would want to turn preschool kids over to Grandma while she works? This is not a "What might have been" caveat. Rather, what can you do now?

Let's go to the point of need, a new washing machine for $500, perhaps. You've wanted one for years, but your old one is still working well. Give the family yours when you buy a new one. But you can do better. Buy the kids with the young children the new washer. Keep the old one yourself, if you are unable to buy two. Some grandmas simply invite the daughter or daughter-in-law over for a twice-weekly laundry, and help with the folding and ironing while helping tend the youngsters.

Subscribe to a diaper service for that young mother, and pay for it yourself. That's about $75 a month, versus about $66 monthly for disposable diapers. Or, if Mom's agreeable to it, spring $75 up front for six dozen cloth diapers and a box of laundry soap.

> *Somehow, American Christians have gotten away from an important biblical principle so common in Asian cultures—that of family members helping each other.*

The concept of kicking the kids out of the nest early and making them rugged individualists is not found in Scripture. "Give, and it will be given to you," Christ stressed in His Sermon on the Mount (Luke 6:38). Give to your grandchildren's needs, and you can expect to be "given unto" in return, in the form of grandchildren who will love you in your old age.

Too often we perceive that we are to give to the church or to the poor, so we may do so to the exclusion of needy family members. The strongest Bible teaching about giving points out that Christians should help other members of the family of God (see 2 Corinthians chapters 8 and 9); and this should include family members in need. Parents are to help children and grandchildren (see 2 Corinthians 12:14). The custom of hanging on to all you've got until you die, then leaving it to loved ones in your will, has robbed many a grandparent of the blessing of helping their grandkids, directly or through their parents, in this life (see Matthew 10:42).

Caring for older children after school hours is a matter largely dependent on the logistics of getting the kids to your house after school either by bus, foot, bicycle, or in your auto. Grandma Hackney, my wife's mother, served as a surrogate grandmother over many years for a child who attended school just a five-minute walk from her house. He stopped at her house for soup and sandwiches until his father could pick him up after work. This young man developed a bond with Grandma Hackney possibly as strong as many natural ties.

If you have built loving bonds with your grandchildren while they were small, stopping by Grandma's house on the way home will come naturally to them. Grandma's home can also serve as a place where an ill child can receive care if he takes sick at school, if this is cleared in advance with school officials.

Should you charge for your baby-sitting services for grandchildren? Whenever money changes hands within a family, in either direction, it should be based on need, not as a business arrangement. Parents who can afford to might choose to pay, of course. Perhaps you might wish to budget that money for birthday or Christmas gifts later. You may wish to help a family from your church in difficult circumstances with some baby-sitting free of charge.

Details of baby-sitting with grandchildren, therefore, need to be mutually worked out in a loving context of family members helping each other. Does the *need* exist? Have all the options been explored? What will be best for the children? Do you—at 55 or 75—still have the stamina for the task? What arrangement will best assure that your spiritual and cultural heritage will be passed on to your grandchildren, rather than have it undermined by secular day-care programs often subtly contrary to godly values?

CHAPTER NINE

The Split-Family Grandparent

A dark family secret when I was growing up was that, years before I was born, Great-Aunt Marcia had been divorced. I learned of this family skeleton only after reading of her prior marriage in an antiquated county statistical report! Of the 30 married adults who lived on our country lane when I was a teen, only three, 10 percent, had ever been divorced. In those days, divorce was a matter of family shame and extreme embarrassment.

Many of you who today are grandparents, like me, noticed as children that few of our elders had been divorced. But by the time you and I were teens, media reports were trumpeting an alarming rise in the divorce rate. In 1969 California liberalized its divorce statutes with the nation's first no-fault law, and divorce rates, already on the rise, jumped another 34 percent in the next 20 years. This paralleled a landslide of easy divorce laws nationwide, not slowed until 1997, when

Louisiana and Arizona offered covenant marriage contracts.[1] Half of the 50 states "have done something to strengthen marriage" in recent years, observed sociologist Steven Nock.[2]

For about a quarter of a century, media reports have regularly repeated statistical evidence making it appear that 50 percent of all homes are fractured by divorce. Christians, it seemed, were even more likely to divorce than the ungodly. For instance, journalist David Crary, writing in an Associated Press story, blames "fundamentalist Protestants" for the fact that, except for Nevada, the nation's highest divorce rates are in several of the Bible Belt states: Tennessee, Arkansas, Alabama, and Oklahoma.[3] *World* writer Gene Veith takes sharp exception. "Controlled studies," Veith noted, "show that conservative Christianity does . . . contribute to strong marriages." High rates of divorce in the states named by Crary, he wrote, are an "economic" and "cultural" problem.[4]

Our parents—today's "greatest generation" of great-grandparents born before 1927—ended their marriages at a rate of fewer than one in five, according to data published by Barna Research Group.[5] Today's grandparents—you and I—born 1927–46, have divorced at *double* the rate of our elders: one in every 2.7 of our marriages.

Now here's the good news. Not only has the divorce rate slowed slightly since 1981, but baby boomers (the parents of today's teens, born 1946–64) have a divorce rate *lower* than ours, the grandparents: one in three, according to Barna's data. Thus far, baby busters (born since 1964) have seen only one of every 14 marriages end in divorce.[6]

As the twenty-first century began, slightly more than one-fourth of all American children lived in single-parent homes,[7] though sociologists a decade earlier predicted that 40 to 60 percent would soon dwell with only one parent. With high divorce rates even among professed born-again Christians, this dilemma has grave implications for Christian grandparents. Neither has divorce escaped the families of Christian leaders. I have personally known several pastors of large evangelical churches and directors of international Christian organizations—respected, gray-headed grandfathers and grandmothers —who have a divorced son or daughter, and grandkids they are trying to rescue from the maelstrom their children's divorce has created.

The responsibility that a grandparent must bear, especially toward a divorced daughter or granddaughter, is great indeed. Divorced women and their children typically experience a sharp decline in their standard of living right after the divorce. Compounding this, no-fault divorce laws have so burdened both parents that the family home must often be sold, and the mother and children must move. The choice for such a mother is frequently between living with her parents and moving into government-subsidized project housing. It's likely she'll need a job and will call upon the grandparents to babysit, whether she lives with them or not.

Children of divorce are more apt to repeat a grade in school than those from two-parent homes. These kids are far more likely to get expelled from school, and without a father at home to encourage them they often drop out without graduating. They are also much more likely to experiment with sex, drugs, and alcohol. The majority of the kids I have seen in trouble with school authorities over many years have come from broken homes.

Remarriage sometimes, though not always, compounds the problem. Runaways are more likely to come from homes with a stepparent or live-in boyfriend than from either two natural-parent homes or single-parent homes. The problem of sexual molestation, now of epidemic proportions, also most commonly involves a mother's second husband or live-in boyfriend, Kennebec County (Maine) prosecutor David Crook told me. Media reports have tended to highlight cases involving natural fathers or grandfathers, wrongly implying that fathers are dangerous to pubescent youth. The facts have often been hidden in statistical reports that lump "father figures" (including mothers' boyfriends) with natural fathers. Blood fathers account for only 8 percent of the sexual molesting cases Crook has seen.

Writing to grandparents, columnist Evelyn Sullivan summarized a study of more than seven hundred students at Central Missouri State University. Sullivan cited Central Missouri professor of family studies Dr. Gregory E. Kennedy, who found that after a divorce these students felt the role of grandparents to be "even more important" in their lives than in homes that remain intact. Most grandparents, whether or not the parents have divorced, do have regular interaction with the grandchildren, Dr. Kennedy's study found. Significantly, most students felt closer to their maternal grandparents than to their paternal grand-parents. This is important to maternal grandparents, since in a divorce settlement the children are usually placed in custody of the mother, notes columnist Sullivan.[8]

Though I can cite examples of grandparents so effectively cut off from grandchildren by divorce that the grandkids don't even know if their grandparents are living, fears of such family disenfranchisement are largely unfounded. If you have dealt kindly and evenhandedly with present and former family members, remembering that "a gentle answer turns away wrath, but a harsh word stirs up anger" (Proverbs 15:1), your light unto these young loved ones can continue to shine brightly.

A June 2000 Supreme Court decision, *Troxel v. Granville,* limiting a Washington State couple to one brief visit a month with their granddaughters, should have little or no effect on the visiting privileges of the Christian granddads and grandmoms reading this book. An AARP *Bulletin* headline in December 1999 blared, "Grandparents' Rights on Trial." But *Bulletin* writer Peter Weaver's fears seem mostly to have been overwrought.

White-haired Justice Sandra Day O'Connor, in writing the majority opinion, noted that the U.S. Constitution protects the rights of *parents.* The court's narrow opinion left intact the grandparents' visitation rights of all 50 states. Yet the High Court agreed with the mother, Ms. Granville, that she was within her rights to limit the grandparenting visits of Gary and Jennifer Troxel to once a month.

The facts of the *Troxel v. Granville* case about this heartrending tug-of-war were largely ignored by the media. Mr. and Mrs. Troxel's son, father of Ms. Granville's two girls, was never married to Ms. Granville. Further, the struggle for the children's attention began right after Troxel, the girls' father, committed suicide—so at the very least, the circumstances of this demand for grandparents' visiting rights were extremely unusual![9]

"Intervention by caring grandparents," writes Dr. Jay

Kesler, "costs something." Kesler notes that helping your grandchild after a divorce may bring disruption of your own tranquil lifestyle and postponement of trips or vacation plans. But when divorce comes, "part of the answer may lie in the wisdom and love of the grandparents," he concludes.[10] Kesler, a grandfather, was once president of Youth for Christ International. He is now chancellor of Taylor University.

Godly grandparents Etta and Ralph (names and certain details have been changed to protect family privacy), themselves the parents of a large family, saw a daughter, the mother of four, go through divorce. The father remarried, though he continued to live in the same community and had regular visiting privileges with the children, two preteens and two teens at the time. The mother—Etta and Ralph's daughter—frequently dated in the evening.

So Grandma Etta was on call whenever the kids were sick (Ralph still works full time). "I felt rather silly, a white-haired old granny sitting with all those young mothers," Etta remembers of one of the first times she went to a school function in place of her daughter who had chosen a party over her child's recital. But her loving interest has been rewarded with grandkids who spent much time in her home and who did well in school.

This divorce took its toll on the grandchildren, particularly in regard to their attitude toward possessions. For instance, the father bought Ralph and Etta's oldest grandson a used Camaro on his 16th birthday over the protests of the grandparents, though the mother did not object when her ex-husband, ordinarily a frugal man, indulged the boy. The teen wrecked the car within a week of getting his driver's license. Wiser, the father required the son to earn his own money for his next auto.

Maxine (another pseudonym) is a paternal grandmother of three children of divorce in a state hundreds of miles from her home. Widowed, but with sufficient means to buy plane tickets, she makes twice-yearly visits to the home of her former daughter-in-law, where she is a welcome guest and a beloved grandma. She seldom visits her son, however, since he has also moved to another state, and she simply cannot afford the extra travel expense.

Grandma Maxine finds, however, that her visits are a means to confirm in person the love she expresses in weekly letters to a teen granddaughter who gains much direction and comfort from Grandma's epistles.

In the following fictionalized case, Grandma Joyce continued with happy family dinner parties for son Earle, Earle's twin girls, and his new wife, just as she did before Earle and his first wife divorced. Birthdays, Thanksgiving, Christmas—they were always together, since the twin granddaughters were with Earle for these occasions, as well as every other weekend, Joyce recalled.

But when ex-daughter-in-law Ruth phoned Joyce and Grandpa Walt to ask them to keep the twins while Ruth and her new husband took a vacation trip, Joyce and Walt refused. There had been angry words between Joyce and Ruth during the divorce process, so Joyce could never visit Ruth's home to see her granddaughters.

Joyce's granddaughters are young adults now. Though they still visit Grandma Joyce, Grandpa Walt died without ever having his granddaughters spend the night in his house.

The circumstances Joyce and Walt found themselves in don't need to play out in your experience after a son or daughter's divorce. In the grace of God, Christian grandparents *can* stay involved, making an important difference in a grandchild's life.

Whether you are raising the child yourselves or are heavily involved as were Etta and Ralph, or even only involved peripherally, as in Grandma Maxine's case, the Lord will bless your loving efforts. But the grandparent so involved must honestly, with the Lord's help, face and correct whatever circumstances in his or her own life might have contributed to the son or daughter's divorce.

This is not to suggest a round of self-condemnation. Parents of adult children who get into family predicaments all experience such negative thinking. We should realize that the adult child is himself responsible before God, society, his church, and his children for whatever decisions led to the divorce. But since we will surely be involved as grandparents (custodial, ordinary involvement, or peripheral), as mature Christians we must seek to serve our grandchildren in the manner that will best bless their lives with maturity and responsibility as they grow.

Grandfathers are especially needed in a split-family situation.

Children of divorce are usually with their mothers and do not suffer as much for want of adult female role modeling. Though my own family was solid and my parents' marriage was never in question, many times it was my grandfathers or an elderly uncle who set an example for me. Grandpa Fuller, after he closed his store, expanded his woodworking shop. I can still smell the pine shavings on his floor as a young teen watching him at work, proud that Grandpa's lawn furniture sprouted behind picket fences—some of which he'd also built—all across our little village. It was the tales of long ago told by Grandpa Wiggin and Great-Uncle Oscar that opened my imagination to storytelling, making it possible for me to write for children, so that several of *their* stories have been retold for thousands in my Sunday school paper series and books.

Christian psychologist Dr. James Dobson warned his supporters in a letter that without "mature, responsible men" as role models, boys without fathers often find "a surrogate family" in teen gangs, especially in the inner city.[11] This is a challenge to split-family grandads to become surrogate dads to their own grandsons. If your grandson has no father at home, it is you, Grandpa, who must attend his ball games and music recitals, take him to church, take him fishing or camping, and listen to his failings and fears, dreams and triumphs. Perhaps, as in the case of one prominent Christian leader whose daughter divorced, you and Grandma may need to take that grandson into your home for a few years when he becomes a teen, or even sooner. That Christian leader's grandson, reared by grandparents from age 10, went on to become a faculty member at a Christian college and coach of a winning basketball team!

> *Granddaughters who are children of divorce need strong, loving grandfathers nearby.*

This is doubly so if the father has become inaccessible. And with grandparents, as with parents, the most important thing you can do for a granddaughter from a broken home is to love her grandmother. There is ample evidence that girls, for good or bad, choose as husbands men like the men who were their mentors and models while they were growing up.

Will you be there when your granddaughter needs you?

If your grandchild is between 8 and 16, take her with you and Grandma on a vacation, perhaps. Give an ear to her fears and musings, whether about things at school, a new boyfriend, moral and spiritual matters, or parents who misunderstand. Mothers raising children alone may become impatient simply from not having a husband to share the burden. A noncritical, nonjudgmental ear from a grandfather in such a case can lift the spirits of a granddaughter and ease the load of a harried mother. Your granddaughter *will* talk with you if you'll listen, Grandpa. There's nothing that a preteen girl with an aching heart desires more than a concerned, interested male listener. Let him be you!

Be careful that you do not come between a grandchild and the parent.

Let's say your granddaughter complains about her mother's fiancé or a grandparent on the other side. You can listen. You can sympathize with her feelings of estrangement. Often, you can give mature advice. But criticize? Bite your tongue, or you may become the one who's lost his influence in that young life. There is a warning from Solomon that the person who bitterly criticizes his parents will have his influence "snuffed out" like a lamp "in pitch darkness" (Proverbs 20:20). Likewise, your influence over your grandchildren may go out like a lamp in a storm if you attack their parents or others whom they love.

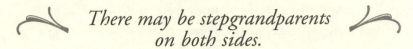

There may be stepgrandparents on both sides.

The problem of involvement in your grandchild's life can become compounded when the parents remarry, and the parents of the stepparent enter the picture as stepgrandparents. They may stay on the fringes or they may wish to get involved. So continue to be available to the family. The grandchild will gravitate to the one with whom he or she prefers to spend time.

Though as a child I had no stepgrandparents, how well I remember Grandma Bickmore, and I felt badly stung when a well-meaning adult pointed out that my cousins' grandmother was not my grandma too. If your child marries someone with children, you can use this new relationship as a stepgrandparent to build love and Christian values into these new family members. But move ahead with caution—both the stepgrandkids and their blood grandparents may get wounded.

Grandparents Joyce and Walt, for example, found themselves with several new grandchildren to entertain on holidays after son Earle's divorce. The stepkids loved it, as did Earle's new wife, their mother. You must, like Grandma Joyce, be careful not to show favoritism to grandchildren related by blood.

Probably your birth grandkids' birthdays—and perhaps their clothing sizes, favorite colors, and books—already appear on your calendar. Their photos are in your "Grandma's Brag

Book." Go ahead and add the stepgrandkids. Nowadays, kids often have e-mail addresses as soon as they can peck out "I luv U, Gramma" on the keyboard. Add these, too.

Be ready to share these new grandkids with their "real" grandparents. Whether or not you and your son or daughter's new in-laws share the same values, these stepgrandkids were *their* grandchildren *first.* Make friends with them and respect their rights and interest as grandparents, while you develop this new ministry from the Lord.

Columnist Sullivan found it "interesting" that the majority of the 700 college students surveyed, now old enough to reflect on the consequences of their parents' divorce, felt closer to their mother's parents than to their father's or to the parents of stepparents.[12] So, if you are the maternal grandparent of a child of divorce, you can expect your responsibilities to increase sharply. Are you ready?

CHAPTER TEN

Grandparents Across the Miles

"You goin' t' *stay*, Grandpa?" I can still remember the urgency in my voice as I stood on the running board of Grandpa Fuller's '36 Chevy panel truck and peered into his lined face, framed with a rumpled straw hat. I knew the answer to that question before I spoke, however. The motor was still idling, and Grandma was clambering out the other side as he reached for the gearshift to put it in reverse.

Grandpa's pleasant "Some other time" was drowned out by Mother's hurried direction to "get off that running board and step back! Your grandfather's got a store to tend."

For my maternal grandparents, grandparenting across the miles meant a five-minute jounce over two miles of potholed graveled road between their place on the main road and our farm home on a crossroad. Whenever Grandma wanted to spend an afternoon with her daughter and grandchildren, Grandpa could put out a "Back in 10 Minutes" sign during a lull in business and expect any customer to be sitting on the steps when he returned. A man of affairs, small as they were, Grandpa got to stay only on holidays.

My maternal grandparents both lived to see all 10 of their grandchildren born. Except when we older ones were in college, we were all nearby until our grandparents' deaths.

But what a change a generation has made! By the time my quiver had filled with our four youngsters, both of their grandfathers had passed on. At the birth of our youngest, we were 575 miles from my mother, and nearly 800 miles from Dot's mother. Both grandmothers could drive, but they restricted their driving trips to local jaunts. Their travels were limited to auto journeys with family members, or when they went by bus, train, or plane.

My mother, who had expected to spend her days in Maine in the farmhouse two miles from her parents' home, has settled with two unmarried daughters in an Indiana city, near one family of grandchildren. The others are scattered in Michigan, Wisconsin, Kentucky, and Texas, with married grandchildren far away in California. In a society where the average American family moves about once every six years, Mother's situation is quite common.

Happily, for grandparents in the twenty-first century, distances are not the challenge they once were. For example, Jack Wyrtzen recalled for readers of this book that "for 20 years our Bible institute in Brazil," directed by his son-in-law, "didn't even have a telephone." But after there were grandchildren in Brazil, he "could call right into my daughter's bedroom," he chuckled. Most preteens and teens today have e-mail addresses. Many, especially girls, have two—one at home and one at school, so you can reach them—with no toll charges or postage stamps!—several times a day if they are half a continent or even half a globe away. Or Grandma can step aboard a jet in Los Angeles in the morning and be in New York or Honolulu in time for supper with the grandchildren.

Write, write, write—write often!

The value of letters to establish and maintain long-distance grandparenting relationships is sadly neglected nowadays. And avoid photocopied, catchall letters. These are fine for general information sent to several families at holiday time. But you should include a paragraph or two of personal greetings to each grandchild and an occasional photograph.

E-mail is ideal for sending quickie letters—or long ones! If computers intimidate you, handheld or desk-model e-mail devices that plug into phone jacks are available for under $100. E-mail will reach your grandchildren—or your church's missionaries in Africa or any place on earth with phone service—in seconds, with none of the lost mail and weeks of postal delay still common in third-world countries.

Be advised, though, your old, pre-Pentium computer, though often fine for word processing or games, will probably not operate a phone modem efficiently enough to be useful for e-mail.

Nearly two thousand years ago the young church in Israel, Asia Minor, and Southern Europe was held together and built up in the faith by *letters,* known in our Bible as "epistles." Some of these were addressed to individuals, such as Timothy and Philemon. Others were written to churches, groups of Christians. Since God saw fit to use letters, from Bible times until today, to bless so many millions of people, can He not still use a letter from Grandma and Grandpa to bless your grandchildren?

Send tapes, both audio and video, if you have the means to produce them. Photos, old and new, can go by e-mail as well, if you have a scanner or a digital camera and your e-mail service is set up to transfer files. But check with your overseas family before transferring photos or files (long documents). Their e-mail reception may not be set up for handling more than letter-length documents. Internet service is not necessary, however. I have listed a free e-mail service in the appendix, as well as several Internet filtering services.

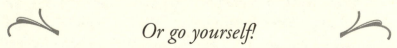

Books will get to your grandchildren with that special message on your heart.

"Auntie—Christmas, 1947" is written in a flowing hand in a book of animal stories given to me as a child, which my four children have all since enjoyed, and which my grandchildren, avid readers, now enjoy. (I have books which belonged to *my* grandparents!) A mind exposed to good literature from childhood is more readily receptive to books on spiritual topics, both then and later on. (But check with your grandkids' mothers to see if the books are actually being read.) Please see the appendix to this book for suggestions of wholesome reading selections.

Or go yourself!

Visiting with grandchildren, especially if the grandparents are elderly or in poor health, often comes about when the children themselves make the trip and bring the grandchildren along. But many grandparents, relieved from employment responsibilities, are better able to take extended vacations not possible when they were younger. And perhaps with more cash to spend they are in a far better position to journey to see the grandchildren than vice versa.

Whether both grandparents are living will affect the type of trip and the length of stay, of course. For instance, whereas a couple may plan a two-week auto tour, with only weekend stops at the grandchildren's home, a widowed grandmother may take a plane, fly direct, and stay with her grandkids for a month.

Here are some suggested trip ideas for grandparents:

 Buy a light camper top for a pickup truck.

The truck can be your second car, if you are still employed. Some folks enjoy pickups anyway, and nowadays they are available with as many options as a sedan, and most of them are just as comfortable. If you buy a light, truck-mounted camper, it can be placed on skids behind your garage during the 11 months or so it won't be used. Air-adjustable shocks will permit a sedanlike ride when the truck is empty. (Caveat: Don't buy a four-wheel-drive or an SUV unless you're going into the hinterlands in mud or driving during the snow season. Such vehicles cost more and generally hog gas. A two-wheel-drive with heavy-duty suspension will handle a camper as handily as a four-wheeler.)

If you limit yourself to a small camper, with bedroom

space only, the expense will be minimal. You can travel when you feel like it, rest when you feel like it, eat in restaurants or at a rest area, and park in a rented lot at a campground with a bathhouse for a fraction of the cost of a motel. This will enable you to park at the grandchildren's for as long or as short a stay as you are welcome. Then, like Roy Rogers' "Tumblin' Tumbleweed," mosey on.

 ## Buy a light camping trailer.

This will give you similar advantages to a pickup camper if you already own a midsized or full-sized sedan adequate to pull it. For trips more than one hundred miles or so, a six-cylinder vehicle is needed. Eight is better, and an older model with a 350-cubic-inch (5.7 liter) or larger engine would be ideal, if you can find one in good shape. A trailer has the added advantage of your being able to unhitch it and drive off, but it can be tricky to tow. With your rolling bedroom you can park in your children/grandchildren's backyard for a couple of weeks in many communities—but clear it with them before you leave home! For variety, let the grandkids camp out in your camper on Friday night, while you sleep in their room.

 ## Furnish a grandparents' room at your own expense.

You will want to clear this with your daughter/daughter-in-law and son/son-in-law ahead of time, of course. You might help them purchase a new or used hide-a-bed for the family room, for instance. Or, if you'll be staying in the children's room while they camp out in the backyard, you may wish to upgrade a child's bed with a box spring and innerspring mattress to replace the link springs and foam slab designed for children. *You* will appreciate it now; the kids will appreciate it ever after.

Consider buying the grandkids a backyard tent and sleeping bags.

Your presence may overcrowd their home, but here is a chance for the kids to have some fun while Grandma and Grandpa enjoy the house with Mom and Dad. But clear this with the parents first, since some neighborhoods are not safe for backyard camping. It may also be necessary to purchase firmer mattresses for the kids' beds, to accommodate adult backs, however.

Buy plane, train, or bus tickets on special offers well in advance.

Tip: Scan the travel section of a Sunday newspaper, as well as your favorite magazine for seniors or families (for example, *Reader's Digest*) for special round-trip fares on airlines, by bus or rail (Amtrak) or for motel discounts. Special fares are posted on the Internet, too—check after 1:00 A.M., when airlines are discounting tickets to get ready for the next day's business.

Also, if you don't mind an auto trip on either end of the flight, travel between major cities becomes much more affordable, and you can avoid many layovers and plane changes. For example, when Grandma Hackney wanted to visit her grandchildren 1,100 miles away in Maine, she found that a flight from western Michigan, with two stopovers and a plane change in a strange metropolitan airport, was more than she could manage. But a direct flight, Detroit to Boston, was manageable and much more affordable. Her daughter drove her to Detroit (three hours), and we drove her to Maine from Boston (three hours), though the flight itself took only two hours! Two weeks later, we reversed the process. A good time was had by all—and the kids got a kick out of knowing that Grandma was getting off the plane in Detroit before we arrived home in mid-coastal Maine!

 Delight your overseas children with a visit.

Such trips can be surprisingly inexpensive and trouble free, if you can get off-peak-traffic rates and have the advice of a seasoned international traveler to help. If your children are doing missionary service, such a trip should be cleared with their mission board, who may help you with customs and will probably furnish accommodations at a modest fee. If you have special skills useful in a third-world country, you might combine such a trip with short-term missionary service. This also must be cleared with the mission board. I'd suggest asking your pastor for advice, as a starting point.

Jim and Shirley Franks, who for years had grandchildren in Niger, West Africa, and for a while in Tokyo, have visited both sets of grandchildren in their overseas homes. The Franks used these trips to supply their African grandchildren, living in a remote, primitive village where their dad is a missionary surgeon, with books and electronic educational materials their daughter can use in homeschooling the grandkids. Not surprisingly, Grandma and Grandpa Franks's home is a favorite spot to visit when the youngsters come to America.

 ### *Grandma, plan your trip with care.*

A lot of grandmothers travel by auto, and this can be happy or hair-raising, depending on your preparation. I suggest you have a towing and road service provision with wide acceptance on your auto insurance policy, or else join an auto club. Have basic maintenance—oil change, belts, hoses, and filters—done to your auto two to three weeks beforehand. This will allow time to work out bugs caused by mechanics' mistakes. One lady left for an extended trip the day after she'd had a cruise control installed. She had to call a tow truck the first day out because of a mechanic's carelessness—a kink left in a small vacuum hose that rendered the car inoperable.

Have a friend who understands autos check everything out.

Even the most competent service garage will overlook small details that could leave you stranded. While helping my grandchildren, I once borrowed my mother's station wagon for a trip of several hundred miles. She ordinarily has her car meticulously serviced, and everything *looked* okay, but I was in a hurry.

A nearly brand-new tire blew late at night on a busy expressway. So Grandpa (myself) pulled the spare from Great-Grandma's wagon and attempted to change the wheel. But the lug nuts were rusty, and the factory-equipment wrench was inadequate. Moral: Have a friend grease those wheel lugs yearly (tire shops almost never do this), and buy yourself a nice, big, star-type universal wheel wrench. Even if you can't change a tire yourself, you need adequate tools so someone else can, and the wrench supplied with your car is very possibly too flimsy. And watch out—one of the most common reasons for getting stranded beside the road is the spare tire. Is yours inflated?

Don't carry more cash than you'll need to get there.

Check with your son or daughter in advance, and be sure he or she can cash a personal check for you, if you're not used to money machines. Warning: Unless you're using your money card for transactions on a regular basis, be sure to try it at a money machine a day or two before you leave. The grandpa who's writing this book was embarrassed to learn, hundreds of miles from home, that his money card wouldn't work—my credit union automatically cancels the PINs of cards not used at least once a year—fortunately I also carried a Visa card. For those who receive Social Security checks, direct deposit now makes it unnecessary for you to be home to collect yours.

If you're past 70, it may be unwise to start a journey requiring night driving.

Older folks often suffer from night blindness, and even with glasses corrected to 20/20 for daylight hours, they can find themselves positively helpless after dark, especially in rain, fog, or swirling snow. If you're traveling far on strange roads, consider investing in a portable CB radio or cell phone to call police or alert a passing truck driver that you need help. By all means, carry a telephone credit card (available free from your phone company) and a list of all phone numbers you'll need at your destination(s) and back home.

Get all prescriptions filled before you leave home.

Be sure to carry sufficient medicines with you to last the trip. Running out of allergy medicine can make your trip miserable; running short of heart medicine could be life threatening. If you're diabetic, carry an adequate supply of insulin and syringes whenever traveling. If you need dental work or new glasses, you'll want your own doctor to do the work. And like auto repairs, dental and ocular work often need adjusting after a week or so.

If you travel by plane, bus, or train, be sure to keep medications and extra underwear in your carry-on bag. It's not unusual for luggage checked through to arrive a day or two late!

Grandmas and grandpas will want to carry small gifts for the younger grandchildren.

Make these unique to your state or region, and they'll be treasured forever, even by children with no sense of geography. I learned as a child that Boston must be a wonderful place.

Though Grandma Wiggin lived right in our house, her sisters—my great-aunts—came from Boston each summer, and the trinkets from their bags, though seldom for children, seemed as exotic as if St. Nick himself had opened his pack on our kitchen table.

 Put the grandkids and their parents first, and you'll all have a happy visit.

I recommend visiting when the kids are out of school, so you can take them to the zoo or other nearby recreation areas. But it's often unwise to plan your visit during their father's (your son or son-in-law's) vacation from work. Four adults, plus kids, in one household for a week or two often get on each other's nerves, though if Dad is working he will enjoy having you around evenings.

If your vacation coincides with your grandchildren's parents', and you decide to follow them to their lakeside cottage in Minnesota, a short visit of a day and a night might be in order. Then leave! At the least, rent your own cabin. Dads, especially, covet vacation times to spend alone with their wife and kids.

Many families plan stay-at-home vacations because they *want* the grandparents around. A full round of family activities, planned and unplanned, is enjoyed by all. The men may work together rebuilding a car or go golfing. The women spend their time in joint activities. Several days are dedicated to the kids. Mature discretion and honest discussion beforehand should determine which approach to take.

Holidays require special planning. Perhaps you're used to having your "kids"—married ones included—eat Thanksgiving or Christmas dinner at your house. But now that there are grandchildren, their parents (your children) will want to establish their *own* family traditions.

Several solutions are possible. You might share one holiday with them at their home; then they could visit you on the other. You could graciously accept the invitation of one family of grandchildren for Thanksgiving and of another for Christmas. Or perhaps you might plan a Fourth of July backyard cookout instead, and bake your special holiday goodies then, when the grandkids are out of school and everybody is free to travel. Christmas fudge goes great with watermelon and corn on the cob!

> *The basic rule in long-distance grandparenting, then, is the "law of Christ" (see Galatians 6:2; Luke 10:25-27).*

That is, to love one's neighbor—grandchild, or that grandchild's parents—as yourself. This requires planning, with their needs uppermost. Put aside the all-too-common concept of purposely using family as free lodging along a larger trip. This may certainly occur, but what is your motive? Instead, consider how you can give of yourself. That's the key!

CHAPTER ELEVEN

When Your Grandchild's Ears Fall Off

My birthday cake for Mother was a crashing disaster. Not only was it heavy and the layers soggy in the middle, but when I tried to frost it, chunks the size of quarters peeled off and mixed with the frosting.

Grandma's handwritten recipe book listed only ingredients. This venerable master cook kept the other directions in her head. And so it was that I ventured into the room where Grandma was entertaining to ask her explanation of a routine step. I'm sure *her* answer was adequate and understandable. But advice was hurled at me by a supercilious bevy of ladies whose baking abilities evidently exceeded their communication skills.

At that moment, my ears fell off. I retreated miserably to the kitchen to mix a cake better suited for Halloween!

"That child didn't hear a thing I said!" I'm sure every grandparent has said this at least once. Grandma's friends would surely have said that had they been on hand when my cake was cut. To this day I don't know what went wrong.

Grandparents and grandchildren fail to communicate for a variety of reasons. Often we blame inattention, TV, or childish rudeness. And these are problems often enough. But a careful physician will seek to eliminate all known causes before he makes a diagnosis. If your grandchild, be he 8 or 18, is afflicted with dropoffsey of the audio orifices, check all problems before fixing blame. Here are several problems and suggested cures for falling ears:

 ## *Commands and instructions instead of loving conversation will tune a child out.*

Forgetting the magic "please" will tell a child that he's of less worth than an adult as quickly as anything. You say, "Do this, Darryl" or "Run next door and ask to borrow a screwdriver." But unless spoken in love and with thoughtful consideration, these requests will quickly reduce your grandchild to one of the Old Lady in the Shoe's "many children." Asking a grandchild to be your "gofer" is one thing. Forgetting to be courteous to him as an individual is quite another. If you've given a child permission to watch a TV show, for example, is it thoughtful to interrupt the most exciting episode to ask him to run an errand?

 ## *Children are deaf to nostalgia.*

Many adults don't have a clue on this one, and they persist in being fooled for years because once upon a time there was a good little child who heard *every* word of your nostalgic tale. And the kid was interested. Nice kid? Or did your story hook that child with a non-nostalgic point of interest that you did not even recognize?

Here's a case in point: When I was a kid, we had a Jersey bull, "old Turk." He had brown eyes, crumpled horns, and a brass ring in his nose. His coat was as ashen as death itself. Turk was the Minotaur reincarnated.

Then one evening Grandpa told me the ox story. As a boy, he'd been sent by his father one December day onto the frozen bog near our farm to fetch an ox-drawn pung (heavy sled) loaded with swale grass, cut with a hand scythe and cocked (stacked) in July. But the oxen broke through the frosty crust and scrambled in terror onto the haycock. Grandpa, a teen at the time, shouldered the yoke and left the dumb, trembling brutes for the night. Next morning, he found them at the barn door lowing to be let inside.

Grandpa loved nostalgia. But having never lived in the past, I had no appreciation for it. It took a gigantic leap of faith, in fact, to imagine my old grandfather carrying a yoke nearly a mile on his shoulder.

And I had never seen an ox. But Grandpa explained they were "something like bulls, but gentler." I loved animals, and fierce ol' Turk I understood. So I found it amusing to imagine creatures "something like" his ilk cowering on a snow-covered haycock. I was interested in the story for the story's sake.

I recall my fascination with learning how to make a wooden whistle from a green willow shoot with bark that could be slipped off. My grandfather's cleverness in making this simple toy amazed and delighted me. Only after the whistle was completed did I learn that "every boy in school had one of these" in the 1870s.

Having never lived in the past, children have no interest in nostalgia. But they are interested in *new* experiences—not new to the world, necessarily, but new to *their* experience. Much of your past as a grandparent is new to your grandchildren, and it can by related interestingly, if given the right perspective. For instance, besides animals, children like humor and adventure.

Grandparents must respect the present, and they must be glad listeners.

Learn from your grandchildren what things impress *them*. Brad, at 15, was impressed with Corvettes. Me, I'd much rather tour a gravel country lane in a '32 Chevy roadster, but to Brad, it's just an old car.

Few youth can appreciate nostalgia until they are older teens. Your "I remember" story of a hard-fought battle driving the Nazis out of France may interest preteens. But your thrill at riding in a victory parade afterward, the second car back from General Eisenhower ("Who was he?") may lose them.

Are you interested in your grandchild's "little things"?

Can you honestly listen to a 14-year-old's contemporary Christian song and appreciate the lyrics with him even if you don't care for the arrangement? Or little Derek has dug up a rusted, nondescript metal object in your garden: "What's this,

Grandma?" Do you impatiently direct him to the garbage can? Or can you share the interest of your budding archaeologist and help him scrape it clean with an old kitchen knife, cementing a bond with Derek that will be rewarded with many happy conversations?

 ## *Do you hear, really, what that five-year-old is saying?*

"I think there's a monster in the closet," little Emma Mae whines. You may insist, "There are no monsters in this house. Go back to sleep, dear." Or do you help Emma Mae find the things that go bump in the night?

A lot of parents miss what their youngsters are saying because too many little tongues are wagging at once. Susannah Wesley, mother of the famous evangelist John Wesley and his hymn-writing brother Charles, is said to have regularly found time *alone* with each of her children, though God had given her 19. Truthfully, most mothers never master this feat. But grandparents can meet this need, both as hearers and speakers.

Emma Mae, at four, may fear closet monsters. At 12, her fears have matured. Being left out of the school social circle is a real fear, which many parents don't understand—or which Emma Mae may not have expressed to a busy mom.

But Grandma can listen. Invite *your* Emma Mae for a weekend alone—no other children. You may be surprised at what's on her mind—and heart.

Kids listen better alone, too. Five-year-old Tessa, a strong-willed child, was spending a few days with Grandma Wiggin and me. Tessa asked me to open a half-pint carton of milk, but

I tore the opening wider than she wished. "That's okay," I soothed, "I'll get you a glass."

"I won't drink from a glass," Tessa tartly announced the moment I poured the milk. She hopped off her stool.

"Back on the stool. Drink the milk—*now*," I said firmly.

Not having an audience to watch her challenge adult authority, Tessa complied at once.

You could be shooting over their heads.

Most kids under 15 (and a lot of adults, as well!) simply lack the knowledge of electrical circuits to understand why opening a window when one is hot isn't as efficient a means of cooling a room as lowering the thermostat. If you've got a 12-year-old grandson with a mind for science, and he sincerely wants to know, explain how a thermostat works. But don't push; most children will have to take it by faith—it's true because Grandpa says so.

Can you tell a child how to tie a shoelace? I can't, though I can tie my laces with my eyes shut. But I can *show* a child how to tie his shoe! Here's a clue to many conversations with children that impatient adults should learn. Often a picture or demonstration will work. Facts are dull and dreary without sufficient points of reference to understand them.

Lying is a sure turnoff.

When Kyle is four he may believe Grandpa's story about the "dangerous old bear" in the tumbledown barn behind the house, concocted to keep him out. At six, Kyle has learned better—and he's learned not to trust Grandpa. So his ears fall off whenever Grandpa speaks.

Tall tales for comic effect—the Paul Bunyan variety—may be okay if they're understood to be fantasy. But bizarre yarns designed to impress kids with one's knowledge of the unusual soon wear thin, especially when told first person, and your grandchild has already heard it elsewhere.

 ## Ask their advice.

They'll listen to this one every time. Grandma's car won't start, so before she calls the garage, she calls on grandson Ryan, 15. She's delighted to learn that Ryan's dad had the same problem and Ryan knows what to do. And Ryan, intoxicated by Grandma's trust in him, suddenly becomes a listener *and* a talker.

 ## Eavesdrop without snooping.

As a frequent substitute teacher, I've learned to tune my ears to bits of conversation by teens who may—or may not—have their work done. Never, ever peek into a child's diary or listen on another line to a private phone conversation. But when your teen grandkids are chatting over the Ping-Pong table or commenting on the Sunday sermon, for instance, you may gain valuable insights into their thought processes by listening in the shadows. Or listen when you drive with teens. Many kids become motormouths in the car, and via their mouths you learn what's going on inside their heads and hearts.

With teens, still water may run deep.

In trying to deal with teen grandchildren on a kid's level, you may have inadvertently ignored their ability to grasp, though imperfectly, weighty concepts of the adult world. Both Einstein and Edison were marked as slow learners by teachers who didn't make the effort to tune in to their thoughts.

Some teens seem interested only in food, clothes, sports, cars, movies, or the other sex, to be sure. But teens can also be concerned about how to curb runaway welfare costs, the Arab-Israeli conflict, starvation in Sudan, or evangelism in Latin America. Try them on these or similar topics. You might find a young intellectual or a youth with great spiritual or social concerns beneath that glum demeanor!

 ## *Be understanding.*

Grandparents, even those who relate readily to younger children, may find themselves dismayed by teens. Here's where the transition from parent to grandparent can be trying, especially if it's been a few years since you had teens of your own.

Twelve-year-old Tabitha, your five-foot-two, blue-eyed darling—she's flat-chested and athletic, but today she's in the doldrums over having loved and lost. *You* see Tabitha on the parallel bars demonstrating her skill at gymnastics, or playing a piano solo, pert, with a black satin bow in her ash-blonde hair at a Sunday evening church concert. *She* sees herself as Cinderella, whose prince has just found another princess!

She'll get over it, you ponder. But how can you convey this to her gently and compassionately without destroying communication? To dismiss her feelings of rejection as a silly crush would only bring a hurt, perhaps angry, response: "Grandma, you couldn't understand!"

Do you understand, really?

At 12, Tabitha—though she may look like a child—is probably capable of the same range of affections and emotions as an adult female. But she lacks the understanding of her emotions that you have or her mother has.

"Carry each other's burdens, and in this way you will fulfill the law of Christ," Paul advises (Galatians 6:2). To love one another is a truth that underscores what Grandma's attitude ought to be toward Tabitha. Have you forgotten your own heartrending first breakup with a boyfriend or fiancé, Grandma?

Perhaps Tabitha confides to you that she has become a victim of contemporary sexual morality. In case you haven't kept pace with the breathtaking changes in moral attitudes, Grandma, "the whole point" of "going all the way" is to do something "pleasurable and special" once you "know your own mind," croons *Seventeen,* a magazine widely circulated in public middle and high schools.[1] Other publications for girls 12 to 18 offer pretty much the same advice.

This issue of *Seventeen* also portrayed a "late bloom[ing]" girl who remained a virgin until college (*yikes!*) as the "last one" in her crowd to "get [her] period and grow breasts."[2]

Another girl caught incurable HPV (human papillomavirus) from sex with two boys. She regrets that she was raised by "ultraconservative religious parents" who had never talked about sex with her.[3] The message is clear: Christian parents, who believe in abstinence until marriage, are uptight spoilsports and dangerous to a girl's health. *Seventeen's* open-minded writers, on the other hand, realize that girls just want to have fun. "Maturity, honest communication, respect [and the] protection [of a condom]"[4] are the only valid criteria for deciding to have sex, according to *Seventeen*.

This is a satanic philosophy aimed at teens by authors like Judy Blume, Erica Jong, and Naomi Wolf, who are long on evolutionary biology. But they are short on even the most rudimentary understanding of the emotional and spiritual implications of sex outside of marriage for humans, created in God's image with sexual natures that transcend the physical realm. Wait until you're "ready" is the world's substitute for godly chastity until marriage. You should lovingly explain to Tabitha that, for several reasons, this is the devil's lie.

Even in these days when sexuality is pushed at them from every quarter, most teens seek the intimacy of a meaningful love relationship, rather than merely casual sex, I have noticed. Here is where grandparents need to tread softly and be very, very sympathetic.

Your grandchild may rationalize early sexual involvement by saying, "But we love each other so much." But here's what most teens don't realize: The inevitable *breakup* is disastrous—*always*. No exceptions. It's like the old saying that "it's not the speed that kills; it's the sudden stop at the end." Those adults who no longer feel pain after a breakup following a relationship involving sex have buried their hearts—emotions, souls—beneath such a heap of moral garbage that, consciences seared, they have become insensitive to romantic love. Sadly, such adults are aggressively advising our grandkids about sex, in the magazines and school sex-ed classes.

One flesh is the Bible's term for a couple united by sex. (See Genesis 2:24 and 1 Corinthians 6:16. Especially notice Ephesians 5:31–32, where Paul likens married sex to Christ's relationship with His church.) The expression is here the Greek word *sarx*, used not only for the body, but for the entire human personality with its affections.[5] Sexual intercourse, therefore, whether the participants are 12 or 22, involves an intimate cementing of two personalities, so that emotionally the two become like Siamese twins. This intimacy was intended by God the Creator as part of a shared lifetime. Sex before marriage certainly corrupts the conscience. Breaking up, however, rends the very soul. Only God can heal this hurt.

Listening, caring grandparents—often better able than parents to distance themselves from the family shame—can feel their teen's pain. They can become God's instruments—His scalpel and sutural needle—to tenderly trim and sew that wound so it may heal. Point your sinning grandchild to passages such as 1 John 1:9: "If we confess our sins he . . . will forgive . . . and purify us."

After your burden-bearing, woman-to-woman empathizing (*not* woman-to-girl!), you may wish to get Grandpa involved, especially if Tabitha's dad is not living in the home. Grandpa could take her out to dinner while Grandma stays home. He may get her to open up by discreetly talking to her about *his* own experiences.

I recall a summer evening in 1959 sitting on a bench beside the Evangeline Chapel in a seaside park in Grand Pre, Nova Scotia, and exchanging parting words of anguish with the young woman of my dreams. The greatest North American epic poem of lost love had begun here in the shadow of that venerable French church two centuries earlier.

Next morning, my last glimpse of this walnut-haired, chocolate-eyed Canadian lass from Acadia was the swish of her salmon-pink skirt as she disappeared through the imposing, brass-hinged doors of the newspaper office where she worked as a typesetter. And I was left facing a solitary 12-hour drive in my ancient chariot to get home to Maine. There had been no sex involved, but our romance had progressed to the point that the agony of the breakup wrenched my heart and reverberated within my soul for several years.

Perhaps someday I'll tell *that* story (every word of it is true!) to one of my granddaughters in love!

Chapter Twelve

Who's That Boy with the Pimples?

Several teens from my growing-up years come to mind as I write this. One we called "Beanpole" was skinny, and he stood six-foot-three by his 14th birthday. "How's the weather up there?" was the smirking greeting the guys met Beanpole with. Beanpole had pimples, and he could often be found doctoring his face in front of a mirror, hunched over the washbasin to get low enough to see his forehead.

Beanpole left our sparsely settled rural community to disappear into a big-city jungle right after high school. Bitter, hurt by childhood schoolmates, Beanpole has not been seen in our town in 40 years.

"Bob" is any of half a dozen guys I knew. He was of medium build, five-foot-ten, which took him $15\frac{1}{2}$ years to achieve. No zits ever scarred his boyish skin, nor did blackheads ever trouble him. If they did, he got rid of them at home before school. Today Bob is successful, respected, and loved by family and friends in the community in which he grew up.

> *Odd things happen to kids at 12 or so that grandparents who do not have regular contact may find surprising, even confusing.*

We tend to measure our grandchildren against our own childhood and the childhoods of our children. We may not have raised a Beanpole. All of our own kids may have been Bobs. But as the gene pool broadens with each generation, the possibilities likewise enlarge. And we're surprised by a grandchild who's different, especially if we haven't seen him since he was small. Watch it, though. "You're taller than your dad already" or, "My, how you're filling out" may bring shame instead of pride, accentuating Brandon or Meghan's secret belief that he or she was mistakenly placed here from another planet.

"We need some of that," a willowy, clever-tongued ninth-grade girl sneered to her equally slender friend. Two flawless complexions smirked cruelly as a third ninth grader, well endowed but with blotchy complexion, hunkered to hide her bosom. She hurried past my classroom to escape her tormentors. Some young teens, painfully aware of their own imagined shortcomings, often will mercilessly tease others of whom they are jealous. A perfectly normal teen may thus learn to believe himself inadequate, a freak, even.

In reality, all of our grandchildren are different, each in his or her own glorious way. And each, in the eyes of the loving Creator, is normal. But each teen grandchild represents a different piece of the mosaic we accept as normal, a piece that perhaps we have not had experience with.

Bob was normal. Beanpole was normal, also. At 15, the flat-chested girls and the bosomy one, too, were fully normal. But neither they nor their schoolmates were ready to accept this.

Growth spurts, like slow growth, are normal. Young people, age 11 to about 17, may suffer excruciating concerns about their "normality" or lack thereof. Younger teens, especially, are extremely peer conscious, and they tend to measure the normalcy of others (including their parents and grandparents!) by the opinions and standards of their peers.

A 14-year-old, for instance, may not think it's normal for granddads to wear hats. And if his granddad, who's bald and doesn't want to burn, insists on wearing a brimmed hat to a soccer game and looking like Calvin Coolidge, he'd better wear it straight, *at least!* More than one fedora-adorned grandfather has had a jauntily cocked felt or straw shade straightened by an indignant grandson or granddaughter on the way out the door. "Grandpa, you look like some kind of ethnic freak with it on *that* way" is the stock young-teen explanation.

The seventh and eighth grades can mark a confusing time of changes for the typical 12- or 13-year-old, and for some few, these changes can be frightening, even traumatic. Your grandchild, used to being in a self-contained school classroom in his K-6 years, with perhaps an outside teacher for music or art, now changes rooms and teachers every hour. Friends he's hung on to during his elementary years may disappear into the jungle that is junior high or middle school, not to reappear again until bus time.

He or she plunges into sexual maturation, which in our culture can have its cruel aspects. Several times a week students disrobe to change for gym and shower, usually in groups. Stages in sexual development become apparent, sometimes painfully so, as insecure bullies make crude remarks about bodily hair, or the lack thereof, or the size of bosoms or private parts.

I've noticed a recent sexual phenomenon in school classrooms and corridors, which has appeared since I began teaching junior high a third of a century ago. Remember when references to the privates was limited to boys-only or girls-only locker-room sessions? Though remarks then were often vulgar, at least decency between the sexes was preserved. Today's youth, urged along by frankly sexual TV shows, teen and adult magazines (*Glamour* and *Mademoiselle* are now found in many high school libraries), PG-13 and R movies, Internet cybersex, and coed sex-education classes, don't see a problem with having discussions about sex in mixed company and have exchanged the old, vulgar four-letter words for privates for the clinical terms for genitals.

A Florida public school teacher wrote Ann Landers to complain of conditions in her school where "fights, thefts, drug sales, and weapons" have become a constant problem. "Threats and filthy language" in the corridors are regular occurrences, and disruptions by "lewd comments, raucous laughter, and loud arguments with teachers" make education all but impossible. This report was contrasted by a letter from a teacher in Dayton who found even inner-city students to be "well mannered and respectful" and gladly accepting of a dress code of the type many other schools find unenforceable.[1]

As a substitute teacher on call in two western Michigan counties, both elementary and secondary, I can take you to schools within 10 miles of each other where either the Florida or Dayton pattern is the norm. It takes a firm, well-balanced staff of administrators and teachers, in cooperation with wide-awake parents, to run a school these days without chaos. Your grandchildren may be enrolled in either kind of school.

> *Today's young teen grandchild may be thrust from innocence into the context of competitive sexuality.*

This includes easy banter from both boys and girls as young as 12 or 13 about sexual experiences. Today's teen is the third generation of American youth to attend the sprawling consolidated schools instituted right after the grandparents of today finished high school. So a teen today is faced with a mind-boggling assortment of attitudes, opinions, and behaviors. These crowd in with relentless insistence that he sample this, look at that, hear this story, learn another thing from peers or teachers that may contradict or compromise the values of his home or church, or even of the relatively supportive environment of the elementary school. These all cry out for him to question old authority and to transfer his loyalty to a new authority—the school and the peer group. This comes on with a rush in the context of his or her wonderfully developing new appetites.

Teens universally suffer the illusion that sexuality is the exclusive domain of folks under 20, who discovered it as a historical first. In a 1998 movie parody, *Pleasantville,* a teen brother and sister are magically transported via a broken TV set back to the 1950s environment of *Father Knows Best* (Robert Young). The world of their grandparents, these teens discover, is in black and white, like this old TV series. These "enlightened" modern youth bring color to the world you and I grew up in, and happiness to the cast of *Father Knows Best*, as they introduce their grandparents' generation to the joys of intercourse and masturbation. The movie is rated—hold your breath—PG-13, "suitable" for kids age 13 and older.

Young teens, informed by the media that their parents were hopelessly repressed, are sometimes incredulous when told that intense, powerful sexual appetites have been around since Adam marveled at the new twists and curves the Lord had given his rib while he slept. This illusion is part of a natural, universally acknowledged God-given moral agency that insists that sex should be a private joy to be shared between two people in the context of: (a) virginity until marriage; and (b) exclusiveness during marriage. Former missionary Elisabeth Elliot, for example, reports that South American Auca Indians, who wear little or no clothing, vigorously protect the privacy of their sexuality.[2]

What too often happens in American youth culture, I believe, is that the sexual loyalty and privacy that God intended for a husband and wife become peer directed. Teens are sharing amongst themselves—bragging, giggling, or at times intensely serious—the thoughts, appetites, and tragically often the actions, that should be saved for a private encounter with a lifelong, covenanted helpmeet. For example, I overheard a snickering teen girl ask a boy, in a stage whisper intended for the indecent vicarious pleasure of classmates around them—but not for the teacher's ears—if he were having regular sex with his girlfriend.

With such shared sexual experience (vicarious or real) comes a wall of exclusiveness and secrecy that draws on the emotions that God intended to make marriage a no-one-else's-business, exclusive relationship. Instead, this exclusiveness is transferred to the peers of teens. Even youth from Christian homes, who may not share these experiences, like Lot's daughters, who learned about sexuality in Sodom, are often drawn into the net.

All too often this exclusiveness shuts parents, grandparents, and pastors outside the youth's circle of privacy. What can ensue is a game lasting three, five, or even seven years in which children try to keep adults out of these private worlds in which youth share sexual experiences with each other—boys talk about experiences, girls pen notes about them. So parents and grandparents are forced to work out a truce with the teens by which both can function with a modicum of civility.

The Beanpoles with the pimples are pretty much left out of this bittersweet society. This can happen to either sex, but girls, with greater social skills than guys, often manage to build bridges with other girls, with younger kids, or even find satisfaction in tending others' babies. And girls' social facility is no doubt one important reason why fewer girls than guys engage in premarital sex.

Christian teens who take a stand for Christ and moral righteousness are excluded, too. Sexually active youth persist—by intimidation ("everyone's doing it")—in including those like themselves, and insist on excluding anyone who dares admit to being a virgin. Many teens will sooner lie about experience than be left outside.

Being left out, however, while it *can* cause a teen to turn on himself in lowered self-esteem, may actually have a very positive side. Joseph, for instance, had been forcibly ejected from the society of his brothers, one of whom—Judah—had unveiled his low moral principles by visiting a supposed prostitute (see Genesis 37:26–27; 38:15–16). Yet solitary Joseph, a slave in a strange land, refused to engage in adultery and as a young adult rose to be second in command in the world's most powerful nation. Strength derived from times alone with God enabled Joseph to become great before man and before God.

 Most youth feel alone part or much of the time.

I believe that's the natural, normal order of things. Adam was "alone" for a while after his creation, for example (see Genesis 2:18). Teens find themselves alone, not so much because they're in a growth spurt that may make them seem like a Frankensteinian freak to their peers, but because they have left the garden of childhood with its vine-hung walls of parental affection, never to return.

When I was a young teen I was an avid reader of Zane Grey westerns. I loved these stories—the man in the saddle, the faithful horse, the marshal who mistook him for a wanted rustler, nights under the stars with the howl of coyotes and the hoot of owls as companions. I sensed my aloneness, yet I couldn't put a finger on its cause. But here was a man I could relate to because, though from an earlier generation (Grey died the year I was born!), he knew how to express being alone as a thrill, a challenge. So I am not surprised to learn that Gary Paulsen, a fiction writer of my generation, has become a best-selling author by writing about boys facing hardships in the northern wilderness—alone!

Zane Grey was onto a timeless need of youth—that Paulsen has since rediscovered. Jacob, alone, wrestled with God under the stars to become Israel, God's prince (see Genesis 32:24–28). Samuel, separated from his parents, alone with God in his room, was called to be the last and greatest judge of Israel (see 1 Samuel 1:24; 3:10, 19–21). Jesus was tested alone in the desert—as were Moses and Paul (see Matthew 4:1; Exodus 3:1; Galatians 1:17). Christ prayed alone at Gethsemane (see Matthew 26:36–46).

Your grandson or granddaughter, whether outwardly the smooth, fit-with-the-crowd Bob, or the awkward, gangly Beanpole, whether guy or girl, has a felt loneliness that he or she is searching to fill. Your task is to direct that search with loving support, compassion, and kindness.

For a teen troubled by the vicissitudes of growing up, grandparents often can offer help that parents cannot.

Having the advantage of a third generation of maturity, and also being in a better position to take a dispassionate look at a grandchild's problems, a grandparent can soothe, console, and win confidences, whereas a parent might tend to alienate.

Judy (name changed), a young teen girl from a home of divorce, was often a guest in our home when I was in college. Judy lived for a time with her grandparents, but she sometimes came to my father, a man of recognized Christian maturity, with her troubles. A Christian teen, Judy very much wanted a father to talk with, and my dad, with seven kids of his own, would lend her his ears from time to time. I'm sure she worked her way through numbers of problems just by having a sympathetic male listener to help her build her self-esteem.

Author Maureen Rank cites a study by psychologist Dr. Daniel Trobisch. In a chapter titled "The Father-God Connection," Rank summarizes Trobisch: *"Every woman* in his study saw God with the same characteristics she observed in her father" (italics hers). Rank concludes that girls, especially, need fathers in order to develop self-esteem and learn to love God.[3]

Secular studies on the influence of the home on youth generally either lump both parents together or focus on the effect of the mother who is away at work. Clichés such as "The hand that rocks the cradle rules the world" solidify the thinking of those who revere motherhood to the exclusion of fatherhood. TV talk shows dealing with teen problems, such as *Montel Williams,* almost never feature fathers confronting these errant teens.

Yet Abraham Lincoln's famous "All that I am and ever hope to be I owe to my angel mother" has much basis in fact: As girls need fathers, so boys need mothers. Adult males normally find the confirmation of their manhood in their relationship with a loving wife. But in adolescence, it is through relationships with their mothers, or another significant adult female, such as a grandmother, that boys develop confidence to court a girl worthy of their charms, courage to keep at it in college, or perseverance in business pursuits when others are quitting.

Your children—your grandkids' parents—cannot meet every need of your teen grandson or granddaughter. Here's where God has put Grandma in the gap to furnish the cheering squad for grandson Brandon while playing role model for granddaughter Meghan; and Grandpa can furnish male counsel for Meghan while being a role model for Brandon.

Dealing with kids' clothes can be a delicate proposition, because clothes are an extension of the personality, the very soul. When you, Grandma or Grandpa, criticize your teens' apparel, they can be hurt because others *they consider important* have taken facts about their clothing—extensions of their souls—and have ground their souls into the dirt by unthinking comments.

Let's say 15-year-old Meghan is spending a week at Grandma's House during the school year, since her parents must travel on business. Your grandchild arrived Sunday evening in fresh Sunday clothes (unlike eight-year-olds, teens *can* stay neat all day!). Monday morning she arrives for breakfast dressed for school. The knees are out of her jeans. Her loafers are worn without socks, and she wears a T-shirt with "Underachiever and Proud of It" in three-inch-high letters. Do you offer a critical comment? Or do you wait until your daughter phones from the hotel that evening, then query her about her child's "styles"?

Let's say you choose the second course. When Meghan's mother calls, her only complaint is that she wore no socks with those unwashable leather shoes!

That evening, after you gently tell Meghan why she's expected to wear socks, she remarks, "Grandma, Dad really gets a kick out of my T-shirt. He says as long as I'm getting A's in chemistry and German he doesn't care what I wear, just so it's decent." You were rewarded for holding your tongue that morning by having Meghan let you in on a family joke. Meghan appreciates your concern, and she has not been put down by what could seem to her an attack on her individuality.

I recall a gentleman who wore a wig that so obviously was not his hair that it could be spotted across a large auditorium. He wore expensive suits and drove late-model luxury cars all the years I knew him. But not once did I question the guy's taste in toupees by suggesting that he toss his el-cheapo into file 13 and buy a fitted hairpiece, which he could certainly afford to do. That's what mirrors are for.

As grandparents, we desire to help usher our Brandons and Meghans across the threshold of adulthood. We can best do this when we realize that those youth, who much of the time are carefree and happy, are also suffering through the most trying years of life—from puberty to young maturity. We gently criticize their behavior when we must. We set guidelines and expectations when they're entrusted to our care. Even as we wouldn't question another adult's toupee or hairdo, we avoid personal remarks about our emerging adult-teens whose souls may have been torn and trampled already in the school gauntlet or by conflicts at home.

But most of all, we support, we listen, we pray. And we love.

CHAPTER THIRTEEN

Grandparents Bearing Gifts

My kids' maternal grandmother, at 90, had more than one hundred descendants spread over four generations, for whom she used to remember birthdays, anniversaries, baby showers, and graduation parties. By contrast, their paternal grandmother, at 83, has a paltry three and a half dozen descendants over three generations, though hers are spread throughout a wider radius of states.

Things were simpler when I was a child. We had four grandparents, and my maternal grandfather was employed. Each set of grandparents had a dozen grandkids, but great-grandchildren, though eventually numerous, for the most part waited until the elders had passed on before being born. As with my children's generation—and my grandchildren's—neither my wife nor I had grandparents who could afford to be heavy spenders at gift-giving times. And since the generations that preceded us all had their roots in agriculture, we knew the value of gifts directly from the farm: a pound or two of honey in the comb, homemade butter, hand-knit socks or mittens, or home-canned mincemeat for pies. Today's grandparent, with mostly urban descendants often of dissimilar lifestyles, must give gifts to suit a wide variety of circumstances and choose from a bewildering assortment of merchandise.

Cross-cultural and cross-social marriages can lead to misunderstanding, even hurt, at gift-giving time. It can help to meet your grandchildren's other set of grandparents on several informal occasions soon after your children's wedding, either by inviting them to your home—to which they'll no doubt reciprocate—or to a modest restaurant where both couples will be comfortable.

Young couples with small children occasionally isolate themselves from the grandparents and may even return gifts sent for the grandchildren, especially where one spouse was reared to riches and the other grew up in a home of more modest means. Pride over an ambition to make it without the aid of wealthy relatives may boil over into resentment when expensive presents are given the children at Christmastime, whereas the other grandparents can afford only bargain-basement specials. This pride may bring on an emotional myopia that wrongly imagines the generosity of the wealthier grandparents to be an attempt to buy love.

Here's where befriending those other grandparents early in the relationship can help. These friendships can provide insight into understanding the mind of your new daughter-in law or son-in-law, as well as build a bridge into his or her heart.

But be sure it's not *your* pride that's been wounded. Did you really expect a grandchild of eight to take better care of the L. L. Bean shirt you bought him than if it came from Wal-Mart?

Wealth intimidates many grandparents
who've never had much for earthly
possessions. Poverty may frighten
some who are rich.

I grew up poor, but as a journalist I've learned some interesting things about accepting and being accepted. A multimillionaire publisher once took me out to lunch—at McDonald's. I had a 60-cent fish sandwich and a Coke. Her meal was only slightly more expensive. We were both satisfied, and neither of us was embarrassed. Weeks before Dan Quayle was elected to the vice presidency, his parents, Jim and Corrine Quayle, were my guests for breakfast at a small roadside restaurant in Michigan. Both were born to wealth, but they are common folks and easy to chat with. I soon found that we shared spiritual values in common.

The comic-strip caricatures of the rich surrounded by servants, or of the poor living in squalor, are made up of about equal parts of myth and anachronism! Grandparents should not let fears of such imagined barriers prevent them from making friends with their grandchildren's other grandparents.

When buying gifts for the grandchildren, don't concern yourself with what the other grandparents, wealthier or poorer, are buying. Clear it with the parents to avoid duplications and inappropriate presents, of course. But if one grandma, who owns a controlling interest in an industrial plant, buys Jason a $400 remote-controlled car, and you send him peanut-butter fudge gift-wrapped in a fancy can—saved from a Christmas past—well, so what? He'll appreciate both, probably equally, for few eight-year-olds can fathom the worth in dollars of a battery-operated model auto versus the goodness of homemade fudge, anyway.

The apostle Paul's teaching about the Lord's Supper, that sacred celebration of God's greatest gift, eternal life through the broken body and shed blood of Christ, is prefaced with some reminders about our all-too-human tendency to celebrate even Christian occasions selfishly and pridefully. Each Corinthian Christian, rather than eat at home, was going ahead with his own lunch in the company of those he met with to celebrate Communion. One family would pig out on the first-century equivalent of pastrami, Swiss, and sauerkraut on rye, while another family had only soda crackers and processed cheese (see 1 Corinthians 11:20–22).

Christmas, in our day, is the celebration when Christians and others in American Christendom sometimes vie with one another for the most attention-getting festivities. It is one thing to enjoy a tradition, such as a 12-foot tree touching the cathedral ceiling of your family room under which the grandchildren can share a joyous occasion. It is quite another to attempt to buy love or attention with expensive gifts. Be sure, however, that you're not pridefully mistaking another's expensive celebration, to which you have been invited, as an attempt to show off. A lot of folks simply enjoy throwing as good a party as they can afford.

Genuine giving must flow out of true love.

This must be *agape* love, the love that always puts that grandchild's best interests first. This is the love of God who gave us His "one and only Son" (John 3:16); whose "gift is . . . eternal life" forever with Him (Romans 6:23).

Gift-giving grandparents tend to have either a surplus of time or a surplus of cash; seldom both. Retired grandparents living on fixed incomes usually have time on their hands to make things or to learn a craft, but grandparents who are still employed, and whose families have grown, can often afford to buy relatively expensive gifts for grandchildren.

"The gifts that touch the [child's] heart are often the least expensive," writes Marilou Booth. She suggests putting together "fun albums" as gifts—collages of childhood photos of the grandparents, parents, and the children at the same age. Kids are fascinated with what their elders looked like as children, she notes. Stationery stores will copy four to six old photos on an 8-by-11-inch sheet in their color copier. Add covers and inexpensive plastic spines, and you've got photo albums your grandkids will cherish. Or instead, give your grandchildren disposable cameras and ask them to snap candid shots of family members, Booth suggests. *You* have them developed to add to their collections.[1] Little ones like pictures, too—picture books and a box of crayons are the "best gifts for any child."[2]

Some grandparents, having more cash than "shop 'til you drop" stamina, may simply get the kids' sizes and order needed clothing from an L. L. Bean or J. C. Penney's catalogue, depending on their budget. A grandmother with limited means and a large tribe can make a baked gift, one for a family. Personally, I prefer fruitcake. But, along with spats, bell-bottom trousers, and accordion music, fruitcakes are held in disdain by a generation raised on pizza, corn chips, and salsa. So check whether they ate (with relish!) last year's gift before baking another. Cookies, sweet rolls, or another type of cake might be more acceptable. And packaging can be as simple as cardboard, aluminum foil, and cellophane tape.

For minimal expense, grandmothers with sewing machines, knitting needles, or crochet hooks—or grandfathers with woodworking tools—can whip up an endless variety of handmade gifts, many destined to become family heirlooms. A visit to a well-stocked supermarket magazine rack will reveal perhaps a dozen "country" magazines, craft magazines, and woodshop journals. These are filled with designs for making stuffed dolls, quilts, cushions, wooden toys, lawn or bedroom furniture, clock cases, bookcases, knickknacks and knickknack shelves, embroidery, stencil work, reusable Christmas wreaths, rugs, baked goods—the possibilities are endless.

For books and magazines on simple, enjoyable crafts for gifts, visit an older, in-town library that has archived back issues of handcraft and woodworking magazines. Some, such as *Popular Mechanics,* go back about a century and carry unique plans that can be easily updated and adapted for modern use. You can also find plans and patterns on CD-ROM or in easy-to-read books in craft shops or lumberyards. Or download plans for your favorite craft from a woodworking Web site. These resources can easily be printed out on your computer's printer or accessed with a public library's computer. See the appendix to this book for suggested Web sites.

My dear old Aunt Gladys had no children of her own,

though she ministered to more than a thousand children during 40-some years as a teacher. The same age as my maternal grandmother, she once told me she thought of my father as the son she never had. And she lived to play grandmother to several of Dad's grandchildren. Using turn-of-the-century patterns from her childhood in the 1890s, she made afghans for weddings and for baby showers, and knitted caps for preschool youngsters—brand-new antiques! Some of her handiwork is now tucked away in Grandma Wiggin's cedar chest for future generations to enjoy.

Books ought to be at the head of a grandparent's shopping list. As with most other gifts for grandchildren, consult the parents; you need to know the child's reading level and interests and avoid duplication. Visit a Christian bookstore well in advance of your shopping trip, and browse the children's, juvenile, and adult fiction sections. "Teen" fiction tends to be aimed at preteens or young teens (ages 10 to 14), so if you have a grandchild 15 or older, he or she will probably prefer a selection from the adult section. Some books, such as C. S. Lewis's and J. R. R. Tolkien's allegorical fantasies, appeal to preteen through adult, however.

Several Christian publishers produce series of biographies and historical fiction to help your grandchild understand God at work in his world. I have included sources for these books in an appendix.

Some grandparents like to add to collections their grandchildren are building.

Grandma Wiggin—my wife—looks for silver charms in the shape of the states we visit on our vacation trips. You, Grandma, may wish to personalize a gift by making a doll or teddy bear with your granddaughter's name sewn onto it. Grandpa may wish to complement a doll collection by building Grand-daughter a fine dollhouse.

Gifts of clothing are usually appreciated, and if Grandma is talented at the sewing machine, dresses for girls, little and big, will look and wear better than the department-store vari-ety. Few teen girls wear dresses to school, though, so the sewing may need to be limited to Sunday wear. "Will she wear this if I make it?" is a valid and often necessary question Grandma should ask the child's mother before buying the cloth and pattern.

Today's computerized sewing machines generally are afford-able and give professional results after a little practice. More than one grandma has eventually found herself drafted to make the bridesmaids' dresses for a granddaughter's wedding!

Consider the age and maturity of your grandchild when buying a gift. If you're tempted to purchase a genuine Swiss army knife (about $35) or a staghorn-handle hunting knife ($100 and up) for a grandson, wait until he's a teen. The usual thing for preteen boys to do with pocketknives is to lose them within a month or so. He'll appreciate a Barlow knife ($3.98), however.

My two oldest sons were teens when they shared the cost of a .22-caliber target rifle at a yard sale held by a grandfather several years ago. Sheepishly, this granddad told me how he'd bought the rifle new for his eight-year-old grandson months earlier—without first asking his daughter, the boy's mother, for permission. Understandably, the mother didn't think her child was old enough for such an adult toy!

I have my own criteria for buying gift firearms for kids, beyond clearing it with the parents. Target rifles (.22's, ordinarily) should never be repeaters. This considerably reduces the chance of kids making tragic mistakes with loaded guns. BB guns (air rifles) are no-no's because children may treat them like toys, though they can put out eyes and may even be fatal. No handguns for kids, ever.

I started my own three boys on a shotgun. The range is far less than a .22, and the kick and roar of a shotgun will remind a kid that he's handling a deadly weapon each time he touches the shooting iron off! Of course many grandparents and parents oppose kids owning guns, period; and that's all right, too. But some grandparents *will* buy guns for rural youngsters or those with access to a target range, so it only seems sensible to establish some guidelines.

It's a common mistake, whether your gift will be books, toys, clothing, or whatever, to wait until the flyers advertising Christmas specials arrive with the Sunday newspaper, then rush off to buy what's on sale. Such buying may address the "thought" in the heart of the giver, but since little thought may have been given to the need of the grandchild who will be the recipient, the gift may be discarded—or returned and exchanged.

 ## But it's the thought that counts, isn't it?

I can hear readers musing on *that* notion, almost in an audible murmur. Yes, indeed! Christ said of the woman of Bethany, who "wasted" the valuable alabaster jar of ointment of pure nard on

His feet, "Leave her alone. . . . She has done a beautiful thing to me" (Mark 14:6). Jesus was not glorying in her apparent groveling, like some earthly potentate who insists on sitting on a chair above his cowering subjects. Rather, looking into her heart, He could see her contrite, thoughtful, worshipful attitude that needed to express itself in this beautiful act of obeisance.

Yet the act of giving, if thought out intelligently, aims first of all to meet the need of the grandchild, the receiver. And in that giving, we should aim to please. Realistically, there was nothing the woman could have given Jesus shortly before His crucifixion that He needed more than this act of worship in preparation for His burial. "She did what she could," Jesus acknowledged (Mark 14:8).

"I don't care what they want; I'm good at fruitcakes, so I'm making fruitcake" is hardly a *thought* of love, though the act itself may be appreciated. Be sure your heart, your head, your purse, and the needs of your grandchildren all coincide. You'll be a glad grandparent bearing gifts at Christmastime—or at any other time!

CHAPTER FOURTEEN

Parenting Is for Parents

"Mother, I've tried that. Amy's rash just *won't* clear up!" Sandy's indignation at her mother's offer of a tube of hydro-cortisone cream for nine-month-old Amy's rash, which had spread even to body areas always kept dry, was largely frustration at the ineffectiveness of salves to stop this scarlet plague.

"When did it begin?" ventured Amy's grandma, casting a worried look toward the baby. The girl looked badly sun-burned, though she had not been in the sun.

"Just over a week ago, when I took her off the breast. I'm following the pediatrician's formula *exactly*," Sandy insisted, anticipating her mother's next question.

"Then you don't think it's in Amy's system?"

"How *could* it be? I mix her formula with bottled spring-water, and her baby food has *no* chemical additives. That's why I quit nursing in the first place. I found out the meat John and I were eating was raised on steroids, and I was afraid my milk would hurt the baby."

Grandma, who herself had become a vegetarian for a

while during a brief fling with the flower children in the 1960s, listened to Sandy elaborate on her favorite topic.

"That little old Yugoslavian lady who's moved in next door—Mrs. Theonas—suggested I try *goat's* milk. Can you imagine?"

"You can buy it at that Greek deli downtown," Mother answered, half amused, half in earnest.

"Mother!"

"Really, now, you had a rash, too. We switched from cows' milk to soybean formula until you were two. It cleared right up."

"I *won't* mess with what I put in Amy's system until she sees the doctor!"

Mother changed the subject.

A week later, Sandy phoned, ecstatic. "Guess what, Mom? Doctor Walcott put Amy on soybean formula. Her rash cleared right up. Even the diaper rash is gone!"

"No goat's milk?"

"*That's* a funny question. The doctor said that should work, too, if I could find it in the stores."

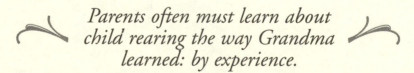

Parents often must learn about child rearing the way Grandma learned: by experience.

Fifty dollars to learn from a doctor what two grandmas already knew, Grandma thought as she hung the phone up. "I guess those kids have to learn these things for themselves," she sighed aloud to nobody but herself.

Grandmas, from little old Yugoslavian ladies to sophisticated suburban dames wise in all the knowledge of American child rearing, are vast reservoirs of knowledge, oozing with advice young mothers ignore at dire peril. Grandpas, also, seem to know more than fathers could ever hope to learn. We made *our* mistakes. Why should our grandchildren suffer when all this accumulated wisdom is on tap?!

"After becoming a grandparent for a few times, one should become an expert. I am that," "Ol' Man Raleigh," an experienced grandfather, wisecracks. Writing tongue-in-cheek to grandparents, he added that if we grandparents hear his wisdom, we won't "make fools of [our]selves, as I did."

On advice to parents, Raleigh says, "Don't give it. . . . New parents will not take it graciously. It's their child." He adds that a youngster's "being your grandchild . . . is really only incidental to the parents."[1]

Does Raleigh's "don't give advice" advice sound extreme? Maybe. My three sons occasionally ask my advice about their cars, for instance. I tried to set a good example when they were growing up by asking others for advice about my auto problems. But baby formulas and child-rearing practices?

Grandma Wiggin and I get *asked* for advice on these, too—by several of our children. Occasionally we offer unsolicited advice—obliquely, phrased as an observation: "Hey, you've taught Erica to count! Would you like us to get her a phonetic reader?" This is indirect advice (with the offer of a gift book!) from grandparents who've helped teach Erica's dad as well as his aunt and two uncles to read: *You should be teaching that four-year-old to read now that she's ready to learn.*

Shirley Franks, mother of 10 and grandmother and great-grandmother of 25, advises that "mostly you think about what you'd like to say or what you'd like to do" when your children are making decisions affecting your grandchildren. Grandma Shirley, in fact, only "hinted about the inadvisability" of letting her newly licensed 16-year-old grandchild have a car to commute to school, though a bus was available. Then "I bit my tongue," she chuckles. Within a few days the parents learned by expensive trial and error that Grandma was right. Grandma, glad that she had not indulged in a lecture beforehand, followed by an "I told you so" afterward, was prayerfully happy that her grandchild was unhurt.

But married children "don't forget how you've brought *them* up," notes Shirley. As the years pass, your children go through the same things with their children that you went through with them. Grandparents who've maintained a happy rapport with their adult children will from time to time find that they "check you out to see if you'd still make the same decisions," she says. This permits grandparents to tactfully have a direct input into family decisions without being offensive.

"No grandparent has the right to take away from fathers and mothers the right to do their own parenting," comments author Charlie W. Shedd, himself a grandfather.[2] Shedd's salient wisdom is based on several important truths: Experience *is* the most effective teacher, though it's often not the kindest! Our children, now parents themselves, have already been "train[ed] up" by us. As Shirley Franks observes, they continue to mature as they apply to living situations what we taught them while they were young, modifying our teachings to suit the needs of a new generation. And while there are many timeless, practical truths not requiring specialized medical expertise—grandmas know that some infants whose systems cannot tolerate cows' milk will thrive on goats' milk or soy formula, for example—life does constantly change. Adult children do often speak the truth when they insist that "it's not the same world we grew up in."

So, how does a grandparent—who really *does* know things about children—go about imparting this wisdom to married adult children with kids (other than by writing a book!)? Here are some hints:

 Don't offer advice on sensitive topics unless invited to do so.

Notice that by suggesting, "Then you don't think it's in Amy's system?" Sandy's mother tactfully drew out Sandy's opinion, while expressing just enough of her own to let her daughter know that there was more on her mind if Sandy wished to inquire.

For grandparents, this rule may change or modify as the grandchildren become teens. Ordinarily it is the *teen* whose permission—spoken or tacit—you must gain. Good judgment must come into play here. Some parents will be very happy to have you help their teens through struggles with sexual temptation, for instance. Others might wish a shared consensus on these matters. Still others might resist your input.

Your son-in-law or daughter-in-law was probably reared by parents with a different set of unspoken signals than yours.

For instance, a young parent reared by parents from the South may have learned that it's impolite to disagree under any circumstances. But in the Northeast friendly disagreements are a means of intellectual stimulation! Does your daughter-in-law's silence mean she is anticipating a friendly debate—or is she trying to avoid what she may perceive to be an unpleasant argument brewing? Learn these differences before you put your ideas, however pertinent, out for airing!

 Learn to separate sensitive, personal advice from impersonal advice.

Realize that what you may consider impersonal may be taken personally by someone with differing thought processes. To point out that your son-in-law's car, which is belching black smoke, probably needs the choke cleaned, may be taken as suggesting he's a polluter and somewhat of a slob. Or he may be grateful to know that a stuck choke might be fixed with a $1.59 can of solvent and an old toothbrush, since a mechanic has just quoted $300 for a carburetor overhaul, which his car probably does not need.

One mother might gladly welcome advice about how to cure a baby's rash, yet she may find advice on educating that same child offensive and overweening. Another mother might be offended at either level of advice; a third, at neither.

Is your grandchild going to be seriously harmed by your withholding advice?

Not usually. "You really should see an orthodontist about Tommy's crooked teeth," you remark. But Tommy's mother has discussed this with the family dentist already. She has valid reasons for *not* spending the $3,000 on orthodontics Tommy's parents have put away for his education. She knows Tommy has lots of friends, so his teeth are no hindrance to him socially. And she has a close friend who, after great expense on her son's teeth, saw him lose several in a ball game.

Do you have constructive solutions, or are you just airing worries?

"I'm afraid for little Justin, with all those trucks rumbling past your house," you may say. But what do you propose? Should Mother keep Justin indoors at all times? Tether him to a tree? Spank him soundly for playing near the road? Teach him to fear trucks (cars, though quieter, are just as dangerous)?

Instead, a happy and appropriate solution to Mother's dilemma with small Justin and traffic danger might be to say, "Could you folks use a fenced backyard? Your father's been wanting an excuse to use that new band saw in the garage. He'll saw the pickets any style you like, and I think we've got enough money in our rainy day account to buy the lumber."

Before you speak, recall advice from a grandparent that you wish you'd heeded when raising your own children.

Mother, my grandchildren's great-grandmother, can't remember a time when she didn't know how to read. Her own mother, a teacher before 1920 when most youngsters were taught reading by the phonetic method, introduced her to letters and sounds. Her earliest memories include reading news reports in the *Daily Kennebec Journal* (Augusta, Maine). Mother began school in grade four at age nine.

So, when our daughter was not quite four, we were introduced to a Christian school pre-K phonetic reading program that had four-year-olds reading third- and fourth-grade books easily and with comprehension. Our Debbie was three years, ten months old when she began school—which her grandmother did not think was a good idea! By her fourth birthday, she could read the King James Bible—and so could most of her classmates.

Would I recommend the same thing for my grandchildren? Not on your life! In an interview with me for a news story, well-known Christian homeschool advocate Dr. Raymond Moore indicated that children should not be inducted into classroom schooling until they are at least 7; 10 is better. Moore pointed out that children gain confidence from parental approval, and that they can effectively be taught to read at home. So my grandchildren's great-grandmother, at nine, began school at an ideal age. And *her* mother made the right choice without the learned advice of Dr. Moore!

Two generations later I made the wrong choice, and Debbie, myself, and her mother—now Grandma Wiggin—have learned a great deal which we'd have missed had we not had the chance to choose, even when choosing badly. Would I have listened to my own mother had she more strenuously advised me not to start my children in school so young? Of course not! I was proud of my college education, but she was *only* a high school graduate. Furthermore, evangelical Christian schools were a new movement, unheard of in most of America when my mother had seven school-age youngsters, their elementary and secondary educations spread over 32 years (1944–76). What, I thought, could she possibly know?

So, if my daughter and daughters-in-law wish to keep their youngsters home until they're emotionally ready, more power to 'em. Grandpa Wiggin may even buy them a phonetic reader and gently, very gently, suggest that four-year-olds can be *home*-taught to read, as was their great-grandmother.

 ## *Give your married children room to grow into their child-rearing responsibilities.*

One day when I, my parents' eldest, was about 16, in an indignant moment of self-pity I asked my father why he allowed one of my younger siblings to get away with thus and so without getting his impudent hide tanned. "I've learned a few things since you were small," he answered archly. Does it surprise you that one of my own older children has asked the same question about why tag-along Brad, who arrived after a seven-year hiatus in our childbearing, once seemed to get away with anything short of homicide?

 ## *Offer them a book.*

Be tactful, however. One young mother told me that she doesn't believe in getting much advice from books.

But our Debbie, with four youngsters 2 to 12, found that their four-year-old Tessie wanted to treat her younger brother like a rag doll. Tessie loved little Zeke, and she could be counted on to hold him and play with him. But Tessie was not to be repressed, even when it was nap time for Zeke.

Then one day Grandpa (myself!) discovered *You Can't Make Me (But I Can Be Persuaded),* a book on rearing strong-willed children by popular seminar speaker Cynthia Ulrich Tobias. *You Can't Make Me* is loaded with practical advice on defusing family conflicts without locking horns.

I phoned Debbie. She was delighted with my offer to order a copy for her and her husband. Their Sunday school class had just been viewing Mrs. Tobias's tapes! So I sent for *two* copies of *You Can't Make Me*—one for Debbie and another for her brother and his wife, who are experiencing their own child-rearing struggles.[3]

   ## *Remember that God is still in control.*

But you can and should pray! Dorothy Larsen organized a Grandmoms in Touch chapter, writes Cheri Fuller.[4] Fuller, author of the book *When Mothers Pray,* noted that answers to prayer for the grandmoms in Dorothy Larsen's circle included improved schoolwork, parent-child relationships restored, and much more (see Matthew 18:19–20). We have listed contact information in the appendix for starting your own Grand-moms in Touch group.

   ## *Our Father knows best.*

Our Father in heaven put your adult child and his or her spouse—opposites in many ways—together to give them a balanced marriage. This will bring about a natural tension, giving them emotionally balanced children also. Grandparents who too intrusively inject themselves into their grandchildren's lives can upset this balance. Can you prayerfully trust our heavenly Father to work out His will in your grandkids' lives?

CHAPTER FIFTEEN

Are Today's Teens Different?

After a third of a century as a teacher, I was told it was time for me to retire by a student who challenged my right to ask him to stop talking so others could work on their math. Of course, not all young people are as brash in their estimation of gray-headed elders as this teen, whom I sent to the principal to explain his concern about my job tenure. This ninth grader might have been surprised to learn that in 1939, the year of my birth, there were no teenagers. His rude reaction to my request, however, was really an extreme example of what Dr. Gary Chapman terms the two "underlying themes" of teenage culture: *"independence* and *self-identity."*[1]

Before about 1929 most American youth remained as *inter*dependent members of their families until they left home to marry or to follow a profession. Farm boys often stayed with their parents, gradually assuming responsibility until the old folks died or were set aside by age and infirmity.

My own parents, of the generation of today's great-grandparents, belonged to the first American wave of youth for which *independence* and *self-identity* were a separate life stage set apart from the gradual merging of childhood into adulthood. After the stock market crash of 1929 (my dad was 13 then) brought on the economic chaos of the Great Depression, the *concept* of the modern teenager emerged, Chapman says.

Teen culture, then, is a phenomenon that appeared in the 1930s, within memory of today's great-grandparents. High schools were created in the nineteenth century as finishing schools for youth without money for college; but for many years only the few lucky ones who did not have to work could attend. Chapman notes that in 1900 only 6 percent of American youth finished high school. By 1939, 75 percent were graduating.[2] My mother, Great-Grandma Pauline Wiggin, born in 1918, recalls that after the Crash of '29 "most" teens in her community enrolled in high school. Modern teen culture, therefore, was born during my mother's youth.

Automobiles became plentiful in the 1930s, and those teens who could afford them snatched them from the used car lots—$10 would buy an older Model T Ford; $50 would get a kid an eight-cylinder jalopy. Talking movies first appeared just before the Crash, and with Technicolor added in 1935, Hollywood stars began seriously to compete with parents and pastors for the attention of impressionable youth. After 1931 car radios began to appear in auto dashes, and teens could listen to the big band sounds of Glenn Miller or Guy Lombardo without having to visit a dance hall. The stage was now set for the emergence of this new social class: the American teenager.

Teen culture had pretty much taken its present shape by

1941, when the word "teenage" first appeared in print, in a *Popular Science* article.[3] Since then, World War II and Korea (1941–45; 1950–53), the Vietnam War with its "make love not war" protestors (1964–75), and the sexual revolution of the 1960s all have impacted teens.

The teen of the 2000s, though, is a world apart from the first 60 years of teen culture. Grandparents should note the important changes affecting the way we relate to our teen grandkids:

 ## Girls are exploited; boys are repressed.

"Girls Kick Butt." This slogan, common on T-shirts worn even by girls from evangelical Christian homes, is the expression of a subtle movement that has smacked our youth with a vengeance. Writing in *The War Against Boys: How Misguided Feminism Is Harming Our Young Men,* Christina Hoff Sommers notes that boys are being squashed down by feminist teachers who squelch normal male behavior and douse masculine creativity by diagnosing it as a psychological malady, then dose it with Ritalin.[4]

But there is a nastier underside to this whole thing. In the name of liberation, girls have become the targets of deliberate sexual exploitation by the media. Feminist writer Naomi Wolf approvingly acknowledges in *Promiscuities* that many girls view such lurid porn as *Penthouse* as primers for how girls should behave toward young men.[5] Add to this the deluge of sex-oriented material in popular magazines for women and girls, and you have a generation of very confused young women.

Chapman, writing about the sexual revolution of the

1960s, notes that baby boomers "rebelled against the traditional mores of their parents. . . . But the contemporary teenager has grown up in a world without sexual rules. Movies, media and music all equate sex with love."[6] Yesterday's baby boomers are the parents of today's teenagers.

Has your grandchild—your granddaughter in particular—been sucked into this maelstrom? Perhaps not. There are encouraging signs that, increasingly, Christian teens are firmly resisting this moral carnage, to live above it. Many Christian parents, shocked by the excesses of their own generation, have successfully thrown a hedge about their children by faithful family devotions, consistent church attendance, and educating at home or in Christian schools. A lot of teens, shored up by strong youth programs in their local churches, stand tall for Jesus in the public schools.

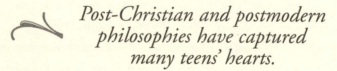

Post-Christian and postmodern philosophies have captured many teens' hearts.

Chapman names "Neutral moral and religious values" as another "fundamental difference"[7] between today's teens and the three generations that preceded them. This is true in general, though not absolutely. High school classrooms have for many years more or less undermined parental values, while attempting to replace Christian principles with evolution and humanism (remember that the Scopes "Monkey Trial," about teaching evolution in a Tennessee high school classroom, was in 1925, *before* there was a teen culture). The nihilistic novels of Jack London (1876–1916), Ernest Hemingway (1899–1961), and J. D. Salinger (b. 1919) have been fed to English classes for decades.

But Walt Mueller, in *Understanding Today's Youth Culture*, puts his finger on the central philosophy that has caused many teens to lay down their moral and spiritual armor and succumb to satanic philosophy: postmodernism. Postmodern thinking outstrips even the angst and nihilism of the 1955 movie *Rebel Without a Cause*, starring James Dean, which presented life without meaning or hope to the generation who today are the grandparents. The postmodernist frankly argues that all opinions are equally valid: the Bible and Christianity; pagan Wicca—gaining popularity with today's teen girls—and worship of Mother Earth; premarital sex or chastity until marriage—you do your thing and I'll do mine. Most of today's teens see no contradiction in this. Postmodernism's politically correct buzzword is "tolerance." Its best-known guru is the late-night talk show host Bill Maher.

Mueller writes that thinking "started to change around the late 1960s" when youthful Baby Boomers were teenagers. "*Postmodernism* began its assault . . . [with] the belief that there is no such thing as objective truth."[8] Mueller cites *Postmodern Times* by Gene Veith: "The only wrong idea is to believe in truth."[9] Pollster George Barna, notes Mueller, "found that about three quarters of all adults reject the notion of absolute moral truth."[10]

 For twenty-first-century teens, electronic entertainment knows no bounds.

Today's teen is the first generation to grow up with the computer, the Internet, and the VCR or DVD player. We grandparents cannot recall a world without automobiles, telephones, or radios, though some of us remember that *our* grandparents predated these inventions. Just as today's parents cannot recall a world without TV, for your teen grandchild a world without computers and the Internet, without video stores where for 99 cents he can rent movies portraying a century of history and entertainment, is incomprehensible.

With the click of a mouse button today's teen can open a world that includes the daily newspaper or French-language foreign periodicals, complete encyclopedias, chat rooms, e-mail from friends around the world, alternate lifestyle news, and Christian theology. He can also view graphic sex 24 hours a day.

Even parents who monitor their children's computers and control video rentals must contend with public library computers. Many of these are wide open to abuse, and even small children can view uncensored pornography.

 Teens of the 2000s fit a unique mold—with problems both similar to and different from those of teens of other eras.

Paradoxically, teens of the 2000s, lacking the explosive, change-the-world philosophy of the "Now Generation" of 30 or 40 years ago, are apt to conform outwardly to adult rules. For every girl with a tongue stud or guy with green hair, a dozen others have neat haircuts reminiscent of the 1940s or 1950s. One study found that perhaps 70 percent attend a church function weekly—worship service, Sunday school, or youth meeting—far exceeding their parents (40 percent) or their grandparents (about 50 percent).[11] Much teen church activity may be for social purposes, however. Only half as many teens claim to be committed Christians, and two-thirds of 13 to 18-year-olds surveyed do not expect to continue the same level of church attendance after high school graduation.[12]

Many of today's teen girls have been caught in the fringes of feminism and women's rights, but few have been drawn into its core. More common, along with WWJD bracelets, teen girls sometimes come to class with "Choose Life" emblazoned on their sweatshirts or notebooks. Teens of both sexes often wear shirts with Bible verses or Christian slogans. Hundreds of thousands of Christian youth annually brave the jeers of their peers to pray, sing hymns, and read the Bible beside their school flagpole on See You at the Pole Day.

In a reflection of student-led spiritual initiatives on school campuses, when Brandon Smith, 16, portrayed the crucifixion at a Mississippi public school skit on April 12, 2000, his classmates joined him in a "full-fledged revival." That's what decisiontoday.org, a Web site of the Billy Graham Evangelistic Association, termed it. Smith, a member of the Pearl River Central High School's Fellowship of Christian Athletes, Carriere, Mississippi, carried a cross in what was planned to be a 90-minute, voluntary school Easter assembly. Instead, 450 of Pearl River's 670 students remained in the gym for five hours, missing lunch as they worshipped the Lord. They sang, they prayed, they wept—and they stood 50 deep at a microphone to testify and confess sins that ranged from premarital sex to being rude. Following a senior awards assembly more than a month later, these kids continued the revival spirit by joining hands to pray.[13]

I have noticed that teen girls today are much more likely to smoke than when I was in high school in the 1950s. This is possibly in response to powerful tobacco ads in women's magazines; but guys appear to smoke less. Teens of both sexes are slightly more likely to have experienced sex than youth of our generation in the 1950s, but less than teens of their parents' generation in the 1970s and 1980s. A January 2001 Centers for Disease Control report shows that overall teen sexual activity declined 8 percent from 1991 to 1999.[14]

 Middle school sex is common.

A 1997 school survey of nearly six thousand teens—about 90 percent of grades 8, 10 and 12—by the Muskegon County (Michigan) Health Department found that about a third of girls who lose their virginity do so at age 11 or 12—as fifth and sixth graders. Most of the remaining two-thirds of nonvirgins experienced their first intercourse between ages 13 and 17.[15]

Boys in the Muskegon County survey most often began sex at age 14 or 15—as eighth or ninth graders. Sixty-two percent of both sexes who had experienced sexual intercourse began before age 14. The usual time and place for teen sex was right after school at home while parents were at work, the survey found.[16]

 Yet teen sex is down.

"Seventy percent" of my teen readers "are still virgins," stated Diane Salvatore, editor-in-chief of *YM*, a girls' magazine popular with younger teens, interviewed April 4, 2000, on NBC's

Later Today show. Salvatore's statistic agrees with the Michigan county survey, which found that of Muskegon County's eighth and tenth graders of both sexes, 68 percent are still virgins. By their senior year, the county survey found, just 38 percent were still virgins.[16] Christian schools and homeschoolers did not contribute to the survey, however.

Encouragingly, teen sexual involvement has dropped over a decade as the new millennium dawns, affecting black teens, whites, Hispanics; godly as well as ungodly. Several factors seem to be at work here: The fear of HIV/AIDS has sobered millions of sexually active adults and teens. Some have restricted themselves to fewer partners. Others have increasingly used condoms. Not a few frightened teens have simply remained virgins or have quit having intercourse. School-based abstinence courses, funded by the 1996 federal Title V Abstinence Education Program, have been shown to result in much less sexual activity.

 Godly purity standards prove most effective.

More than a million Christian teens have taken True Love Waits pledges to remain chaste until marriage, according to a spokesperson for that program at Lifeway Christian Communications, Nashville, Tennessee. The Southern Baptist Convention's True Love Waits program, begun in 1993, is now used by at least 87 denominations, including many who are not Baptists, Lifeway reports. Teens of both sexes increasingly sport "True Love Waits," or a similar proabstinence slogan, on T-shirts and sweatshirts worn to school.

Sex Respect, a Catholic organization, is hard at work promoting virginity among teens and encouraging youth who have already experienced sex to abstain. Sex Respect's Web site promotes *Love and Life: A Christian Sexual Morality Guide for Teens,* a program aimed at youth 12–17.

The divorce rate has slowly declined for two decades since 1981, according to the National Center for Health Statistics report for 1998.[18] Fewer divorces mean fewer kids from broken homes; and fewer teens without daddies at home means fewer teens experimenting with sex to salve empty hearts.

Some authorities question that virginity is again gaining wide favor, however. Highlighted by the media is the decline in the *pregnancy* rate, with little emphasis on the *chastity* rate.

ABC News commentator Peter Jennings, on July 13, 2000, told his *World News Tonight* audience that the "teen pregnancy rate dropped 8 percent between 1995 and 1997." *Seventeen* magazine, which tacitly approves of premarital sex, cites a Kaiser Family Foundation survey, dated August 10, 1998, that teen pregnancy "has *decreased* [italics theirs] by 15 percent."[19] The Maine Department of Human Services Bureau of Health found that from 1980 to 1996 pregnancies for 15- to 19-year-olds fell by a third in that state—from 67.9 to 45.6 per 1,000 girls.[20]

The point many secularists wish to make is that birth control, not abstinence, is primarily responsible for the decline in teen births. The editors of the *Maine, 1980–1996* report note that "the percentage of males and females aged 15–19 years [in Maine] who ever had sexual intercourse was 58% in 1991, 49% in 1995, and 52% in 1997." This 6 percent overall drop in teen sex elicited a cynical snort from the editors: "The changes in these percentages were not statistically significant."[21] Further, these editors ignored the fact that the teen pregnancy figures from the Maine Vital Statistics Office represent *all* Maine girls 15 to 19. But the "statistically [in]significant" sexual experience decrease noted in the *Maine Youth Risk Factor Survey* represents *state-licensed* schools only. Maine's Department of Human Services and Planned Parenthood have for years linked hands to push a powerful "practice safe sex" program in 85 percent of Maine's public schools. "You can't teach chastity and hand out condoms," cautioned Bettina Dobbs, RN, MS, in an interview. Dobbs is president of Guardians of Education for Maine, a public school watchdog group, and a former consultant to the U.S. Department of Health and Human Services.

Yet Maine also has a thriving private religious school sector—Catholic parochial schools, church-run evangelical Christian schools, besides a burgeoning homeschooling movement. These, which promote virginity among their students, were not represented in the sexual activity data.

The Centers for Disease Control and Prevention (CDC) reports also that not only is pregnancy falling among teen girls, but "the prevalence of sexual experience" decreased 11 percent overall 1991–97: from 50.0 percent to 43.6 percent among white students; and from 81.4 percent to 72.6 percent among blacks during these six years.[22] The Kaiser Family Foundation was even more optimistic: 60 percent of the 13- to 19-year-olds it surveyed in 1999 were still virgins, reports *Seventeen*'s Web site. "A lot of people talk about sex, but they really aren't doing it. They just want to fit in," Katie, 18, told Kaiser's researchers.[23]

A February 10, 1999, study supported by the two-thousand-member Consortium of State Physicians Resource Councils tackled the professional sexperts' pooh-poohing of abstinence, with its own conclusions. "The decline in overall teen birthrates is primarily attributable to abstinent adolescents," these doctors concluded. But condom education, said the Physicians Resource Council, had caused a "dramatic increase . . . in the out-of-wedlock birthrate" for girls already sexually active.[24]

As a means to slow or stop teen sexual activity, decency groups for many years have combated pictorial porn aimed at men and boys, but printed pornography has quietly slipped into the women's novels and magazines found on newsstands, in public libraries, as well as in many school libraries. Many girls are heavy readers of this type of salacious diversion as early as grade seven, which may partly account for the fact that for the first time in memory, fewer girls than guys are remaining virgins.[25] Graphic *Cosmopolitan, Glamour,* and *Mademoiselle* articles introducing young girls to explicit details of bedroom love are commonly passed around in study halls in middle and high schools—indeed, I have seen the latter two magazines on school library shelves.

But today's girls still say "thank you" if you hold the door for them, and they wear skirts to church and other dress-up occasions. They are still given to feminine hairdos and romantic fantasies about proms, silk gowns, low lights, and loud music.

Hugging and other nonsexual touching are "in" with teens of the 2000s. During a stroll through the corridors of a high school between classes you notice girls hugging both girls and guys, and guys reciprocating. This is often accompanied by friendly squeals of joy or occasionally tears.

Divorce, though slowing down in the 2000s, still wreaks

havoc in the lives of the kids it affects. Such youth may find themselves unable to bond in a marriage relationship. Not a few confuse sex with love. Your teen grandchild, though he may not have had parents who were divorced, is nonetheless a part of this culture, and he shares much of the mentality common today. Lacking long-term commitment, many pair off in housekeeping arrangements short of marriage.

> *The teen from a divorced home, notes Focus on the Family, suffers a "diminished ability to form lasting relationships."[26]*

He is more likely to divorce later; or before marriage to drift into cohabitation, which sets him up for a much higher than the average divorce rate. Perhaps typifying this sad phenomenon, Stephen Lyons writes that, "I did not meet my grandmother until I was 37 . . . because of divorce." When Lyons was nine, he reports, his parents split up. Twenty-eight years later Lyons, his father, his mother, and an older brother had averaged three marriages each—twelve marriages, seven divorces, and one death.[27]

Two sets of divorce statistics seem at odds with each other, however. The divorce rate of all *marriages* (about 50 percent for the past 30 years)[28] evidently reflects multiple marriages and second or third divorces, to a large degree among the same population. A Barna Research Institute study recently found that only a quarter of all married adults, nationally, have ever been divorced.[29] Barna's findings agree with an earlier Harris Poll study that concluded that barely 20 percent of marrieds have ever divorced. In 1981 the number of divorces in the U.S. was roughly half the number of marriages: 1.2 million and 2.4 million. Hollywood and media personnel, notorious for divorces and eager to disguise their own shame, latched on to this statistic to announce that the rest of America was living as portrayed on the silver screen: busy at bed-hopping and wife-swapping.[30]

Surprisingly, fewer of today's parents than grandparents have been divorced, Barna found.[31] I believe that this is already showing up in stronger families, as baby boomers, born 1946–64, rear their children.

I have noticed more gallantry among guys and less boorishness toward girls today than 20 or 30 years ago. Compared to the 1940s and 1950s, however, when many boys were patterning their manners after the likes of Clark Gable and Humphrey Bogart, boys today are less outwardly romantic. Among some there's a nasty undercurrent of sexual pursuit that on the surface seems to come straight from the *Playboy* philosophy. But if you look behind the scenes, it's apparent that a lot of today's attitudes are a reaction to role switching between Mom and Dad at home, which, in turn, may be a product of young mothers denying their maternal instincts in favor of outside employment. Thankfully, organizations such as Promise Keepers and Focus on the Family, are helping to slow or reverse this trend.

I ran into a startling phenomenon among girls' attitudes a couple of years ago, after *Titanic* played in the theaters.

A housewife in Grand Haven, Michigan, made news by viewing this 3-hour, 10-minute melodrama more than 20 times. So I began to ask schoolkids, "Have you seen *Titanic?*" Nearly all girls in grades 5, 8, and 9 through 12—where I was a substitute teacher—had seen it. Many three or more times!

"What did you think of the movie?"

"Great!" screamed the girls.

Boys' responses ranged from "Okay" to "Boring." Only about half the boys had seen the film, many of them dragged into the theater by a girl.

One eighth-grade girl said she had viewed it in the theater 16 times until her mother bought the video. She then watched *Titanic* every afternoon with her sister, age 18. Several from eighth grade up—in different schools—had seen *Titanic* 6, 8, even 12 times.

So, what's the big deal? The one scene that the girls, without exception, enjoyed the most was when actor Leonardo DiCaprio drowned so that Kate Winslet, drifting on a flimsy raft, could be saved. Some girls sighed with unashamed pleasure while telling this. I recall my own boyish shock at learning that my mother's favorite poem as a teen was "The Highwayman," the tale of a gallant bandit shot to death while trying to elope with the landlord's daughter. Wow!

Here is a universal truth about girls from about age nine to adult—your granddaughters and mine: They desperately, passionately want someone to love them to the death. And they will search out this unconditional love, even if it's only a poignant, vicarious experience in a movie or poem. Could this craving serve the dual purpose of opening young hearts to Christ—and to the love of the man God may have for their "till death us do part" husband?

Yet many young girls in today's world seem to have lost this capacity—as a result of their parents' divorce, emotional and physical abuse, or premarital sex.

Perhaps because of parental divorce, today's youth of both sexes are more peer dependent than ever before.

And they have more money to spend than ever—or their parents do. Guys and girls both will compete with the crowd and spring hundreds on prom clothes, a chauffeured limo, and a fancier party than a wedding, if possible. For many youth today, the prom has become *the* rite of passage into adulthood. For some, it ends with beer and sex in a motel room. A lot of parents give tacit assent to such all-night parties, closing their minds to what obviously goes on in a rented motel room. In summer 1999 an R-rated comedy film aimed at teens, *American Pie*, exploitatively introduced kids to a high school world where boys competed to lose their virginity before prom night.

Few of today's teens are addicted to drugs, but current news reports on actual levels of teen drug usage appear contradictory. Many have tried marijuana, though, and one or more types of pills. Alcohol—usually beer, but sometimes wine coolers or spiked lemonade—is still the drug of choice for teens.

Young people today have access to more knowledge than any prior generation. For instance, according to recent news reports, more scientific data has been accumulated during my lifetime than was discovered and compiled during the preceding thousands of years of recorded history. Yet, paradoxically, the typical 17-year-old knows less about the world around him than did his recent ancestors, according to the book *What Do Our 17-Year-Olds Know: A Report of the First National*

Assessment of History and Literature by Diane Ravitch and Chester E. Finn, Jr.[32] And I have discovered that many teens, introduced to calculators in the primary grades, finish high school without learning to multiply or divide.

Today's high schooler is exposed to tons of propaganda that passes for education; the curricula in many classrooms I have monitored is thin on facts and larded with political opinion—written and taught, not surprisingly, by the Now Generation activists of the 1960s. In schools where I work, environmental activism or speculative studies of dinosaurs have in many classes replaced the solid facts of science you and I were required to master in ninth grade. Kids from primary grades through high school are being "shamelessly propagandized" with political "pseudo-science," writes Joel Belz, publisher of *World*. Much classroom time is lost as millions of young brains are left confused, while kiddie mags like *Time for Kids*, a juvenile version of *Time*, promote untested environmental theories in classrooms, rather than scientific knowledge about how the real world functions. In an age of color television I have found entire classes of secondary students unable to supply a valid explanation of the relationship between light and color.[33]

Journalist Cal Thomas points to a possible motive for these "tree and whale worshippers" messing with our grandchildren's minds. "Their goal," he writes, "is expanding government power"[34] by manufacturing crises, which youth are then educated to solve.

Many of us recall Billy Graham preaching against materialism in the 1950s—our generation! Materialism is popular again, and youth with all their idealism have not escaped it.

That the Dow soared from under one thousand to over eleven thousand in less than a generation should cause us to ponder. Today's teens have no memory of an era when industrial and commercial expansion were *not* growing like Jack's beanstalk.

It's comparatively easy to teach a child the value of money in economic terms, though. He may understand for instance, that a $200 used, high-quality bike is a better deal than one that sells for $99.95 new, which will self-destruct within a year.

But to teach a teen eternal values in regard to family, love, sex, eternity, and a myriad assortment of other issues is the real challenge. What your grandchildren and mine are seeking answers to, though many of them can't put words to their feelings, are not the social causes of the 1940s and 1950s when we struggled to build an economic kingdom to avoid a repeat of the Depression of the 1930s or the Nazi holocaust of the 1940s. Nor do today's youth seek the answers of the 1960s and 1970s when youth—today's parents and teachers—sought to "make love, not war." Nor do the politically correct issues of the 1980s, 1990s, and 2000s—the extinction of species in Tibet or depletion of the Amazon rain forests—touch the real concerns of twenty-first century youth.

Rather, more than at any time in life, teens—from Cain and Abel millenia ago, to Michael and Jason who perhaps are tossing layups in your backyard basketball court right now—seek to have their lives make sense; to find meaning, purpose, and identity. In this need, teens never change; nor does the answer—submission to the claims of Christ on their lives.

Grandparents are encouraged when teens like Jonathan Wyrtzen, grandson of Word of Life founder Jack Wyrtzen, accept the challenge to be different in the face of an often-hostile public school environment. As valedictorian of his senior class at Midlothian High School, near Dallas, Texas, Jonathan had a solid Christian testimony going back to his grade school years.

On graduation day Jonathan stood to give his speech to a crowd of some two thousand parents, students, and friends—and his grandparents, Jack and Joan Wyrtzen. After warming his audience with several teen-style jokes, Jonathan turned serious. "Everybody is looking for one thing in life to make them happy. I have found that one thing," he said. "That one thing is Jesus Christ as my Lord and Savior."

The crowd of mostly nonbelievers gave Jonathan a standing ovation!

I met and chatted with Jonathan's dad, Dave Wyrtzen, in the summer of 2000, just after the U.S. Supreme Court ruled that Texas teens like Jonathan can no longer lead in prayer or offer their testimonies to crowds at school functions. Wyrtzen is a pastor who ministers to youth at Word of Life's camps part of the year. He feels that today's Christian teens are more upbeat and committed to Christian testimony than in the recent past.

Two teens we read of in the Old Testament illustrate the need for grandparents in the lives of teens: a girl who went wrong though she had her parents' affection; and the girl's teen half brother, who did right, although hundreds of miles from home.

Fourteen-year-old Dinah was confused at her father's cowardice when he was confronted by his brother and disturbed by the duplicity and bickering amongst her father and the two women in his life. Dinah strayed into premarital sex so vile in her brothers' eyes that they murdered her boyfriend and his family (see Genesis 34:1–2; 25–27).

Dinah's half brother was Joseph, about her age at the time of this episode. Too young to have joined the older boys in their bloody raid to retrieve their sister, you can be sure he pondered this occurrence and its side effects for years afterward. Scorned by Dinah's brothers, Joseph was sold by them to a caravan of traders bound for Egypt.

About five years later, Joseph, now 19, rugged and handsome and overseer of wealthy Potiphar's household servants, was seduced by his employer's wife. Though it could have cost him his life, Joseph slipped her forced embrace and ran out without his cloak. Angered at Joseph's apparent betrayal of his trust, Potiphar had him jailed.

For Joseph, sexual immorality was a sin, not only against Potiphar, who trusted and respected him, but against God who created sex and set bounds on its use (see Genesis 39:7–20). That we are created in God's image, notes talk-show host Dr. Laura Schlessinger, is the main reason to avoid sexual immorality.

Yet God remembered Joseph, so that eventually he became wealthy, successful, and able to repay his wicked half brothers—good for the evil they had done him (see Genesis 45:1–8).

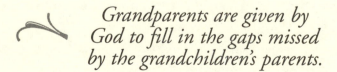

Grandparents are given by God to fill in the gaps missed by the grandchildren's parents.

Some of us may have seen a daughter or granddaughter go the way of Dinah, flirting with guys not worthy of her, fooling with sex to fill the emptiness within her soul. Then we have our Jasons or Janies, teen grandchildren of the 2000s who,

perhaps because of being misunderstood by their own generation and parents, as Joseph was, or for longings that they can
put no words to, open up to us.

Our opportunity is to hear what their parents did not
hear, to see what their busy parents missed. Perhaps it is only
a pat on the back they need, or a word of encouragement from
the Bible. Perhaps, like Potiphar, we've seen in that grandchild
a youth whose potential needs our direction on a long-term
basis. We may hire them to weed our garden, to wax our car.
Or we take them hunting or fishing, or become their tutor in
homework during a difficult year in high school. Perhaps, like
Pharaoh, we can be used of the Lord to give a grandchild a
boost on the climb to successful living before God.

Other grandparents need only to e-mail or write letters, to
phone, to pray, and to be on hand for graduations and other
special occasions, because Mom and Dad have built into that
grandchild's life the courage to be positively different!

CHAPTER SIXTEEN

When Love Must Say No

ᔛ

Fifteen-year-old Mark waited outside his Grandma Wiggin's front door, a perturbed but polite police officer behind him in the shadows. "This your grandson?"

"He sure is!" Grandma was concerned, though looking Mark over she could spy no signs of injury.

"We got a call from one of your neighbors that a prowler was shining a flashlight onto their house." The policeman produced a two-cell light.

"That's my flashlight. I loaned it to him," Grandma affirmed quickly. "What were you doing?" she addressed Mark.

"Minding his own business, near's I could tell," the officer answered for him. "But lots of people get suspicious if they see someone outside with a light. Figure they might be setting them up for a burglary."

"But Mark's only—"

"I know. He's from out of town, and he's hardly a burglary

suspect. But it might be best to leave the flashlight in the house from now on. Thank you, ma'am." The cop handed Grandma the flashlight and strode off to his patrol car.

Having a grandson brought to your door by a uniformed officer is an unnerving experience, and fortunately it rarely happens to most of us.

Mark is the father of four of my grandchildren now, and this vignette from his past is a family joke. He had grown up beyond the streetlights, and when he went out at night he often carried a flashlight. Visiting Grandma in a strange city neighborhood, he asked to borrow her flashlight, and she lovingly said yes without hesitation. He'd innocently cast a light beam on a stray cat scurrying after a mole. So now she'd have to say no.

Not a few grandparents lock horns with teen grandchildren visiting in their homes. This can easily occur when the teens have grown up miles from the grandparents, and neither teen nor grandparent knows what to expect of the other. Misunderstandings may range from problems with innocent but inappropriate behavior, to actions that startle or shock the sensibilities of a grandparent, or even to conduct that flouts morality.

Generally, kids act much better for teachers and grandparents than at home. There's something about a new relationship that causes even the child who's a dickens at home to behave better for a person with whom he's not yet plumbed the depths of their authority. I think it's a combination of family respect that subconsciously wishes to protect the parents' good name, and respectful fear of unknown authority, that makes this so.

For a child under age 11 or 12, your control must be *in loco parentis*—in the parent's place. Behavior standards should be worked out beforehand, either tacitly or explicitly, with your grandchild's parents. Grandma may wish to adjust rules to suit circumstances, of course. For instance, a nine o'clock bedtime for a nine-year-old may be enforced at home because Mom and Dad, who rise at six, wish to be alone for an hour before bedtime. But Grandma, who sleeps until eight, may wish to let little Jeremy stay up until 10:30 to beat her at chess, if there's no school the next day.

Puberty, however, brings on a new set of standards for dealing with children. A preteen or teenager is struggling with a combination of childhood dependency and emerging adult independence. One day Stacey, at 10, is a child, playing mother with dolls. At 11 or 12, she's preening herself for boy-ish glances, and she has put her dolls on the shelf. But she still sleeps with her teddy bear!

By age 15 or 16 youth of both sexes think adult thoughts, and they sense that they have been caught between adulthood and childhood. They are vulnerable to impulsive, sometimes surly behavior to demonstrate their independence. Unless given an uncommon amount of parental support, they may vent this frustration in inappropriate ways.

When teens or college-age grandchildren are your house-guests, therefore, it's up to you to help them set boundaries. In some instances you'll need to consult their parents. Here are some situations that may require you to say no.

Church attendance should be required of teens visiting grandparents.

This should be understood in advance, so the teen will bring clothing appropriate to the occasion. It's probably unfair for you to expect your teen grandchild to attend church if his carry-along wardrobe consists of a pair of jeans with the knees out and a bathing suit. But if he's used to wearing jeans to church, in good humor let him wear them. "It's no skin off your nose to wear a tie," I once told Mark when he protested a regulation at his Christian high school that neither of us agreed with. Conversely, it's no skin off Grandma's nose if Jeremy—or Stacey—wants to go to church in jeans. Isn't the important thing that they be exposed to the spiritual environment and the teaching of the Word of God?

Make allowances for denominational differences and established church-attendance habits.

Courtesy is a two-way street. If you are a Baptist or Assemblies of God churchgoer and your son or daughter has married an Episcopalian or Lutheran (or vice versa) and is rearing your grandchildren in this denomination, compassionately realize that your grandchildren may be uncomfortable in a worship service with practices that are strange to them. Don't require them to accompany you to every service, though you should insist they keep the biblical principle of worship in the house of God at least once weekly. Try this: Offer them a choice among Sunday school, morning worship, or evening service. They may surprise you and choose all three!

Don't push clothing requirements.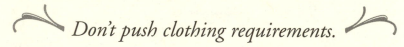

Kids should be able to relax when they visit grandparents, but you should let them know of any house rules. In my home I require young men to remove their caps or hats and wear shirts at mealtime. But that's a table rule, not a clothing rule. (I don't let them sit on the table, either!)

If you find 15-year-old Stacey's bikini or high-cut one-piece suit too brief for public beachwear (another issue that should be discussed with her mother beforehand), insist that she wear something more modest. In a pinch, she might wear shorts or cut-off jeans with the suit, for example. Stacey is probably not unreasonable to want to wear a skimpy suit in the backyard pool if there are no men around and she agrees to dress or wear a robe when she is done with her swim.

Grandmothers who grew up when girls covered up simply because they were told to do so may not realize that young people today expect more explanation for rules than in the past. And even with the exposure to sex that teens get in girls' magazines, and in the movies and school, many girls do not actually realize what they are doing to males—16 or 60—by such casual dress. It's entirely appropriate for Grandma to speak to Stacey in private and point out what Christ said about lust (see Matthew 5:28), or the result of Bathsheba's careless bathing and King David's longing looks (see 2 Samuel 11:2–5).

Grandmothers will be happy to know that modesty is coming back in style once again. Jewish writer Wendy Shalit, in *A Return to Modesty*, comments that "our society makes fun of modesty, and then we are surprised to find our men behaving abominably." Shalit's efforts while a college student (she was born in 1975) have started a movement that has caused several large universities to rewrite their policy on coed dorms. "How can we expect men to be honorable," Shalit wonders, "when . . . women . . . send them the message that they do not have to be?"[1]

If your granddaughter thinks that the girls of *Baywatch* set the standard for beachwear, tell her to look about her. Commonly—at least here in the conservative Midwest—girls buy brief bathing suits to be in style. Then they cover them with gym shorts before going to a public beach or pool. A teen girl turned my classroom TV on to *Baywatch* during lunch hour. Another girl quickly changed channels—*Baywatch* is fun, the girls agreed, but not with boys in the room! In still another instance I listened as several senior girls admonished one another to be sure to set modest dress standards for the younger girls.

 Smoking, drinking, and drugs are not permitted in Grandma's house.

It should make little difference whether it's Jeremy, now 17, or his father, 47, on this one. But precedent sometimes must be honored to keep family peace. If there are smokers in your family, and you've permitted them to smoke indoors over the years, it may be too late to change the rules without hurt and anger. About all you can do is ask the parents if they permit their teens to smoke at home, then make them smoke outside until they reach the legal age for smoking. But if their parents have a "no smoking" rule at home, they should not even be permitted to smoke outdoors. And if you've never permitted smoking in the house, there's no reason to let it start—ever. So if Jeremy, at 20, comes home from college with a pipe in his mouth, insist he take it outdoors, even if it's 20 below zero.

But no booze—beer, wine coolers, or hard liquor—is permitted under any circumstances. Even 21-and-over college-age youth, who may drink legally, should not be permitted to go out and drink, say, at a bowling alley with a bar, while they are visiting Grandma and Grandpa.

 ## *Music, TV, and videos should be controlled.*

Here's where younger teens, even from otherwise solid Christian homes, will run over you, if you let them, and in some respects it's an iffy situation for grandparents of teens. You will not permit morally objectionable music and television programs, nor PG-13 and R-rated videos, of course. But say you've got cable TV because Grandpa likes historical documentaries, and the package comes with MTV, BET, and late-night R-rated movies. State up front that MTV and BET, with their suggestive, often lewd visuals and lyrics, are not to be turned on, and no movies after the 11 o'clock news. Post this rule conspicuously on every TV set in the house, and remind the teens that it will be enforced. And grandparents should set the example by not tuning in to the daytime soaps. Perhaps Grandpa could miss a few TV ball games to build a relationship with Jeremy by playing ball with him in the backyard!

Rock music is an addiction with many teens that grandparents frequently must deal with. Dr. James Dobson observes that "a steady diet" of hard rock "will pollute the minds of even the healthiest teenagers."[2] While Dobson's observation has to do with lyrics that he finds often violent and explicitly sexual, the music, with or without the words, will drive a lot of grandparents to near insanity. It should be part of your teen's maturing process to learn to respect the rights of others who do not wish to be subjected to his or her favorite sounds. Insist that he shut it off, or at least wear headphones. Medical reports have shown that a radio or CD player cranked up to where it can be heard by those not wearing the headset is damaging to the listener's ears. That's the bottom line on volume.

So, must Grandma scrutinize each and every CD Jeremy and Stacey play in their portable players? It's not feasible. But this may require parental contact, and in some instances, a truce. Try limiting the teen to Christian music only when at Grandma's house. If it's a modern piece that grates on your nerves, listen to some of it anyway, and let him explain what the words mean to him. Then relegate it to earphone-only listening.

 ## Computers can be filtered, controlled.

A responsible grandparent will say no to unrestricted computer use when Jeremy or Stacey is visiting. We've all heard horror stories about how easy it is for your grandkids or mine to access raunchy sex Web sites or violence and demonic horror on the Internet. This may happen quite by accident, or your grandchild may have been given the address of unclean material by a schoolmate. In writing this book, for example, I learned that a national women's organization has had to change its name. The acronym for its former name had become the Web site of a pornography distributor.

Any child who can peck out www.(name).com on the keyboard—and that's any kid who's learned to read—will, sooner or later, log in to some pretty nasty stuff, if he or she has access to a computer with an unfiltered Internet service; and most Internet services are not filtered.

But here's good news. *You*—Grandma or Grandpa—can log in to www.family.org. Then, when Focus on the Family's Web site comes up, type "Filtered Internet access" into the box, and hit the "Go" button. You'll find articles dealing with filtered Internet, as well as a lengthy list of services from which to choose.

You might also try Broadman & Holman/Lifeway's Lifewayonline Web site at www.lwol.com. Some Christian bookstores distribute Lifeway's Web site content on a free CD for people who do not yet have Internet service. Or you can phone them at 1 (888) 454-5965. Their fee is $19.95 monthly, or just $15.95 monthly if paid a year in advance.

With a filtered Internet service, Stacey can access the Hotmail account she's probably set up at school to communicate with friends. Or Jeremy can do online research for his homework right from Grandma's family room. Filters do have their limitations, though. Students have complained to me that their school's Internet filter also keeps them out of some valid, wholesome Web sites.

If you use your computer for a home business you may prefer not to permit grandchildren to use it. That's okay. But so that your visiting grandchildren may have a computer to use, you might invest in a used computer suitable for games and word processing. There are plenty of good, older 486 or Pentium I models available for $100 to $200; occasionally a good laptop. These will run games, as well as DOS and Windows 95, to handle older versions of WordPerfect or Microsoft

Word, compatible with the newer versions in your late-model high-speed computer. Most of these vintage computers are too slow for Internet access, however.

If possible, buy your used computer from a dealer in second-hand electronics who can do setup and repairs.

 Teens must keep regular hours at Grandma's house.

And they should be expected to phone if delayed by an emergency. "But Grandma, I'm almost an adult. *You* don't call when you're late!" is Stacey's accusation at 17. She's just gotten her license, and you let her drive to the supermarket at eight in the evening to get a box of cereal for breakfast. She met a friend she hadn't seen all summer, and they stayed at McDonald's until after ten.

First, shame on Grandma for not setting a better example. Jay Kesler, chancellor of Taylor University and former president of Youth for Christ, told me in an interview that his secretary can reach him on a half-hour notice even when he's traveling overseas. If *you* went to the store and got delayed two hours, you owe Stacey (or Grandpa!) a call out of ordinary courtesy. Then be back when you say you'll be back.

Try this. Point out to Stacey that if you didn't love her you wouldn't be concerned. And make your own good practice an example. Teens often perceive curfews as an unfair means to control them. "You wouldn't want someone telling you what to do" is an indignant, immature objection.

So appeal to their sense of responsibility. Insist that they call home. And when they do, don't snap, "You come home this minute!" Ask, "When will you be home?" Then don't let them go out again for a while if they don't keep their word. This is an appeal to the maturity they profess to have, rather than the exercise of your real or imagined urge to control.

Say no to letting a grandchild under age 25 drive your car until you've cleared it with your insurance agent.

And if your grandchild is under 18, clear it with his or her parents. You may be held legally responsible for any damage he or she may do. In most cases your insurance will probably cover your visiting grandchild to the same extent as you are covered, without paying an extra premium, but state laws and insurance policies vary. If a grandchild who is licensed to drive is living in your home, however, you *must* pay extra for insurance, whether or not you permit him to drive your car—unless he also owns a car. You should not be bashful about asking him to pay it.

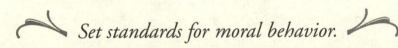

Set standards for moral behavior.

No grandparent should ever let his house or apartment become a crash pad where teen or college-age grandchildren can carry on premarital sex. This can be a problem, especially if your grandchild's parents are divorced or your grandson or granddaughter has had ongoing troubles at home. Teens sometimes seek recourse from their problems by having sexual encounters. Your grandchildren should know, or you should

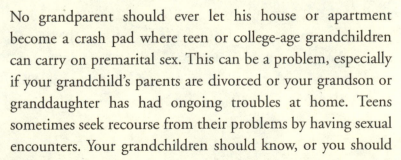

tell them, that they are expected to refrain from sex, including petting and prolonged kissing, until marriage; and they must understand that this is a rule that will be enforced while they're your guests.

Grandchildren should not be permitted to entertain guests of the opposite sex in their bedrooms, ever, no matter how old they are. Nor should they be permitted to sit in a car in the driveway for extended periods—and make this clear in advance. (Stock answers from teens confronted for spending two hours alone in a parked car: "We weren't *doing* anything—we were just talking"; or, "Nobody uses a car for *that* anymore!")

Either of these answers may be honest enough. Whereas when we were teens the most common place for a premarital sexual encounter was an automobile, nowadays, with so many mothers at work until hours after the kids get home from school, the teen's own room is by far more common. Many teen couples do sit and talk for long periods without getting physical, so it's unfair to assume the worst. You may alienate your grandchild by even a tacit accusation, so gently head off trouble by stating the rules in advance.

If your teen is visiting with a girlfriend or boyfriend at your house, let them alone to watch the moon from the porch swing, if you have one. Or give them reasonable privacy in the family room. Don't try to police every move, but be sure you're not a party to behavior they or their parents would later be ashamed of.

"Don't you trust me?" a teen grandchild may ask. "Yes, honey, I trust you. But I also love you more than you can imagine, so we've got to have rules," you could answer. Then let her or him help you formulate those rules.

Help your grandchildren say no to sex before marriage.

It may be that Stacey and Jeremy have sought out Grandma and Grandpa because their parents are so taken up with their own troubles that they have little emotional and spiritual strength left to share with their children. Love and compassion toward a teen grandchild who is developing into adulthood will often open the door to your helping her with relationships with the opposite sex. Grandparents who obviously truly enjoy each other's company, and who really do enjoy being around teen grandchildren, are well on their way to helping teens realize that adults can relate to each other sexually in happy, wholesome relationships. If grandparents have an affectionate and caring relationship they can help teens understand that sex is okay and beautiful, but that it must wait for marriage.

Questions such as "Grandma, when did you and Grandpa first kiss?" or "Tell me about your first date" can lead to gently pointing out that you were a virgin when you married Grandpa, and you've never regretted it.

Daytime talk shows have even produced panels of mothers (fathers are seldom seen on these shows) who state that it's all right with them if their kids have sex, so long as it's at home while their parents are there to supply the condoms. Montel Williams, that warm, caring guru of troubled teens, frankly stated that he wants his daughters to read *Promiscuities*, a book in which author Naomi Wolf encourages all manner of sexual experimentation short of intercourse.[3] And sweet-faced show hostess Jenny Jones carried on with the help of authoritative, grandmotherly Dr. Joyce Brothers. Together they encouraged

a group of smirking, snickering, middle-aged female enter-
tainers in pajamas to tell Jones's TV audience—many of them
teen girls on summer vacation—about their exciting premarital sexual encounters (for example, "on the football field with
my boyfriend"). Is it any wonder that today's teens of both
sexes face major confusion about morality?

Wendy Shalit cites a *Redbook* magazine survey of one hundred thousand women that found "the most strongly religious
women"—virgins when they married—to be "more responsive
sexually" than all other women surveyed.[4]

And no wonder. When a couple unite in a sexual union—
and you should tell Stacey this—they become "one flesh," literally *one self* (see Genesis 2:24; Ephesians 5:31). When a man
and woman give their bodies to one another they have irretriev-
ably given that person a piece of themselves (see 1 Corinthians
6:15–16). Adam "knew" Eve and Eve "knew" Adam; they came
to each other "naked . . . and not ashamed" of their bodies in a
union of precious carnal knowledge not reproducible in any
other human relationship (Genesis 2:25, KJV).

And what about Jeremy? Possibly the most neglected passage in the New Testament is 1 Thessalonians 4:3–8, which
ties holy living with sexual purity. Verse 6 stands as a somber
warning against anyone who "take[s] advantage of"—
"defrauds" (KJV)—another person sexually. When a guy takes
a girl's virginity before they marry, he has not only cheated the
girl, but also her parents, who entrusted her into his care. Such
a young man has despised the girl, her parents, society, and
God as well (see v. 8). This "no" that Jeremy needs to learn is
God's standard for holy living.

Love may have to say no to future visits.

If basic codes of courtesy and conduct are not met, you may need to firmly refuse to permit overnight stays by Jeremy and Stacey. Such decisions are excruciating and should certainly be made with prayer and reflective consideration. And be sure to make allowances for misunderstandings, of course.

But you have a responsibility, before God, to "restrain" (1 Samuel 3:13) that teen or young adult grandchild from morally objectionable behavior when he or she is in your home. You cannot condone wrongdoing by giving a grandchild a place in your home to carry it on. This kind of tough love can cause a youth to examine his or her behavior and shape up. Columnist Ann Landers reports, for example, instances where teens left off using drugs or running around at night when parents drew a line and refused to back down. Grandparents can take a lesson from a slogan popularized by the antidrug campaign: "Just say no" to behavior that violates the high standards you set for yourself and your family, to the honor of the Lord.

Grandparents are in a unique position to help parents set boundaries.

Grandparents can lift their emerging adults from the disappointments that too often weigh them down with discouragement. "Catch Your Teenager in the Act of Doing Something

Good" is a chapter in *Understanding Your Teenager*, by Wayne Rice and David Veerman. This chapter warns that parents, harried by the responsibilities of earning a living, balancing a budget, and rearing several children, "have built in 'botch detectors' that go off" whenever their teen makes mistakes. Parents may alienate their children by appearing to be "blind to anything good that their teens do," the authors caution.[5]

Rice and Veerman are on target, I can readily affirm—as a parent of four, with teens from 1978 to 1996—and as a grandparent of 10 who's observed his own married children overreacting to the faults and mistakes of their children. Watch it, though, Grandpa and Grandma. You may not know everything that is behind that parent's corrective reaction. Rather, when Stacey or Jeremy is visiting your home, try to appraise that teen's behavior in this neutral environment. You can thus lovingly reinforce the limits set by parents to mold your grandchild's daily actions into conformity to the "likeness" of Jesus (Romans 8:29).

Chapter Seventeen

How to Invest in Your Grandchildren's Future

Grandpa Hackney collected pennies in a piggy bank, and whenever my wife and I would visit her parents' home with our children, the bank would be dumped onto the kitchen table and its contents counted. Those pennies bought ice cream cones, zoo tickets, and rides on the plastic horse at the supermarket. They furnished the seed money for a myriad assortment of gifts ranging from plush monkeys to rocking chairs.

The two of my four children who remember Grandpa Hackney are now parents themselves. Most of the gifts were worn out long ago and discarded, but the memory of their modestly indulgent grandfather is with them yet.

Grandma Hackney, who passed on at 90 having more descendants than years, did her best in nearly 30 years of widowhood to keep up with family birthday gifts. There were grandchildren, great-grandchildren, and great-great-grandchildren—half of whom were born since Grandpa

Hackney died. Understandably, having nearly two family birthdays a week, she did miss one occasionally.

America's some 55 million grandparents spend more than $1,000 per couple every year buying gifts for fewer than three grandchildren, or on phone calls and travel to visit with grandchildren. For most of the past half century, our nation's population has been aging and the birthrate sharply declining. So when today's grandparents pass on, their children and grandchildren will inherit more cash, investments, and real property than any generation in human history.

Our culture is a dichotomy where young families, many of whom have known only prosperous times, have overburdened themselves with consumer debt. Yet grandparents—those who remember the Depression, or who were influenced by parents who did—have set themselves up with tax-sheltered retirement plans, in part in response to Reagan-era tax reforms. Speaking to the grandparents reading this book, Christian financial counselor Jim Rickard, director of Stewardship Services Foundation, said, "By the time parents become grandparents, with these corporate pension plans that have been in existence so long, retirees are becoming the strongest financial power bloc in the country."

My own grandparents, though all of them owned property, passed little cash to their grandchildren while living, and they left none when they died. Their real estate was passed to their children in return for care in old age. What possessions were left—a few pieces of furniture, books, bric-a-brac—were given to the grandchildren in oral wills during the last days of their lives.

My grandparents made some mistakes in investing in their

children's and grandchildren's futures, but for the most part, given their circumstances and the economy at the time, I believe they made very good decisions.

My paternal grandparents were themselves from farm folks of several generations back, and they both grew to adulthood in the nineteenth century when a farmer could expect his sons and his sons' sons to follow in his footsteps. Grandpa Wiggin built a modest farm, which included a new, nicely furnished house—even indoor plumbing was installed some 20 years before the power lines ran out our way. He saw the passing of the horse and buggy, bought a new car in middle age, and helped both his sons with new or late-model wheels of their own. Old enough to be grandparents, Grandpa and Grandma Wiggin had a baby boy in the same year they bought their first new car, a 1917 Willys-Overland touring car.

That baby was my dad. At 22, on the eve of World War II, my father was given the farm in exchange for a life-lease in which he agreed to care for his parents to the end of their days. No cash was involved, nor did Grandpa Wiggin have any savings to speak of. And Grandpa stayed on the farm in his sunset years as advisor and helper.

Those halcyon days are gone forever. The twentieth century saw more rapid economic and social changes than any other period in history, and the practice of father passing to son the farm or small business merely by scratching his signature on a piece of paper is no longer adequate to deal with inheritances. But from the good features of this time-honored practice, we can glean lessons for grandparenting that will take us on into the twenty-first century.

"In the eyes of a grandchild, many times, a grandparent is

put on a higher pedestal than even Mom and Dad," says Jim Rickard. This will occur only when grandparents, as mine were, are accessible on a regular basis. I'm sure I idolized my grandparents, especially Grandpa Wiggin. And as a young adult, I was often troubled by the fact that during the 13 years that our lives overlapped, I put him "on a higher pedestal" than Dad. Grandpa was successful; Dad was still struggling to get there. Grandpa had a great past; Dad, to an extent, seemed to live in Grandpa's shadow. Only years after they both had passed on did I fully accept that both men did pretty much as well as could be expected in the context of the opportunities in which God placed them.

"If you want to raise children of integrity, be a model of integrity."

This is financial counselor Rickard's paraphrase of Proverbs 20:7. Since grandparents *are* often looked up to as greater than their parents in the eyes of grandchildren, as grandparents we must accept this mantle of role modeling. Grandparents must be men and women of their word in the presence of their grandchildren in regard to financial dealings. Whenever we handle money, there are impressionable eyes watching!

An example Rickard mentions is the frivolous use of credit cards before grandchildren, especially for buying them gifts. I seldom knew the price of anything my grandparents bought me, except a five-cent helium balloon at a fair, or a bottle of pop from my maternal grandfather's country store. Maybe that's not so good, either. Grandkids need to learn that neither cash nor gifts grow on trees!

Rickard gave the example of the indulgent grandparent who cruises the aisles of a department store with a child in tow, pushing a shopping cart. Gifts for the grandkid tumble into the cart. A plastic card is used to cover the bill at the cash register.

Suppose you *can* afford it. But can the grandchildren afford such a materialistic lesson? "The kids have no idea whatsoever that somebody's got to pay, that there's a day of reckoning," Rickard says. "They look to Grandma and Grandpa for freebies, for fun, instead of for reality."

Older youngsters do realize that credit card purchases must be paid for. But the easy-come–easy-go attitude of a grandparent sets an example of treating with frivolity the goodness of God from whom "every good gift and every perfect gift" originates (James 1:17).

 Grandkids should learn that gifts cost money, for which someone had to work.

When you take a grandchild shopping, lay out in advance how much you plan to spend. Let the child see the money and perhaps count it. Pray with your grandchild, asking the Lord to lead you both to find your needs within the limits of available cash. Let him know that when it's gone, it's gone. If you can't trust yourself to stick with this decision, leave the rest of your cash, your checkbook, and your credit cards at home.

I recall that I had an appreciation for my grandparents' limited resources rather early in life. Grandpa Fuller, a part-time deputy sheriff, got paid five dollars for five or six hours' work keeping order at the local dance hall each Saturday night. I quite easily found myself seeing how his expenditures on his grandchildren reflected his modest stipend as a bouncer, a sum I could readily understand.

 ## *Do you live with eternity's values in view?*

"I'm spending my grandchildren's inheritance," read the bumper sticker plastered on the rear of a motor home with Florida license plates—a recreational vehicle costing more than many parents could spend for a home in my childhood. I'll admit I was not amused.

This is not an indictment of owning a motor home or wintering in Florida. Both practices raise some questions, though, which I have dealt with in another chapter. However, what does a grandparent's conspicuous consumption say to the grandchildren? To me it says, "You only live once. Get all the gusto you can. Tomorrow we die—there's no hereafter."

Grandparents who are alarmed at their grandchildren's indulgent living should not wrap themselves with the self-righteous cloak of, "He's spending it all when he's young; he won't have any left for old age" if they are themselves living as though old age were just a final vacation before annihilation. Can we live with eternity's values in view before our grandkids? In 1 Timothy 5:5–6 the Lord warns merry widows against living in pleasure, because a life of indulgence is really death in life. What will such a life of pursuing the things of a dying world do to our grandchildren's attitudes toward money and possessions?

Maturity is required to appreciate the value of a large inheritance.

Another serious mistake is to give children or grandchildren large sums of money while they are young. A young son was left substantial endowments from his father's life insurance. This boy collected his endowments at age 18, about $75,000, which he spent within two years on new pickup trucks, motorcycles, and partying. Then, having no funds left for college, nor any particular training, he took an entry-level job.

Years later, this young man, now married and the father of two, regrets not having the education necessary to pursue a better-paying job. He was unable to manage money that might have paid for a college or trade school education, or have bought his family a house. Rickard tells of a Christian dad who's having second thoughts about the $500,000 he's stashed away for his four-year-old to receive at age 21—perhaps $2 million with interest by then.

There are many opportunities for grandparents, with means to do so, to help grandchildren with judiciously given gifts, even substantial ones:

Invest in their college education.

College tuition has increased much faster than the rate of inflation over the past 30 years. It's tough for families in the lower- to middle-income level to put away money enough to pay their children's way, and in most cases nowadays it's impossible for a college student to pay his entire bill with a part-time job—community colleges excepted. Many youth today finish college with a greater debt in student loans than we carried in mortgage when our families were young. Children from poor families do qualify for many free grants at state and federal levels, however.

Particularly if your children are in full-time Christian ministries, they may be unable to put away much toward a son or daughter's college expenses. It is entirely appropriate to help with their tuition bill, either on a regular basis or with occasional lump-sum gifts, as needed. Let your grandchildren know in advance how much to expect and when, so they can plan accordingly.

 Some grandparents pay their grandkids' way to a Christian day school.

This is an investment in your grandchild's future that can reap eternal dividends. Be sure that your grandchild really wishes to be there. A common mistake is to wait until the child is ready for middle or high school, then try to get him or her into a Christian school to avoid the coarse influences of public secondary schools. But by then the child has already made close friends and developed loyalty to the public school system. He may also have developed a negative attitude toward Christian school education that immersion in a Christian school will only tend to reinforce. To coerce a child to attend a Christian school will create resentment unless that child has had a life-changing experience with Christ.

One grandfather gave his granddaughter a nice car for her commute to college.

He and Grandma didn't need the trade-in value of their older, well-maintained vehicle, and the girl, newly graduated from high school, needed a reliable vehicle.

This can work particularly well if, like a lot of older men, you have learned auto repairs during your retirement years, and have maintained the car yourself over a number of years. Have your granddaughter bring the car by regularly. Change the oil for her. Replace the brake pads, belts, and hoses as needed. Don't let the old car become a liability instead of a blessing!

I don't recommend giving a high school student an auto, though it might be all right to sell him one below market value with the parents' wholehearted permission. An exception might be made for an older teen who's shown himself responsible and needs a car to drive to work while he saves his earnings for college.

Consider making your married grandchild's down payment on a house.

If you can afford it there's a lot to be said in favor of helping your grandchildren avoid a lifetime of servitude to the banks and other moneylenders. And while you're at it, here's a chance to show them the huge financial advantage of paying off a mortgage in 15 years instead of 30. Remember, mortgage brokers typically use pressure to get young buyers to sign up for long-term mortgages. And first-time homebuyers often are incredulous when shown the modest increases in monthly payments that are possible merely by cutting the length of terms in half.

 ## Help grandchildren over genuine emergencies.

This can range from loaning them your car while theirs is in the shop, to helping with medical bills, or even to letting them live in your home while attending college.

Again, I would give first priority to children or grandchildren struggling under the often-inadequate salaries paid to Christian workers. For example, a young couple were in their first year teaching at a Christian school when the wife gave birth. This church school's insurance policy fell short, and they were left with hundreds of dollars in unpaid medical bills. But another family, whose father teaches in a Christian school, is not able to put away money for a down payment on a home of their own while they pay rent. So the grandparents, who live in their home only part of the year, allow their married daughter, son-in-law, and children to live there rent-free.

The principles outlined in 1 Timothy 5:9–10 for aiding only deserving, destitute widows should be applied to your grandchildren.

Grandchildren who are to become recipients of substantial financial aid should have shown themselves responsible in handling day-to-day financial commitments, such as credit cards. And they should have shown themselves generous toward others in need (see Luke 6:38).

Grandparents sometimes have to deal with adult children who, because of selfishness and egalitarian notions of fairness, may expect to see every nickel left by their grandparents divided equally amongst the children, needy or not, deserving or not. I know of one man who felt that helping one child (his wife) less than her siblings was flawed reasoning. He thought that his in-laws should have given equal amounts to each child regardless of his or her needs.

The writer's complaint is valid if, as he asserted, his wife's brothers and sisters had squandered their livelihood on "laziness, gambling, and poor judgment." But that is for the giver to decide, not other family members.

Give on the basis of need to those who will use it responsibly. Grandparents who have taught their own children love, sharing, and generosity when they were growing up will not have to face these jealousies later.

 ## *What should you do with cash and investments left at death?*

Should you: (a) leave it all to your children; (b) leave it all to your grandchildren; (c) leave it all to the Lord's work; or (d) combine the three approaches?

Counselor Jim Rickard points out that often the grandchildren are in greater need of help than the children, who may be 50 or 60 years old and past their financial struggles at their parents' death. So, "give the grandkids a nudge" based on *need*, he counsels. They may need help setting up a new business, for example.

In the case of a father and son in business together, if the son wishes to continue the family business, make provision so that he will not be financially hurt by his father's death. I've seen too many sons and daughters financially wiped out, or left without a needed line of credit, because of inheritance taxes and the claims of other family members on a family business or farm in which the one in partnership with the parent has made substantial investments in both time and money. Make firm decisions while you're able. Otherwise ungodly wrangling (sometimes by people professing godliness), hurting your family's testimony, may continue for a generation or more. In many cases, it is wise to transfer ownership while the parent/senior partner is still alive and healthy and his ability to do so is not in question.

 One Christian businessman is giving his investments to the Lord's work.

This man plans on having his bank account at zero at his death, if possible, said Rickard. He's having fun and receiving countless blessings in giving his money back to God, who gave it to him in the first place! This man is truly laying up treasures in heaven.

There is a danger of taking Old Testament passages about patriarchs passing their farms on to each succeeding generation out of context. There is no biblical mandate for such a practice for Christians; this was for ancient Israelites, the people of the land. But common sense should prevail, I believe. Have your children and grandchildren been taught biblical principles of giving? They especially need to hide in their hearts those principles relating to Matthew 6:33 to "seek first [God's] kingdom and his righteousness, and all these things [food, clothing, shelter] will be given to you as well." If they have learned sound principles of money management, and if you can leave them enough money to keep them from servitude to the banks, they can build God's kingdom by plowing that money back into Christian service. I know several Christian leaders, with inadequate salaries, who got substantial portions of their livelihood by managing estates left them by parents or grandparents. The apostle Paul, great as he was in the ministry, helped support himself by sewing tents.

But all children and grandchildren, godly or ungodly, ought to have a token remembrance of Grandma and Grandpa, if feasible. An unsaved grandchild may be inspired to turn to Christ in later years by a possession that helps him remember a godly grandparent.

A postcard with a motto, crudely hand-framed under a piece of window glass, hung on my grandmother's bedroom wall during my childhood. I found that motto among some of her things more than 20 years after her death. It now hangs above my office desk where it gives me courage more than a third of a century since she went to be with the Lord:

"Be Strong! We are not here to play, to dream, to drift; /

We have hard work to do and loads to lift. /

Shun not the struggle—face it, 'tis God's gift!"

My younger brothers and sisters remember Grandma Wiggin, in her 90s, feeble and old, confined to a wheelchair. I remember her well as the big-boned, strong woman of 70-something, who though "old" to me, nevertheless worked untiringly at housework and gardening in and around our Victorian farmhouse, little changed from the nineteenth century. It is not the motto that inspires me to go another mile when I am ready to quit nearly so much as the memory of Grandma this motto evokes!

 Consider a family trust.

Finally, Jim Rickard suggests setting up a living trust, rather than a will, if you have a substantial estate. This will enable you to continue to give to the Lord's work and to your children and grandchildren while you are living. Under present state and federal laws, a trust can, unlike a will, enable your children and grandchildren to escape most taxes and probate entanglements on money passed on to them, because your assets continue in the trust; only they, rather than you, are now the trustees.

CHAPTER EIGHTEEN

The Grandparent and Eternal Values

As a small girl my wife, Dot, now Grandma Wiggin, often visited her grandmother, who has since gone to be with the Lord. She would hear this dear, uneducated lady from the hills of East Tennessee praying aloud late at night for her children, including Dot's parents, who did not then attend church.

Great-Grandma Mary Hackney's prayers were answered. Dot's parents eventually came to follow the Lord, as did their children and grandchildren, most of her aunts and uncles, and dozens of Mary Hackney's descendants, now extending to six generations.

One of our married sons and our daughter, Debbie, were visiting Dot and me overnight with their spouses and children. I led the families in evening devotions, and I asked my son-in-law, Lew, the eldest among them, to lead in prayer. I heard his words with interest as he asked the Lord to help him and Mark, our oldest son, to be faithful in their responsibilities as "priests in our own families."

That prayer was a beautiful observation, but it must be understood in the context of Bible teaching. The New Testament teaches the individual priesthood of every believer before God, rather than the Old Testament concept of a priest in the temple, standing between God and the worshipper. In Christ's church, therefore, all Christians—men, women, and children—are "a holy priesthood" and Christ is our High Priest (1 Peter 2:5; see Revelation 1:6).

But there is a priestly responsibility within the Christian home, apart from the local church. Fathers are to take this leadership, and grandfathers are to set the example in leading their families in the ways of Christ. There is an example of a godly grandfather as priest beautifully illustrated in the earliest-written book of the Bible (see Job 1:4-5). Job's married sons and daughters took turns holding feasts (v. 4). Grandpa Job, knowing the human tendency of even believers to forget God when in a party mood, offered burnt offerings to the Lord, Old Testament fashion, on his children's behalf. This is not a suggestion that Christian families return to burnt offerings; rather, the principle is that grandfathers have a priestly responsibility in family worship.

In an important sense often overlooked in our day when the value of fathers is downplayed by the media, fathers and grandfathers really do stand as priests between young children and God. The child who does not perceive his father as loving, for example, may not perceive God as loving, either.

Moses instructed the people of Israel to "impress . . . on your children" the Word of God, and to be so faithful in this, that whether sitting at home with the children or walking along the road with them, God's truth was continually taught the youngsters (Deuteronomy 6:7). Years later, Moses repeated this warning, so that the "children who do not know this Law" of God might be taught the Bible and the ways of the Lord (Deuteronomy 31:13).

Grandparents need to teach their families Bible truth so that their grandchildren may grow into the "whole measure of the fullness of Christ" (Ephesians 4:13). My maternal grand-mother had been a schoolteacher before her marriage, and for perhaps a quarter of a century late in her life she was a Sunday school teacher. Grandma Fuller was also a teacher to her grandchildren, and when my brothers or I visited overnight, she would read us a chapter from a child's story Bible and pray with us before bedtime.

Grandma took this responsibility because Grandpa did not become a believer until we older grandkids were young adults. We children understood this; at any rate, on Saturday, our usual day at their home, Grandpa was absent during the evening on his duties as a part-time sheriff.

> *As a grandparent seeking to strengthen a grandchild's devotional life, you should build on the parents' foundation as much as possible.*

If the parents have laid no foundation, build anyway. I recom-mend using a child's story Bible for kids under 12 such as *365 Children's Bible Stories*, which is an excellent, heavily illustrated resource for reading to all children. The old standby Bible story books by Hurlbut[2] and Egermier[3] are good, too. For older children, or for when the entire family is present, read an easy-to-understand chapter of the Bible, preferably from a modern translation, followed by prayer requests and one or more family members leading in prayer. For Grandpa himself to lead such family devotions, whenever possible, lends respect and authority to God's Word and the spiritual, eternal values you cherish.

Jack Wyrtzen, at 80, was a great-grandfather and grandfather to 21, ages 3 to 33 in his family and that of his wife, Joan, whom he married after they both were widowed. As founder and for over 50 years director of Word of Life International's far-flung youth ministries, Jack was in a spiritual sense a grandfather and great-grandfather to millions of young Christians around the world. Yet despite the heavy demands on their time of the Word of Life ministries, Jack and Joan planned to see each of their grandchildren, except for those in Brazil, "on the average of two to three times a year," Joan told me.

Chuckled Jack, "During the summer they'll all be piling in on us."

I asked them how a grandparent can pass the eternal values of a Christian heritage on to grandchildren. "I think the greatest thing a grandparent can do is to be involved in their grandchildren's lives," replied Joan. She mentioned that she and Jack arranged their schedules to attend every grandchild's high school graduation. For example, the Wyrtzens flew to São Paulo, Brazil, to attend the graduation of Jack's daughter's children. And we "try to call them every week," she said. If the grandchildren are at home, she and Jack talk to them, or "at least we talk to the parents."

Jack Wyrtzen was a letter writer, though he admitted he

didn't "get as many as I would like" in return from their grandchildren. But one grandson, in particular, when in college on the West Coast, was separated by three thousand miles from his grandparents in Schroon Lake, New York. He was a quiet teen, the Wyrtzens remembered, and he found it difficult to talk with them. But Grandpa Jack wrote letters to this grandson, who "just seemed to open up and blossom" in his letters in return, remembered Joan.

Jack read a portion of this grandson's letter in which he writes, "I really want to thank you guys for all you've done in my life. . . . Thank you most of all for the spiritual example. I couldn't have had a better example when I was growing up. . . . I just wanted to let you [Grandpa Jack and Grandma Joan] know how much I appreciate you for what you've done."

Letter writing has nearly become a lost art in our day. Only a few older grandparents still prefer writing to making a phone call. For just a few cents your message can be shared and cherished for days or weeks; but phoning may cost several dollars a call for a message often forgotten within hours.

My paternal grandparents got their first telephone in 1907, when they were both nearly 40, and letter writing was already their established habit. Grandma Wiggin continued to write my aunt until shortly before Grandma's death, though they lived only five miles apart, and both had phones. Most American homes had phones by 1950, and personal correspondence has declined sharply since. So the letters I best remember as a college student were from my aunt and from Grandma herself. Grandma Fuller's letters, in particular, were filled with spiritual encouragement and hints of her prayers.

Electronic communication has taken a new twist in recent

years, though: e-mail. My son-in-law is a Christian school teacher, and he, my daughter, and their four children live on a limited budget. So when a friend gave them a nearly new computer, I quickly bought the family a modem and helped them set up a free e-mail account with Juno. Granddaughter Katy, a seventh grader, loves to type out letters to send electronically, as does Hannah, in third grade. We get instant communication, though they live two hundred miles away in another state. Katy now corresponds at the speed of light by e-mail with a friend in Uganda, Africa—a girl who had been Katy's classmate in grade five in Indiana until her parents became missionaries.

A theme Jack Wyrtzen repeated,
both by word of mouth and in
his letters to his grandchildren, was
"Quiet time, quiet time, quiet time!"

Jack said, "We keep after our kids—grandchildren, children, all our staff members and everybody else on this theme, because you're never going to be filled with the Spirit unless you're filled with the Word of God."

"The primary function of grandparents," write Stephen and Janet Bly in *How to Be a Good Grandparent*, is to "pray for your grandkids."[4] The Wyrtzens prayed often for their grandchildren, and God's resultant blessing has impressed the Wyrtzen grandkids with the efficacy of Grandpa Jack's prayers. "When my granddaughter called me after her first child was born," remembered Jack, "she said, 'You know, Grandpa, this is the fourth generation—this is wonderful! Pray for my kids, just like you prayed for us.' I think most of our grandchildren feel that way," Jack added.

The Blys recommend keeping a "picture prayer journal,"[5] using a notebook with your grandchild's latest photo, and pages to keep records of birthdays and other occasions requiring special, specific prayer. A purse-sized Grandma's Brag Book, leaving every other page open for notes, might work for this. Grandpas could use a similar book to keep in their desks. A notebook kept on the shelf with your family Bible makes easy reference for evening devotions and prayers.

So be faithful to maintain family devotions. Your consistent example, especially when your married children visit overnight with your grandchildren, will encourage them to be faithful in family worship also. Pray for your grandchildren. As He did with Great-great-grandmother Mary Hackney's prayers, or Jack Wyrtzen's prayers for his grandchildren, God will honor these prayers with yet another generation that follows the Lord.

And write often, offering spiritual encouragement. Younger grandchildren are often not at home when the phone rings. But a letter will get there every time, to be read, reread, and cherished. Hearts will be encouraged. You will be remembered as the grandparent who cared about your grandchild's spiritual welfare.

Use e-mail, especially in writing to grandchildren in college —or in schools where kids are permitted to use the Internet. Though most students will not have Internet or e-mail service in their dorm rooms, Hotmail is available to anyone with access to an Internet-connected computer in a school, college, or a neighborhood public library. Many girls develop dozens of "pen"—e-mail—pals, and they check their electronic corre-spondence whenever they use a computer—which can be sev-eral times a day.

So whether it's 12-year-old Tabitha in the sixth grade, or her big brother Jacob at State U, if you have e-mail service on your computer, write them. Kids, who may assume that e-mail is the exclusive domain of children and teens, will be sur-prised—and delighted!

And if you don't have e-mail? Drop them a note of encour-agement in the mail. And don't forget to pray for your grand-kids daily, *by name!*

How Grandparents Can Let Go Without Losing Their Posterity

Grandpa Wiggin sat down heavily on a chunk of curly rock maple long ago that Saturday morning in January. He pulled a mitten from one gnarled hand and fished a grimy handkerchief from a deep pocket of his mackinaw.

At first I had not been alarmed with Grandpa's coughing and sneezing during the two hours we had spent splitting and stacking stove wood since breakfast. But his coughing had progressed to spitting, and when I saw a red stain in the snow at his feet, I became worried. He rose, and 10 more minutes of work with the maul and wedges brought on more violent coughing. "Grandpa, I'll finish the woodpile. You go inside," I finally insisted in frightened exasperation at his determination.

I watched Grandpa's rheumatic hobble as he mounted the shed steps. I took up the sledgehammer, and after splitting half a dozen chunks into kitchen-stove size, I went indoors to check on him. I found Grandpa Wiggin already abed, and Grandma rubbing his chest with camphorated oil. He rose from that bed only once in the three bitterly cold winter weeks he lingered in the warmth of a house he had built himself half a century before, heated by wood he had helped saw and split during the fall and winter months. At age 84, Grandpa Wiggin died on Dad's 37th birthday, January 30, 1953.

I suppose that my having been with him during his last earthly labors impressed me indelibly with the concept of Grandpa Wiggin as a man who valued hard work. Over the years as I have matured, the impression that incident left on me has a few times induced me to tackle tasks beyond my means. (I began one summer between college years driving a farm milk truck, which required wrestling 115-pound cans onto chest-high shelves. After two 12-hour days, I had to quit!) But all in all, far more often his example has given me impetus to press on through discouragement to the euphoria of a job well done.

Rarely does a value held by a grandparent impress itself into the mind of a child with a lesson as poignant as the death of my grandfather impressed me with the value of work. More commonly, we teach our grandchildren here a little, there a little, leaving marks on their minds and spirits as we interact with them.

I learned much from my grandparents, and if you have a solid relationship with your grandkids, you can teach them much as well. For example, I found in Grandma Fuller a quiet, modest woman who was always courteous and thoughtful, a model of kindness. Grandma Wiggin, a Maine farm housewife from a generation older than my maternal grandmother, was the epitome of frugality, practicing home arts alongside my mother, ranging from canning to soap making to knitting, which kept our large family supplied through long New England winter months. So what if the creamery's check was needed to pay off last spring's seed and fertilizer bill? If we had barrels of Northern Spy apples, bushels of Kennebec potatoes, canned beans and beets on the shelf, and bacon and hams hanging on a cellar floor joist, we would eat.

Both my grandfathers taught me truthfulness. To utter an untruth was morally abhorrent to them. I remember that Grandpa Fuller, a sheriff, had only contempt for a man whom he'd arrested then heard perjure himself at a court trial. "The first word that fellow ever uttered was a lie," Grandpa declared.

Grandma Fuller and Grandpa Wiggin were students of the Word. I can still see Grandma preparing a Sunday school lesson for her boys' class as she sat beneath a lamp in her rocker, or Grandpa marking his Bible in the glow of a kerosene Aladdin.

Our heritage of American family values has taken a beating during the past half century, and the destructive processes attacking our grandchildren are accelerating.

Strangely, some cultures that do not share Bible-based beliefs nevertheless successfully transmit many positive values of their heritage to succeeding generations, such as the careful conservation of cash and other resources, as well as family cooperation in entrepreneurship. Orientals such as Korean and Vietnamese immigrants, refugees from two wars, are well known for this.

Until recently, crime was virtually unknown among these peoples, transplanted to America.

Most Japanese young people claim to be agnostics, and have abandoned the religious beliefs of their parents and grandparents. Yet social and family traditions are much more a part of life in Japan than in America. Most young Japanese still give homage to the old ways, not only in the pageantry of colorful centuries-old dress for special occasions, but also in the habits of daily living, as well, reports Paul Horlits in the ABWE *Message*.[1] Though not a religion, Confucianism, borrowed from the Chinese some six hundred years ago, supplies an unwritten code of behavior on which most Japanese draw for their traditions of social behavior, morality, and family relationships, Horlits noted.

American culture is not as devoid of old-fashioned positive tradition based in a Judeo-Christian ethic as the media report, or as even many ministers of the gospel would have us believe. Anyone who's spent time in cultures where Judeo-Christian ethics have not been felt, or have been suppressed, such as Africa and the former Soviet Union, can attest to this. In Moscow, for instance, free enterprise is slow to catch on, whereas it is accepted as the norm in the U.S., Canada, and Western Europe. Consumer goods routinely displayed for customer inspection in American stores are kept locked behind the counter for fear of theft. Mutual trust, based in biblical morality, has made it possible for Western industry, merchandising, and banking to flourish.

But values which are specifically *familial* in nature, such as sexual monogamy, the leadership of the husband-father in the home, respect for elders, and obedience to parents, have taken a beating since today's grandparents were kids.

Pastor's wife, mother, and writer Lola M. Williams interviewed Christian men and women, ages 20 to 32, from a wide variety of backgrounds and lifestyles. All had been reared in Christian homes and are all now "serving the Lord in some capacity," she wrote in *Confident Living*.[2] Based on the answers to her survey, Williams compiled a report on the common characteristics of these homes where family values and a heritage of Bible-believing Christianity have been carried to the second generation. Though the comments of her respondents are primarily of value to parents, these answers will also prove useful to grandparents seeking to preserve their heritage in their grandchildren. As a refresher course in parenting—for grandparents—I have restated and organized in outline form several principles from Williams's article "Keeping Them in Church," adding some from my own observations:

1. Most successful parents take time to listen to their children, even when it means putting aside an important task, the newspaper, or a favorite TV show.
2. Parents of Christians who later become church workers regularly take time with each child alone, one-on-one. These children are praised for doing well more often than criticized for making mistakes (see Ephesians 6:4).
3. Both parents in the home are united in discipline. One parent will not undercut the authority of the other, leaving the child confused.
4. With small children, the most common discipline used by parents successful in carrying their heritage into their children's lives is spanking; with teens, it is grounding (see Proverbs 13:24; 19:18).

5. Eighty-six percent have a curfew.
6. The children are exposed to other Christian youth in a variety of circumstances, such as summer camp or a Christian school, in addition to Sunday school.
7. Most such homes have daily devotions.
8. Most parents require church attendance, unless the kids are ill. This usually includes Sunday services and mid-week attendance at a prayer service or a Christian children's club, such as AWANA.
9. Sex, religion, and politics are openly, sometimes fiercely discussed in many homes. Most children can politely disagree with their parents on such issues. The repressive attitudes that ungodly child experts often claim characterize Christian homes are found in only a minority of cases. Teens are also permitted to discuss their own discipline measures with their parents.
10. Consistency in lifestyle and in dealing with the children, Williams found, is the most common characteristic of a home that sees its values carried on for succeeding generations.

Except in those unusual cases where the grandparents have custody of the grandchildren, and can rear them as their own, the grandparents' role is pretty much to be supportive of parents as they seek to implement the principles mentioned above. "The best thing is to be an example" to the grandchildren, says Grandpa Jim Franks, who describes himself as "the only guy my wife knows who talks back to the television."

"He not only talks to it; he never stops," adds Shirley Franks.

"Why do Hollywood and Broadway deliberately try to

destroy family values?" ponders Jim, who views much of TV fare as bad examples for kids. And his grandchildren know where he stands on issues ranging from sex to fatherhood, from socialism to the causes of famine in Africa. "I just tell my grandkids it's baloney," he says of antifamily opinions expressed on TV.

"How do you say that without being thought an old grouch?" I asked him.

"I'm smarter than those guys in Hollywood," Jim says, his eyes atwinkle. "They wind up in the junkyard physically and spiritually," he points out. Jim's 25 grandchildren and great-grandchildren respect his opinions, and they know Grandpa's right.

> *It's not realistic to expect your children and grandchildren to copy your parenting practices as if cut out by Grandma's gingerbread-boy cutter.*

Nor is it possible. The Franks reared their children in a Christian heritage that shared both Baptist and Christian Reformed evangelical convictions. But one child married a Roman Catholic, and so this set of grandchildren is being raised Catholic. So Grandma Shirley, who frequently has seen the Lord work in the lives of her children, prayed. And "the priest was saved through the testimony of an evangelical minister," she says. She and Jim went to a granddaughter's first communion at the Catholic church, and "they sang all our songs and the music was Spirit-filled," Shirley remembers. "Our daughter loves the Lord, and she prays with her children, and the family studies the Bible together," Shirley says.

The practice of praying with the children, Shirley says, has been passed down through at least four generations. She recalls waking up at night with what her mother called "growing pains"—leg cramps. Her mother would rub Shirley's little legs and pray with her, and they'd pass the time praying for the pain and for family members until the cramps were relieved. Shirley herself passed this practice on to a daughter who also had nighttime leg cramps as a child.

Shirley's daughter had a daughter of her own with the same problem. Both mother and grandmother had sessions with this four-year-old, rubbing her legs and praying for family members. Once when the small girl was asked to say grace at a family picnic she prayed around the family circle, remembering aunts and uncles and cousins by name before she finished!

Grandparents who would hand their heritage of spiritual, moral, and social values on to their grandchildren should seriously consider the words of Paul the apostle to the church in Corinth. Christ "died for all"—grandparents and grandchildren —"that those who live should no longer live for themselves, but for [Christ] who died for them and was raised again," Paul wrote (2 Corinthians 5:15). This implies that a grandparent should avoid a materialistic lifestyle. I watched an elderly, 70-something couple in a Cadillac, a new one, the big four-door Fleetwood with all the bells and whistles. It never ceases to amaze me that many folks wait until the kids are grown to buy a big car! Instead, use your resources to prepare Grandma's House for the grandkids. Build Grandfather's Mountain as a family refuge, so that, like old Caleb's, your heritage can pass on to a third generation (see Joshua 14:11–14).

My kids' Grandpa Hackney, who passed away before the birth of our fourth child, was known by his grandchildren for his generosity. The neighborhood kids knew him for this, too. He gave away cookies and treats to neighborhood children, who as adults still remember his kindness. And when his own children were young parents struggling with finances, Grandpa, not mindful of laying up for old age, sacrificed to buy his grandchildren shoes, socks, winter coats, or school clothes. Like the woman of Bethany, Grandpa Hackney is remembered for his giving heart by several dozen grandchildren who have become givers themselves. As your grandchildren see that your values are eternal rather than temporal, they'll want to emulate you and the heritage you seek to pass on.

Author Maureen Rank, writing in *Dealing with the Dad of Your Past*, speaks of "launching" one's children "from a childish dependence . . . into a healthy *interdependence*" (italics hers) with others they encounter in their adult lives.[3] Ready for it or not, Grandpa and Grandma, even as our own children grew into maturity and feathered their own nests, our grandchildren will repeat this process. They will be launched like arrows throughout the wide world (see Psalm 127:4).

We must let them go, releasing them to build their own lives. But can we be assured, as they move out of Grandfather's Mountain into the well-watered plains below, that they will carry with them the heritage, both goodly and godly, with which we have striven to endow them? I believe we can, as we entrust them into the Lord's care.

> *Our most important responsibility*
> *as grandparents is to pray for*
> *our grandkids each day,*
> *says Shirley Franks.*

Grandparents Jack and Joan Wyrtzen and Jim and Shirley Franks attested that God does answer prayer in regard to their grandchildren. Pray *for* them and *with* them, says Grandma Shirley. "Later they can say to their own kids, 'Grandma prayed and Grandpa prayed, so we pray as a family.'"

CHAPTER TWENTY

The Grandchild
Who Climbs Trees

A small boy many years ago raised up on one elbow in his bed to watch the glow from the grate of an old stove piped into a closed-off fireplace in the master bedroom of a pre-Civil-War-era country inn. The rattle of a stove poker and the squeak of cast-iron hinges had caught the child's attention, and silhouetted in the glow from the fire, an old man in slippers and flannel nightshirt stuffed the stove at the foot of the bed with wood to keep the drafty room cozy against the snow-laden winds of a northern New England winter night.

The old man crawled beneath the quilts on the opposite side of the double bed, and the child, satisfied that Grandpa had not abandoned him to the vagaries of a night in a strange room, fell back asleep. I was that small boy, and the old man was my grandfather, Bill Fuller.

Much is made by some family counselors about parents—and grandparents—telling offspring they love them. Many children *need* to be told, I'm sure. But I can never recall feeling insecure in the love of either my parents or my four grandparents—not once. Grandpa loved me, though I don't recall that he ever put into words his feelings toward me. He loved me enough to rouse himself at two in the morning to refuel the bedroom stove, and I was satisfied with that.

Like the dog hears "His Master's Voice" from the Victrola in the famous old ad, I can hear Grandpa Fuller's voice in the squeak of the door of a century-old stove that sits in my living room. I'm not sure whether the fact that that stove had sat for many years in Grandma's House before it came into my possession has anything to do with it or not!

The influence of loving grandparents on grandchildren is profound, reaching beyond mere belief to shape behavior, affecting destinies. Children need a proper balance of security and dare if they are to become effective soldiers of Christ in later life. My grandparents, as well as my parents, offered me security that I never questioned, either as a child or as a teen. They also taught me to climb "trees"—both literally and figuratively—giving me a sense of dare.

A happy melding of this security and encouragement came in my teens when I helped Dad shingle the back of a three-and-a-half-story hillside house. We erected the staging, course by course. As the work progressed, I mounted along with him. Nearly 40 feet above a rock-strewn Maine hillside, we stood on a plank catwalk with several shingles just out of reach, high in the gable. I agreed to go up, providing Dad would agree not to let go of the ladder while I nailed the final shingles in place. "Don't look down," Dad warned as I started up. I didn't. And I got the job done.

But not all parents and grandparents are as confident of their children's ability to climb as my dad was. Consider the following anecdote, based on fact:

"Jeffrey could break a leg!" Eva Jones was emphatic. A grandmother with years of experience in raising children, she felt she had ample grounds to warn Theresa Thompson about her grandson's dangerous behavior.

Theresa explained as patiently as she could that she really *didn't* mind if grandson Jeff climbed the tall pine in the Thompson backyard near the Jones property line. "He'll survive—*my* kids all climbed it," she remarked pleasantly as she hung up the phone.

Have you ever wondered why some children become leaders and step confidently out of the family nest to pursue rewarding careers, while others, though they may settle down to a steady job, never seem to rise above the daily routine of running with the nine-to-five herd of wage earners?

Man, created in the image of God, is creative (see Genesis 1:27). He is not bound, like the beast, to his instincts. Yet many folks, even Christians, find themselves forced into such a mold of conformity that creativity is effectively stifled, or at least misdirected.

The transformed life of which the Bible speaks seems far from the daily existence of many Christians. "Do not conform any longer to the pattern of this world," Romans 12:2 advises. This implies, among other things, trusting God to help us break mindless habits that curtail creativity. As grandparents, we must not get ourselves into a rut while guiding our grandchildren.

The New Testament Greek word chosen by Paul for "conform" in Romans 12:2 is *suschematizo,* meaning to shape one thing like another, as with a mold or cookie cutter. Peter uses the same Greek verb in 1 Peter 1:14–15: "Do not conform to . . . evil desires . . . in ignorance. But . . . be holy in all you do." Creativity, then, coupled with clean living, makes a grandkid a climber who slips the surly bonds of earth to soar and serve his Creator-Savior!

Would-be visionaries and winners are constantly warned by the world to "squat down in the trenches. Keep your head low. Don't climb above the level of the crowd." Grandparents who dish out this type of advice do so at the peril of their grandchildren, who like pinioned Canada geese may never leave the stagnant farm ponds of mediocrity. We want our grandchildren to fly. In God's image, we wish them to climb trees!

Let's take another look at the Jones and Thompson grandchildren. Though the names are fictitious, their circumstances represent several real-life Christian families who have faced similar episodes in child rearing.

Eva Jones had had a discouraging time raising her family, with little help from her husband. Her oldest son had not returned to high school after a motorcycle accident nearly took his life. It was he of whom she had been thinking when she called Theresa Thompson about her eight-year-old grandson, Jeffrey. Her next, a daughter, had quit high school to marry, then taken a job as a waitress while Grandma Eva tended her two babies. Only her third child finished high school and found a good job.

But her youngest, Brittany, still at home and the same age as Jeffrey Thompson, was her mother's darling. Susie would never cause her mother concern—Mrs. Jones saw to that.

Even as her mother called Mrs. Thompson, Brittany had been safely ensconced before the TV filling herself with cookies and Coke while feeding her young mind on a steamy soap opera.

But God wants your child to develop his full potential. Psychologists estimate that the average human being uses only about 3 percent of his brain capacity in his lifetime!

Brittany Jones' indolence is apparent to most grandparents reading this. And her mother's indulgence is an all-too-common reaction to the stress of bringing children up in modern times. Our society has gone, within the memory of older grandparents, from a work-oriented culture in which boys and girls had chores to fill their spare moments when not in school, to a leisure- and consumer-oriented culture in which the pursuit of fun and goods fills a child's time and imagination. Hanging out in a shopping mall with other youth has become the number-one pastime for millions of American kids, ages 11 to 16. Many of today's grandparents are poorly equipped to uphold their married children in child rearing in a society so unlike the one in which they themselves grew up.

Though the drudgery of yesteryear certainly stifled creativity, the vacuum left by the plunge of the American family into materialism is even more deadly to the growth of human potential. But the Christian grandparent enjoys an advantage which grandparents in the world around him do not have. Grandma and Grandpa have in the Bible the resources to help guide their grandchildren to an adulthood that will glorify God. And as the believing grandparent draws on God for strength, his grandchildren will recognize their own spiritual, mental, and physical capacities.

For some grandparents the directive in Proverbs 22:6 to "train up a child" (KJV) means merely to take their grandchildren to Sunday school, pray for or with them, and when they are guests in your home, lead them in family devotions. Spiritual training is foundational to the upbringing of children, certainly. Having helped Mom and Dad lay the foundation, these grandparents often expect the child to construct the "building" of his life with little encouragement other than to warn him with the usual social taboos and moral restraints. Need we be surprised that most adolescents emerging into adulthood build one-story houses—huts, even—of their lives, when God's plan is for them to build skyscrapers?

How, then, can grandparents help their grandchildren build their lives in accordance with God's plan? Several principles follow:

 The principle of acceptance: God loves us in spite of what we are or do.

A grandparent's responsibility begins with showing the grandchild that he can be "made . . . accepted in the beloved" because Christ's death made this possible (Ephesians 1:6, KJV). The Greek verb is here *charitoô*, meaning to be given grace or special favor, in this case from God, based on Jesus' sacrifice.

Children crave unconditional acceptance. Your small grandchild will best learn of the Christ who has graciously accepted him as he sees Christ in you. He needs to know, for example, that the paper he brought home from Sunday school is every bit as important as Grandpa's Sunday newspaper. In terms of the future of his young life, it is far more important. If your grandchildren see that their grandparents are pleased with the small things they shove under adult noses, they'll consider themselves to be of worth before God and before the world, and act accordingly, realizing their full potential as adults. Reinforce their efforts by taking that little one on your lap to read his Sunday school stories to him, an act of more value to the child than the content of the paper itself. So what if your newspaper never gets read?

As a child I used to vie with my brother George for a turn to sit on Grandpa Wiggin's knee on the way to church in our 1937 Dodge sedan. I recall that I wore short pants and that the car was upholstered in mohair. I'm not sure which was roughest on my little bare legs—Grandpa's wool serge pants draped over his bony knee, or the bristly goat-hair seats! But sitting there was a twice-Sunday privilege, once coming and once going, and I felt important and loved seated on his lap.

The principle of encouragement is expressed in 1 Thessalonians 5:11.

The King James rendering is to "edify one another." The New International Version renders this "build each other up."

"You can do it, Jeffrey," he often heard, both from parents and grandparents. But "Why bother to try, Brittany? You can see that the teacher is playing favorites" was Eva Jones's unfortunate response to Brittany's complaints about her school grades. Success in adult life is in many ways directly a product of attitudes one acquires about his abilities while still a child. These positive attitudes are largely derived from encouragement by *adults* whom the child admires and attempts to model, especially parents and grandparents.

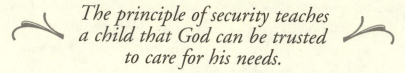

The principle of security teaches a child that God can be trusted to care for his needs.

The secure child will become an adult who can serve God, confident that he'll not be left helpless. Many adults yearn for the satisfaction of a more rewarding career, only to be held back by childhood-learned fears which make it impossible for them to risk losing the benefits of their present employment. Preferring their retirement pay and guaranteed raises to using their creativity to climb towering "trees"—with occasional rotten branches—they stick with routine jobs that offer little room for personal growth.

Grandparents who are constantly fussing in front of children about money matters may be damaging their grandchildren's faith in God's loving care. Grandparents and grandchildren should pray together, committing their daily needs to the Lord and thanking Him for His blessings (see Matthew 6:25–34). They should provide a love so transparent that a child can never question it. My grandparents offered me the security of a love I never doubted as a child, symbolized in my memory by the glow of that old stove's grate and the squeak of cast-iron hinges interrupting the whistle of a north wind on a winter night.

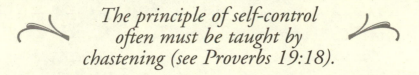

The principle of self-control often must be taught by chastening (see Proverbs 19:18).

Jeffrey had to learn that lesson. Against explicit instructions not to do so, he spent all the money in his pocket for candy. The chastening he received afterward—a spanking by Grandma Theresa and strictly rationed sweets for several days—hurt for a while, but in later life it might save him from financial disaster.

Grandparents should clear disciplinary measures with parents, of course. You can easily alienate a daughter-in-law or son-in-law, or confuse a grandchild, by varying drastically from patterns established at home. While grandparents can teach a parent firm disciplinary measures (how often I've heard a grandmother say, "That kid needs his sit-down warmed up!"), sometimes the wisest recourse is isolation or loss of privilege. Grandma is probably not hurting Jeffrey by giving him two cookies whereas Mom might give him one. But Grandma would surely harm him by letting him raid the cookie jar whenever he pleases.

The principle of creativity separates leaders from followers more than anything else.

The leader innovates. He dares. He may not have the inventive genius of an Edison; he may have only the willingness to try something different at the risk of being laughed at.

David expressed creativity when he went to meet Goliath armed with only a sling and stones. Offered the ready-made armor and weapons of Saul, he chose to use just the bare essentials (see 1 Samuel 17:38–40). And God later used David, the innovator, to lead a nation!

Ready-made toys, I think, are often creativity-stealing culprits. Watch your two-year-old grandson become a highway engineer with a truck, a tiny shovel, and a sandbox. (My oldest granddaughter and grandson *both* loved to build things inside the sand-filled tractor tire in our yard when they were small, as do their younger siblings.) Give the same child a battery-operated gizmo, and he'll put it through its paces until bored, then smash it. Why? His creativity has been frustrated. Destructiveness is nothing more than misdirected creativity, I believe. Give a child tools and teach him to build, and you have equipped him for a rewarding life. The tools in my shop that I now cherish most belonged to my dad and my grandfathers—I have Grandpa Fuller's toolbox.

My best Christmas ever when I was a child was the year my dad's crops dried up and there was no money for toys. Dad spent hours for many evenings in the cellar with his tools. Under the tree on Christmas morning, in dazzling varnish and glorious red paint, was an assortment of wooden toys, including a kid-sized slide of lovingly planed and sanded maple planks mounted on the frame of an old barrel churn.

Grandpa Fuller spent many hours each day in his woodworking shop behind his country store. Many times I saw him brush the sawdust from his mattress-ticking overalls to slice cheese or bologna. How many of Grandpa's customers may have tasted pine or maple sawdust in their sandwiches the next day?! I learned the joy of following creative urges from watching Grandpa, from helping him assemble a piece of lawn furniture or loading it into his panel truck for delivery. Exactly how much he or my father, skilled at husbandry, carpentry, and mechanics, added to my urge to create, I don't know. But I do know that watching them, helping them, and enjoying the fruits of their labors gave me a push to try my own creative urges.

 ## *TV is a killer of creativity.*

The grandparent who succumbs to the urge to let the television set be Grandma's baby-sitter is helping that grandchild form a lifelong habit of preferring lazy, vicarious experience as a substitute for real life. With TV, a child doesn't have to think; he just absorbs. But with the radio on—remember *Little Orphan Annie, Inner Sanctum, Dragnet,* or *The Lone Ranger?*—the child's mind supplies the pictures. And with a book, the child must *think,* sort over facts and ideas presented, and creatively furnish his own conclusions.

How pleased I was recently, when driving four of my grandchildren home after church, to have them ask me to turn the radio on to "listen to our story." It was a dramatized serial of a Christian juvenile novel loaded with Bible truths and moral lessons. Episodes from *The Sugar Creek Gang* and other wholesome tales are aired on weekends on Moody Network stations. My grandkids love these, as their fertile young minds fill in the imaginary video. These are the very same adventure stories that I *read* on Sunday afternoons half a century ago!

 ## *Let your grandkids climb trees.*

Challenge your grandchildren to excel in whatever field they enter. But tailor the tasks you give them to the reasonable limits of their abilities. "Train up a child," said Solomon. Note the direction. Plants and people naturally, by creation, grow *up*ward. Neither should be constantly beaten down, though both need pruning and direction.

Mrs. Jones continually scolded her sons whenever they climbed above their heads. So she should not have been surprised when, after several years at his job, her third child, the only one who had finished his education, passed up an offer of a managerial position on a commission basis as too risky. Often put down by his parents whenever he sought as a child to express himself, he now preferred a secure, salaried slot in his company. The risks inherent in a chance at greater creativity were too great for a man whose parents had failed to build his faith and courage during childhood.

Jeffrey Thompson, on the other hand, became an executive with a large nonprofit Christian organization. His parents and his grandparents are satisfied with their child who climbed trees! Will your grandchildren be among those few who climb confidently over life's difficulties, their eyes fixed on the Son through the leafy shadows of doubt and fear? Or will they remain on the ground, content to nibble on what acorns are knocked loose by the tree climbers? It's largely up to you!

Chapter Twenty-One

When Grandparents Must Be Parents

"I'm gonna stay here until they give me away in marriage." Fifteen-year-old Cheri Allison's eyes shone with pleasure as she spoke. Yet as I listened to her, her mouth at times betrayed the sad circumstances that had brought her to live with her grandparents, Jim Allison, 61, and his wife, Edie, 59, in their idyllic lakeside cottage in Michigan. Before Cheri was two, her unmarried mother had taken a new lover, dumped the toddler on the girl's semiemployed, alcoholic father, Jack Allison, and moved to another state.

Her father married after Cheri's mother left. Jim and Edie were alarmed by his drinking, stints in jail for drunken driving, and by Cheri's constant verbal abuse from an overtired, worried stepmother with two babies. One day when their son came to get her after he completed a six-month sentence for driving under the influence, these caring grandparents simply refused to give Cheri back. And so she has lived with her grandparents since age five.

This story of Cheri, a teen being reared by loving Christian grandparents who would like to adopt her, is true. Names and minor details have been changed to protect the Allison family's privacy. Across America some 4 million of our nation's 71 million children under 18 live in homes headed by a grandparent. Nearly one and a half million of these, like Cheri, share a home where the grandparents are the only adults.[1]

Occasionally, as in the case of the Allison family, it is the mother who abandons the child or children. In such cases the father often opts to keep his child and perhaps move back with his parents or his widowed or divorced mother. With Cheri, her father's verbal abuse when drunk, the harried stepmother's letting little Cheri know she was unwanted, and a home in economic chaos led to Jim and Edie's determination to be to Cheri the responsible parents they had failed to be for their son, Jack.

Cheri Allison's case is pretty typical of abandoned or abused kids taken in by grandparents. Writing in *Parade*, newsman Bill O'Reilly notes, "Parental substance abuse . . . divorce and teenage pregnancy . . . are the leading reasons that grandparents take over the care of their grandchildren."[2] Death of parents has not been an important cause of child abandonment for about a century. The orphans romanticized by Dickens and Twain in the nineteenth century, and by L. M. Montgomery and K. D. Wiggin at the beginning of the twentieth century, scarcely even exist at the dawn of century twenty-one.

O'Reilly interviewed actor George Kennedy, 75, and his wife, Joan, 68, who have adopted their 5-year-old granddaughter, Taylor, and taken her into their Los Angeles home. Taylor's mother, Shauuna, had been "involved with drugs since she was 12," Kennedy told O'Reilly. The mother is now in a California penitentiary as a chronic offender. Shauuna, when small, was herself adopted by the Kennedys, and the Kennedys admit that they'll "never understand" what went wrong. But with little Taylor, "we have another chance," Kennedy said, happy that God has given him and Grandma Joan "another shot" at child rearing.[3]

Drugs, alcohol, divorce, premarital sex, jail sentences—these factors, often in combination, are ordinarily the elements that bring about a child being left to grandparents. Many situations are more mundane than that of Taylor or Cheri, however. Kirsten's (a pseudonym) parents were teens when they married, and they tried hard to make their marriage work. But petty quarreling and the failure of Kirsten's father, Ray Shaw, to lead his young family brought Kirsten's mother, Shirley, to where she simply gave up, packed up, and left. She returned to the turmoil of an undisciplined home that she had married to escape in the first place.

For a time Kirsten was passed back and forth between grandparents. Then her dad remarried, this time to a strong woman who took charge. Kirsten returned to her father's home, where she stayed until she was 12. But as she entered puberty the war of wills escalated between Kirsten and her stepmother.

Ray, meanwhile—hardworking, sober, successful in his profession—came home late each evening. Then he would hide behind his newspaper, letting his wife manage the kids. Ray's parenting skills pretty much consisted of being a good provider and from time to time attending a school function or

Sunday school program in which his children were involved. Otherwise, Ray was seldom seen in church.

Then came the summer Kirsten spent with her father's parents, Luke and Ellie Shaw, in another state. She enjoyed the tranquillity and freedom—no stepmother to boss her around, no younger siblings to mess up her room. And she enjoyed unhurried hours with her grandparents; her favorite times were helping Grandpa Shaw in the garden when Grandma Ellie was at work. Between them, the Shaws enjoyed Ellie's salary and Luke's ample pension, so Kirsten placed no strain on their finances. When Labor Day came, Kirsten, now 13, begged to stay and go to school in the town where her dad had grown up. Kirsten's father, seeing an opportunity for an armistice between his wife and oldest daughter, readily agreed. He offered to help his parents with Kirsten's expenses.

Kirsten went with neighbors to church and Sunday school, as she had when living with her dad. She trusted Christ as her Savior, and seemed to be growing spiritually. But the male examples in her life left much to be desired. Like her dad, Grandpa Luke Shaw enjoyed having kids around—so long as he didn't have to be bothered to leave his newspaper or TV ball game to entertain them. Kirsten eventually met a young man at school who paid attention to her. At 17, with Kirsten pregnant, they married and dropped out of school. Things went fairly well for several years while the couple lived rent-free in a house belonging to Kirsten's grandfather.

Today Kirsten is a responsible, productive adult. But she repeated some of her parents' mistakes—marriage to a man who didn't know how to love her fully, divorce—before she grew wiser and stronger.

Should *you* take a grandchild in to raise as your own? Are you prepared—spiritually, financially, physically, emotionally—for the task? Answer the following questions honestly between yourself and the Lord before you commit yourself:

1. *Do I have the financial resources?* This may not be as big an issue as you think. Loraine and Peter Pearson of Denver are full-time parents of four granddaughters—five-year-old triplets and a seven-year-old—on an income of about $24,000 a year, plus Medicaid benefits to help with the kids' medical bills. The Pearsons say they are making it. They refuse to consider applying for state foster-care benefits, which could double their income, because of the intrusion from Colorado social services workers that would go with the aid.[4]

A lot of grandparents do not have mortgage payments. Many can add their grandchildren, as dependents, onto their pension's retirement medical insurance policy at a modest additional cost. In many instances, federal benefits such as Medicaid, and often food stamps, will supplement the expanded family's income, with very little intrusion from social workers. Frequently the parent—like Kirsten's dad—is able to help with expenses.

2. *Do I have the physical stamina to rear a child?* Many grandparents find themselves partly handicapped with arthritis or a heart condition. But the perception—shared even by a lot of seniors—that over 50 is over the hill belies reality. Medical news reports often point out that men and women of 50 to 70, if not burdened with a geriatric infirmity—and most of us are not—have more long-term, steady stamina and fewer sick days than younger adults. Having outlived most common

viruses, we simply are not ill so often. And what grandmother suffers with PMS?!

So your knees won't let you jump with Jason on the basketball court? Take him fishing instead.

3. *Do I have the time and the readiness to put aside adult pursuits and nurture a child at this stage in my life?* A lot of grandfathers are at the height of their careers and working longer hours than when their own children were growing up. Even when Grandpa is retired, Grandma may have taken a job right after her own children left for college. She's finally worked up to the top of her department and plans to stay until she's 65 and can collect full Social Security benefits, and perhaps a pension.

4. *Am I ready for the emotional stress?* Many children taken in by grandparents are already teens or on the threshold of the teenage years. James Dobson, who has himself reared kids through the teen years, notes, "Raising boisterous teenagers" can be "frustrating," with "the noise, the messes, the complaints, the arguments . . . the missed curfews, the paced floors . . . the jilted lover, the wrong friends, the busy telephone . . . the rebellion . . . the tears."[5] I spent nearly two decades raising my own teens, and Dot and I went through everything that Dr. Dobson describes.

I recall only too well the phone call in the middle of the night from a mother angry because her son was sitting on her porch steps smoking—with *our* son.

"But he's in his room upstairs," I explained.

"Oh, yeah?".

He had climbed out a bedroom window, using my painting ladder, placed there before bedtime!

These episodes now seem to me like a surrealistic dream

from a life once lived by someone else in a Narnia long ago and far away. Grandpa and Grandma, you *do* know what I'm talking about. And like me, you may prefer not to repeat those days.

5. *Am I ready to assume the role of a father?* Dobson writes of a "desperate need for fathers."[6] When you're faced with deciding whether to rear a grandchild, I believe, this is possibly the prime consideration in your choice. The vast majority of kids I've seen who grew up to become confused adults—alcoholics, drug addicts, sex offenders, promiscuous women—grew up in homes without a strong, responsible dad present. Others had abusive fathers who were losers in adult relationships, so they took their frustration out on the kids.

America's homes need *fathers*—dads who are respected by moms who don't cut them down, or quarrel with them in front of the kids. Real dads, who will put down the newspaper, turn off the TV or computer, and play checkers or Monopoly or chess with Jason and Aleesha. Men who will skip the golf tournament to take the kids to the park, to the zoo, to a museum. Fathers who think more of their sons than they do of their businesses, so they won't miss a child's ball game or recital.

America's teen girls need loving, doting dads, men who will tell them they're beautiful—and mean it. Men who will kiss their daughter's mom and say "I love you" in the kitchen when the kids are present. Men dedicated to developing their daughter's mind by helping her with homework; who are committed to shoring up her soul by taking her to Sunday school and reading the Bible to her each evening.

Girls need daddies who think enough of their daughters' bodies and moral development so that they will never pick up a *Playboy* magazine or open a skin-photo Web site to gaze at the naked body of another man's daughter. They realize that they wouldn't be leering at the centerfold if it were *their* daughter selling and disgracing herself for fame and money and mistaking shame for pride. Daddies are needed who acknowledge that such displays stink in the nostrils of a holy God who made female bodies beautiful and precious for private viewing by an "until death" husband. Then he can be the father (grandfather!) who one day hands her off in marriage to a young man who will love her as Daddy loved her, as Jesus loved His bride and died for her (see Ephesians 5:32–33).

 ## Grandpa, are you ready to become that daddy?

George and Joan Kennedy recognize that they must "do differently" with little Taylor than they did with her mother, Shauuna. "We're careful not to argue in front of her or create unnecessary tension," Kennedy, wiser now, and mature in years, remarked.[7]

The Allisons, too, were prepared to "do differently" before they took in small Cheri. Like her father, Jack, they had been alcoholics. One day friends invited them to church. Trusting Jesus' sacrifice and filled with His Spirit, Jim and Edie left off drinking. Happier now both with themselves and each other, they were ready to respond to Christ's urging to take Cheri in and rear her as their own.

Cheri sees Jim and Edie as her parents, though they have not been able to adopt her, since neither her birth mother or her father is willing to sign adoption papers. The Allisons' custody of Cheri withstood a challenge in court, however, when Cheri firmly told the judge that she wished to remain with her grandparents. They are sending Cheri to a Christian school, and she plays violin in a civic symphony orchestra. Grandpa Jim expects to one day fulfill Cheri's teenage wish to have him give her away in marriage.

There are no guarantees that Cheri, or any child reared by loving grandparents, will turn out okay. Kirsten Shaw followed pretty much the same route as her mother—teen pregnancy, early marriage to a man not ready for responsibility, divorce—before she finally got her feet firmly planted. Yet Kirsten spent five years with grandparents who wanted her, and who supplied her with a peaceful home environment. Her grandfather was sober and responsible, though gruff and sometimes surly.

It's unfair to blame grandparents for their grandchild's behavior. Kids in such situations are often haunted by the ghosts of their first (birth) parents' quarreling or boozing. The skeleton of their parents' divorce, which left that child insecure and feeling unwanted, is with them yet. Only the acceptance of Christ's death in redemption can heal these wounds; and they do take time to heal.

The Lord has given us a few more years to love our grandchildren. Whether we are raising our grandkids or are grandparenting across the miles, let's do so for the blessing of our grandkids—to God's glory.

Notes

CHAPTER 1

1. Neil Postman, *The Disappearance of Childhood* (New York: Delacorte Press, 1982), p. 138.
2. Postman, p. 144.
3. Postman, p. 67.
4. *Statistical Abstract of the United States for 1999,* 119th edition (Washington, D.C.: U.S. Census Bureau, 1999), pp. 31-32.

CHAPTER 3

1. Charlie W. Shedd, *Grandparents: Then God Created Grandparents, and It Was Very Good* (New York: Doubleday, 1976), p. 5.

CHAPTER 4

1. *Statistical Abstract,* ibid.
2. Allan Carlson, "Domestic Partners," *World,* May 10, 2000, p. 30.
3. *The World Almanac 2000* (Mahwah, NJ: World Almanac Books, 1999), p. 889.
4. "Christians Are More Likely to Experience Divorce Than Are Non-Christians," *Barna Research Online,* December 21, 1999.

5. As quoted by Gene Veith, "Bible Belt Breakups: Does Evangelicalism Cause Divorce?" *World on the Web,* November 27, 1999.
6. *Barna,* ibid.
7. U.S. Census Bureau, February 11, 2000.
8. *Statistical Abstract,* pp. 15, 144.
9. Douglas Wilson, "It's a Family Tradition: Grandparents Are a Nice Supplement, But No Substitute," *World on the Web,* February 1, 1997.

CHAPTER 6

1. Timothy Lamer, "The Value of Work," *World on the Web,* November 28, 1998.
2. Bernard Gavzer, "Retire from Life? Never!" *Parade,* June 18, 2000, p. 14.

CHAPTER 7

1. Elisabeth Elliot, *The Liberty of Obedience* (Waco, TX: Word, 1968), p. 62.

CHAPTER 8

1. U.S. Census Bureau, as cited in *USA Today,* February 9, 2001.

CHAPTER 9

1. Joe Loconte, "Louisiana Puts Right and Wrong into Divorce Laws," *World on the Web,* June 13, 1998.
2. CBN's *700 Club,* June 8, 2000.
3. Crary is cited by Gene E. Veith, "Bible Belt Breakups: Does Evangelicalism Cause Divorce?" *World on the Web,* November 27, 1999.

4. Ibid.

5. "Christians Are More Likely to Experience Divorce Than Are Non-Christians," *Barna Research Online,* December 21, 1999.

6. Ibid.

7. Bureau of Census, U.S. Department of Commerce, cited in *The World Almanac 2000,* p. 392.

8. Evelyn Sullivan, "Divorce Separates Kids from Their Grandparents," *Muskegon* (Michigan) *Chronicle,* October 13, 1991, p. 5B.

9. From various media reports.

10. "The Wisdom and Love of Grandparents," *Smart Families,* spring 2000.

11. James Dobson, *Newsletter,* June 1992.

12. Sullivan, ibid.

CHAPTER 11

1. "Are You Ready for Sex?" *Seventeen,* "Love Issue," summer 2000, p. 75.

2. Patty Hoffman, "The Flowering of a Late Bloomer," *Seventeen,* "Love Issue," summer 2000, p. 42.

3. Alex Reagan, "The Summer of My STD," *Seventeen,* "Love Issue," summer 2000, p. 67.

4. "Are You Ready for Sex?" p. 75.

5. W. E. Vine, *Expository Dictionary of New Testament Words* (London: Fleming H. Revell, 1966), pp. 107-108.

CHAPTER 12

1. Ann Landers, *Muskegon* (Michigan) *Chronicle,* July 1992.

2. Elisabeth Elliot, *The Liberty of Obedience,* pp. 16-17.
3. Maureen Rank, *Dealing with the Dad of Your Past* (Minneapolis: Bethany House, 1992).

CHAPTER 13

1. Marilou Genereaux Booth, "Grandloving Those Grandkids," *Smart Families,* fall 1999, p. 12.
2. *Bottom Line Personal,* May 15, 2000, p. 15.

CHAPTER 14

1. "Ol' Man" Raleigh, "No-No's for Grandparents," *Alive,* May 1994, p. 6.
2. Charlie W. Shedd, *Grandparents: Then God Created Grandparents, and It Was Very Good* (New York: Doubleday, 1976), p. 19.
3. Cynthia Ulrich Tobias, *You Can't Make Me (But I Can Be Persuaded)* (Colorado Springs, CO: WaterBrook Press, 1999).
4. Cheri Fuller, "Interceding on Behalf of Your Grand-children," *LifeWise,* April/May 2000, p. 21.

CHAPTER 15

1. Gary Chapman, *The Five Love Languages of Teenagers* (Chicago: Northfield Publishing, 2000), p. 7.
2. Ibid., pp. 253-255.
3. Ibid., p. 254.
4. Christina Hoff Sommers, *The War Against Boys: How Misguided Feminism Is Harming Our Young Men* (New York: Simon & Schuster, 1999). Cited by Alice Cary, *Bookpage.com,* June 30, 2000.

5. Naomi Wolf, *Promiscuities* (New York: Random House, 1997).

6. Chapman, p. 25.

7. Chapman, p. 26.

8. Walt Mueller, *Understanding Today's Youth Culture* (Wheaton, IL: Tyndale House, 1999), p. 46.

9. Gene Edward Veith, Jr., *Postmodern Times: A Christian Guide to Contemporary Thought and Culture* (Wheaton, IL: Crossway Books, 1994), p. 196. Cited by Mueller, p. 46.

10. George Barna, *Generation Next: What You Need to Know About Today's Youth* (Ventura, Calif.: Regal Books, 1995), p. 31. Cited by Mueller, p. 46.

11. *Barna Research Online,* "Teenagers Embrace Religion But Are Not Excited About Christianity," January 10, 2000.

12. Ibid.

13. David Van Biema, "The Day God Took Over," *Time,* June 5, 2000, p. 61.

14. *Fact Sheet: Youth Risk Behavior Trends, 1991-1999,* Centers for Disease Control Web report, January 23, 2001.

15. *Health Survey on Teen-Age Risk Behaviors,* conducted by the Muskegon (Michigan) County Health Department, 1997.

16. Ibid.

17. Ibid.

18. *The World Almanac 2000,* p. 889.

19. "Who Knew? The Spin of Teen Sex," *Seventeen* Web site, July 13, 2000.

20. *Assessing Adolescent Pregnancy—Maine, 1980–1996,* Centers for Disease Control Web report, June 5, 1998.

21. Ibid.

22. CDC's *MMWR Weekly Web site* report for September 18, 1998.

23. "The *Seventeen* Sex Survey," *Seventeen* Web site, July 2000.

24. Cheryl Wetzslein, "Drop in Teen Birthrates Attributed to Abstinence," *Washington Times National Weekly Edition,* February 15–21, 1999 (Web site report).

25. William Mattox, "The Next Hip Trend: Saving Sex for Marriage," *Washington Times National Weekly Edition,* February 22–28, 1999 (Web site report).

26. *Focus on the Family* magazine, April 19, 1992.

27. Stephen Lyons, "Recouping the Steep Cost of Divorce," *Newsweek,* May 8, 2000, p. 12.

28. *The World Almanac 2000,* p. 889.

29. News item, *Baptist Bulletin,* March 2000.

30. "The Myth of the Fifty-Percent Divorce Rate," *The Lookout,* July 20, 1997, p. 15. (This article cites *Inside America,* a 1987 study in which pollster Louis Harris concludes that the actual divorce rate is about 20 percent.)

31. "Christians Are More Likely to Experience Divorce Than Are Non-Christians," *Barna Research Online,* December 21, 1999. (While I accept Barna's data as accurate, I believe his conclusions are off base. See discussion of this phenomenon on page 114, second paragraph.)

32. New York: Harper and Row, 1987.

33. Joel Belz, "The Propaganda Rolls On," *World on the Web*, February 20, 1998.

34. Cal Thomas, "Environmental Theology Is Expanding Government Power," *World on the Web*, August 30, 1997.

CHAPTER 16

1. Wendy Shalit, *A Return to Modesty* (New York: Free Press/Simon & Schuster, 1999), pp. 104–105.

2. James Dobson, *Focus on the Family* magazine, August 1992.

3. Naomi Wolf, *Promiscuities* (New York: Random House, 1997).

4. Shalit, p. 171.

5. Wayne Rice and David Veerman, *Understanding Your Teenager* (Nashville, TN: Word, 1999). Cited by John Bethond, "Insights for Parents of Teens," *Youthculture@ 2000,* spring 2000, p.12.

CHAPTER 18

1. Mary Batchelor, *365 Bible Stories* (Colorado Springs, CO: Cook Communications, 1990).

2. Jesse Lyman Hurlbut, *Hurlbut's Story of the Bible,* rev. ed. (Grand Rapids: Zondervan, 1967).

3. Elsie E. Egermier, *Egermier's Bible Story Book* (Anderson, IN: Warner Press, 1992).

4. Stephen and Janet Bly, *How to Be a Good Grandparent* (Chicago: Moody Press, 1990), p. 173.

5. Ibid., pp. 174–175.

CHAPTER 19

1. Paul Horlits, ABWE *Message*, summer 1992, p. 2.
2. Lola M. Williams, "Keeping Them in Church," *Confident Living*, May 1991, pp. 12–14.
3. Maureen Rank, *Dealing with the Dad of Your Past* (Minneapolis: Bethany House, 1990).

CHAPTER 21

1. U.S. Census, *The World Almanac 2000*, p. 392.
2. Bill O'Reilly, "Their Labor of Love," *Parade*, March 26, 2000, p. 4.
3. Ibid.
4. Tina Traster, "When Grandparents Are 'Parents' Again," *Parade*, March 26, 2000, p. 5.
5. James C. Dobson, *Parenting Isn't for Cowards* (Waco, TX: Word, 1987), p. 155.
6. Ibid., p. 156.
7. O'Reilly, p. 5.

Books

Note: Of the following list of books, videos, magazines, Web sites, and organizations, some will be of direct help to grandparents. Others are intended for grandparents to read, then offer gently to their children—the parents who struggle with rearing your grandchildren. You will also find sources for sound Christian fiction and biography you may wish to purchase for your grandchildren.

The Five Love Languages of Teenagers stands alone in that it deals with today's teens from a unique perspective—what makes that teen tick, and how you, the grandparent, can best address the heartfelt needs of your grandchild. Get a copy. Read it. Lay its concepts next to your own child-rearing experiences as you turn them over in your mind. Make it your goal to love your teen as Christ loved you.

BOOKS FOR EXTRA HELP

1. Linda Burton et al., *What's a Smart Woman Like You Doing at Home?* rev. ed. (Fairfax, VA: Mothers at Home, 1992), 174 pages, paper. ISBN 0-9631188-1-1.

This book is addressed to that "whole new generation of mothers" who are "savvy to their rights and aware of their choices," educated, and experienced in the business world, but nevertheless have chosen to "devote more time to tending the hearth and caring for their children." These women, the writers attest, have "enormous conviction about the importance of what they do." *What's a Smart Woman* will be of interest to the grandmother who wishes to encourage her daughter or daughter-in-law in her decision to be a homemaker rather than a career climber.

What's a Smart Woman, though written from a secular point of view for a broad audience, is in no way offensive to Christian mothers and grandmothers. For example, it deals gently with the mother who feels guilty because she is not contributing to the family income or is not using her college education; or who, pressed by circumstances (divorce, widowhood, single motherhood, a disabled husband), must take a job while her children are growing up.

Employing a lighthearted anecdotal approach, the writers deal with the challenges of child rearing and the financial and emotional advantages of staying at home, against a background of cultural changes in attitudes toward women's roles over much of the past 50 years. This is not a how-to-do-it book. Yet it is loaded with real-life examples and encouragement from life experience that will challenge and invigorate the mother to press on in God's calling to nurture her own precious jewels.

To order: Phone: 1 (800) 783-4666. Web site: www. Mothersathome.org; or log on to your favorite book-ordering Web site.

2. Heidi L. Brennan et al., eds., *Discovering Motherhood.* (Vienna, VA: Mothers at Home, 1991), 80 pages, paper. ISBN 0-9631188-0-3.

This beautifully illustrated, folio-size book is a collection of 48 essays and 15 poems that deal with breastfeeding (much healthier physically and emotionally for both mom and baby), money (moms who work realize only one dollar gain for every three they earn), memories, loving moments to cherish, practical tips, postpartum blues, getting enough sleep, and the first year of a child's life. Enjoying a three-year-old, illness, adoption, keeping a journal—there are a host of topics dear to a mother's heart.

This timeless work of art is still in print and definitely worth the price ($8 to $10). As with *What's a Smart Woman,* a grandmother might use *Discovering Motherhood* to encourage a stay-at-home mom.

To order: Phone: 1 (800) 783-4666. Web site: www. Mothersathome.org; or log on to your favorite book-ordering Web site.

3. Larry Burkett, *The Complete Financial Guide for Young Couples* (Colorado Springs, CO: Cook Communications, 1993), 228 pages, paper. ISBN 1-5647613-0-4.

This planning book will help your grandchildren's family plan a workable budget and live within it. Authored by well-known radio financial advisor Larry Burkett, his organization, Crown Ministries, recommends this as a starter for young families having difficulty making their money go around. *The Complete Financial Guide* deals with choosing insurance, teaching kids about money, and diagnosing financial danger signs in a marriage.

To order: Phone: 1 (800) 722-1976; Web site: www. cookministries.com or www.ChristianBooks.com.

4. Arlene Rossen Cardozo, *Sequencing*, rev. ed. (Minneapolis: Brownstone Books, 1996), 330 pages, paper. ISBN 0-9651238-0-4.

Dr. Cardozo is a Jewish mother who writes from both sides of the fence: the home and the job. In the decade and a half since *Sequencing* first appeared (1986), it has met with such phenomenal success that, surprisingly, reviews have appeared in several periodicals more commonly associated with feminism: *The New York Times, The Washington Post,* and *Vogue,* among others. Arlene Rossen Cardozo, Ph.D. has represented women's issues in appearances on NBC's *Today* show and CBS's *Evening News.*

Sequencing, based on interviews with 350 mothers, is for the mother with professional experience and training who moves in and out of employment as she gives birth and rears children. Examples: One mother and her husband moved to a smaller house to get relief from a heavy mortgage so she could stay home with their children. Another wife saved much of her salary for four years at a professional job so she could quit work to have a baby.

Like *What's a Smart Woman, Sequencing* is written from an anecdotal though scholarly point of view. I recommend *Sequencing* as a gift for educated mothers seeking in-depth answers to insecurities that may have arisen from radical changes in their lifestyles.

To order: Phone:1 (800) 767-9276. Fax: 1 (612) 623-3231. By mail: Brownstone Books, 127 5th Street N.E., Minneapolis, MN 55413. Also available through several book-distribution Web sites.

5. Arlene Rossen Cardozo, *Woman at Home* (New York: Doubleday, 1976; Lincoln, NE: iUniverse, 2000), 172 pages, paper.

Dr. Cardozo is a mother and founder of the Woman at Home Workshops, Minneapolis, Minnesota. This newly rereleased book is more down-to-earth than *Sequencing*. *Woman at Home* gives an excellent anecdotal overview of the battles fought by stay-at-home moms during the early years of the women's lib movement. If the mother of your grandchildren is a serious reader seeking practical and moral support for her choice to put motherhood ahead of a career, she will find *Woman at Home* a stimulating read.

To order: 1 (800) 767-9276 or 1 (877) 823-9235. E-mail orders: custservice@iuniverse.com. Web site: www.iuniverse.com.

6. Gary Chapman, Ph.D., *The Five Love Languages of Teenagers* (Chicago: Northfield Publishing, 2000), 259 pages, hardcover. ISBN 1-881273-83-0.

Gary Chapman's vast experience as a parent, grandparent, pastor, college instructor, marriage counselor, and conference minister shines through in *The Five Love Languages of Teenagers*. The book begins with an overview of teen culture at the beginning of century twenty-one, "Understanding Contemporary Teens." This chapter should be read alongside "Appendix One, How Teenagers Got Their Name." The reader will be surprised to discover that when many of today's grandparents were small children, the word *teenager* had not yet been invented, and the concept of a teen culture was still emerging.

While other writers discuss what makes a teen respond to parental and grandparental love, Chapman—with humor and illustration—*shows* us how to love our teen grandchildren: with words of praise, friendly touch, quality time, selfless service, and thoughtful giving. Though Chapman's book is directed to parents, this is a "must read" for grandparents. Not only does he write with understanding about teens and their problems, *The Five Love Languages of Teenagers* is stuffed with the kind of practical advice that makes grandparents ponder, *Why didn't I think of that years ago?!*

To order: Web site: www.MoodyPress.org or www. ChristianBooks.com; or visit your favorite Christian bookstore.

7. James C. Dobson, *Parenting Isn't for Cowards* (Dallas: Word, 1997), 240 pages, paper. ISBN 0-8499-3342-0.

"Parenting," notes Dr. Dobson in this lighthearted yet dead-serious approach to child rearing, "isn't for cowards." Readers know all too well that grandparenting isn't for cowards either! Dobson deals with all stages of parenting—from toddler through adolescence—in this engaging book. His anecdotes at times rise to the level of parables. Drawn from both observation and experience, they liven the book so that you keep remarking, "Yeah, just like my kid." Grandparents looking for a refresher course in child rearing need to read this one.

To order: Phone 1 (800) A-FAMILY/(232-6459). Log on to www.family.org. Or visit your local Christian bookstore.

8. Margaret J. Meeker, M.D., *Restoring the Teenage Soul: Nurturing Sound Hearts and Minds in a Confused Culture* (Traverse City, MI: McKinley & Mann, 1999), 199

pages, paper. ISBN 0-9669894-0-6. Foreword by Elayne Bennett, founder of Best Friends.

Restoring the Teenage Soul is an excellent overview of the problems—physical, sexual, moral, and social—that war against the souls of today's teens. Author Meeker is a Christian physician and mother, and she approaches her topic with thoroughness and understanding.

Dr. Meeker writes as a physician rather than as a psychologist, so some readers may complain that *Restoring the Teenage Soul* seems written for a secular audience rather than an evangelical Christian audience. Nevertheless, Meeker's heart for teens shines throughout, and the book is packed with data and facts useful in helping grandparents get a grasp on the needs of teenagers in the twenty-first century.

To order: Phone: 1 (877) 800-7567; Write: McKinley & Mann, 940 Pine Ridge Drive, Traverse City, MI 49686; also available on the Internet at www.teenagesouls.com.

9. Walt Mueller, *Understanding Today's Youth Culture*, rev. ed. (Wheaton, IL: Tyndale, 1999), 461 pages.

Mueller's collection of data and advice about the plight of today's teens will be highly useful to the grandparent who is heavily involved in a teen ministry. But many readers may be overwhelmed with the reams of information—all of it useful in proper context.

Pick up a copy of *Understanding Today's Youth Culture* if you're looking for serious, in-depth details about the broader scope of high-school and college-age youth. Mueller does a thorough job of laying out the negative peer pressures today's youth face about sex, materialism, clothing, drugs, and alcohol.

Mueller also deals with the underlying philosophy of our age: postmodernism—that there is no right or wrong; that everything is relative. From his book one can easily get the impression that all teens have accepted the world's philosophy. In fact, movements such as "True Love Waits" show that many Christian teens and college-age youth do shine their bright lights above the sordid actions and notions of a spiritually bankrupt world.

But Mueller has produced a well-written exposé, and he has documented it with recent data. It needs to be read by grandparents who are heavily involved with youth, or who simply wish in-depth material about the problems perplexing their older grandchildren.

To order: Phone: 1 (717) 653-1950; or on the Internet at www.cpyu.org, or www.ChristianBooks.com; or by e-mail: cpyu@aol.com.

10. Donna Partow, *Homemade Business,* rev. ed. (Wheaton, IL: Tyndale House, 1999), 304 pages. ISBN 1-56179-713-8.

This manual has ideas for two hundred home-based businesses, worksheets, and testimonies by mothers who have stayed at home and helped their families' cash flow. It is written for mothers who want a career but not a job outside the home. A grandparent may wish to purchase this for a daughter or daughter-in-law struggling with making ends meet. Grandma herself may wish to start a small business!

To order: Phone: 1 (800) A-FAMILY (232-6459); Internet: www.family.org, www.Tyndale.com, or www.christianbooks.com; or visit your local Christian bookstore.

11. Cynthia Ulrich Tobias, *You Can't Make Me (But I Can Be Persuaded)*. (Colorado Springs, CO: WaterBrook Press, 1999), 208 pages hardcover. ISBN 1-57856-193-0.

You Can't Make Me deals with a common, often misunderstood child-rearing phenomenon, the strong-willed child (SWC). Though I personally believe that this book could use a biblical discussion of corporal punishment, I strongly urge grandparents to purchase and read it. *You Can't Make Me* contains an array of practical, workable techniques for dealing with the SWC—probably one of your grandchildren fits this category.

Here's where some grandparents may miss what's going on—I speak as a father of 4, grandfather of 10, and oldest sibling in a family of 7. I have watched child discipline for three generations now, and I have had considerable experience in dealing with youth as a pastor and teacher.

First, I have been wrong in my dealings with kids more often that I'd like to admit. Thanks to Cynthia Tobias for pointing this out. Second, you, Grandma and Grandpa, share much of this misapprehension with me.

Here's what too often happens. Remember Little Hernia in the old "They'll Do It Every Time!" comic strip? She gave her mother fits. But a lot of kids like her are perfect angels (well, almost!) when alone with their grandparents. As a teacher I've noticed the same phenomenon in the classroom. The child who merely throws spit wads or abuses his restroom pass may at home try to burn the house or stay out all night with a gang. The point is, kids act better with those whom they hold in awe—teachers, grandparents—than with their own parents. I did. So did you as a child. Remember?

So, before you blame your "weak-nerved" daughter or son for failing to take that out-of-control kid to the woodshed, read *You Can't Make Me*. You may be surprised.

Importantly, Tobias points out that much of the childish behavior that frustrates parents may cause teachers and school psychologists to label the SWC with the Attention Deficit Disorder/ADHD paradigm, then resort to Ritalin or another mood-altering drug. Yet SWC behavior is very likely normal, creative activity programmed into your grandchild's system by the Creator-God. Our job, as grandparents and parents, is to learn to channel that energy and determination to the glory of the Creator. So—get and read this book!

To order: Phone: 1 (253) 862-6200; Write: P.O. Box 1450 Sumner, WA 98390; Web site: www.applest.com. *You Can't Make Me* is also available from the publisher, from your Christian bookstore, or from your favorite on-line book distributor.

BIOGRAPHIES YOUR GRANDKIDS WILL LOVE

1. Christian Heroes: Then & Now

A series of mostly missionary biographies, 16 titles and still expanding. Published by Youth With A Mission (YWAM).

To order: Phone: YWAM, 1 (800) 922-2143; Write: Youth With A Mission, P.O. Box 621057, Orlando, FL 32862-1057; E-mail: info@ywamorlando.org; God's World Book Club, 1 (800) 951-2665; Christian Book Distributors, 1 (978) 977-5060; Web site: www.ChristianBooks.com.

2. *The Sower Series*

This Mott Media series was begun by the late George Mott, an entrepreneur with a heart for home schoolers. *The*

Sower Series has expanded to 26 titles and growing. These books highlight famous Christians in business, missions, and government whose lives will challenge your grandchild to achieve greatness. For grades five through eight.

To order: Phone Mott Media, 1 (248) 685-8773; God's World Book Club, 1(800) 951-2665; Christian Book Distributors, 1 (978) 977-5060; Web site: www.ChristianBooks.com.

3. *Men & Women of Faith*
Bethany House offers a total of more than two dozen titles in the sixth-to-ninth-grade level as well as ninth through adult. Mostly missionaries, such as John and Betty Stam and Jim Elliot, whom we older grandparents remember were martyred in China and Ecuador during our lifetime for their dedication to His service.

To order: Phone: Bethany House, 1 (800) 328-6109; God's World Book Club, 1 (800) 951-2665; Christian Book Distributors, 1 (978) 977-5060. Web site: www.Christian-Books.com.

Grandparents may help their grandkids enroll in God's World Book Club by phoning 1 (800) 951-2665; Web site: www.gwbc.com.

Magazines and Periodicals

The Focus on the Family Group of Periodicals

1. *Focus on the Family*
This is Focus's main magazine. It contains family-oriented articles and news of Focus on the Family ministries. Twelve complimentary issues a year. Web site: www.family.org/fofmag

2. *LifeWise*
For seniors, grandparents—you and me. Great stuff about relating to the grandkids. Six issues a year, by subscription. Web site: www.family.org/focusoverfifty

3. *Citizen*
Political, social, and moral issues of concern to Christian families. Twelve issues a year. Web site: www.family.org/citizen

4. *Clubhouse, Jr.* (ages 4–8); *Clubhouse* (ages 8–12) (www.clubhousemagazine.org); *Brio* (teen girls) (www.briomag.com); and *Breakaway* (teen guys) (www.family.org/teenguys/breakaway)

Focus on the Family's top-quality magazines for your grandkids. All are loaded with special features and up-to-the-minute reader interest—not preachy. Kids' book reviews, teen fashions, advice, jokes.

Hint: Most kids read; a few don't. Ask Mom's opinion first. And don't be alarmed if the subscription to *Breakaway* you bought for Zeke, 15, winds up in the hands of Aimee, his 13-year-old sister! Just subscribe to *Brio* for her and suggest that she let Zeke read his *Breakaway* before she grabs it!

5. *Plugged-In*

Both teens and parents will find *Plugged-In* useful as it examines current youth culture, and includes reviews of music, movies, and TV. Web site: www.family.org/pluggedin

6. www.*Boundless.org* is Focus's Web magazine for college-age kids—and it's free. Your grandchildren will love it, if they haven't discovered it already. It has well-written, sometimes controversial, always thoughtful articles on moral, social, and spiritual issues of interest to your university grandson or granddaughter.

To order: Log on to www.family.org, or call 1 (800) A-FAMILY/(232-6459) to subscribe to any Focus on the Family periodicals.

OTHER PERIODICALS

7. *Youthculture@2000*

This is the newsletter of the Center for Parent and Youth Understanding, the folks who distribute the book *Understanding Today's Youth Culture*. Walt Mueller, author of *Understanding*, is the organization's president, and he is a heavy contributor to *Youthculture@2000*. Published quarterly, this magazine gives news updates in cultural trends—secular and Christian—affecting teens.

To order: Phone: 1 (717) 653-1950; E-mail: cpyu@aol. com; Web site: www.cpyu.org.

8. *Youth Walk*

Published by Bruce Wilkinson and Walk Thru the Bible Ministries, *Youth Walk* is a pocket-sized magazine for Christian teens. *Youth Walk*'s emphasis is spiritual—relationship with the Lord in prayer, Christian obedience, service, and Bible study. It also discusses teen culture and music, as well as moral issues. *Youth Walk* seems to address sex less than many teen magazines, perhaps trusting spiritual truth to keep its readers above moral sin. *Youth Walk* is a balanced approach to Christian living for teens.

To order: Phone: 1 (800) 763-5433; Write: Walk Thru the Bible Ministries, 4201 N. Peachtree Road, Atlanta, GA 30340; Web site: www.walkthruthebibleministries.org.

9. *Smart Families*

Topics ranging from "How to Handle a Child's Bad Report Card" to "Loving a Kid at College" to "Long-Distance Grandparenting" make *Smart Families* a veritable smorgasbord of practical parenting and grandparenting ideas. It is not an overtly Christian magazine, but well-known Christian authors and evangelical publishing houses are well represented in articles and book reviews.

To order: Phone: 1 (800) 255-3237; Write: Family University, P.O. Box 500050, San Diego, CA 92150-0050.

10. *At-Home Mother*

This slick, full-color, beautifully illustrated magazine is packed with practical ideas for child rearing, home industry products, purchasing at discount, computerizing the family finances—the list goes on. *At-Home Mother* is the official publication of the National Association of At-Home Mothers. Membership also includes a newsletter.

To order or join: Write: National Association of At-Home Mothers, 406 E. Buchanan Ave., Fairfield, IA 52556; Fax: 1 (641) 469-3068; Web site: www.AtHomeMothers.com.

11. *Welcome Home*

This is the magazine of Mothers At Home, founded in 1984, which bills itself as "the nation's largest and oldest national nonprofit organization supporting mothers who have chosen . . . to be at home to nurture their families." This 32-page monthly is filled with "personal essays, informative articles, poems and art created by and for mothers," the editors affirm. Softer in tone than *At-Home Mother, Welcome Home* is filled with warm photos and artwork featuring children, flowers, and homey scenes.

To order or join: Phone: 1 (703) 352-1072; Write: Mothers At Home, 9493-C Silver King Court, Fairfax, VA 22031; E-mail: mah@mah.org; or Web site: www.mothers athome.org.

12. *Forum*

This is the members-only publication of Mothers and More, an organization of eight thousand "sequencing" mothers—"women who move in and out of paid employment and opt for a variety of flexible work arrangements," according to the Web site. The organization states its purpose as "to change workplace culture so adults can live up to their commitments at home while still living up to their potential at work."

To join: Phone: 1 (630) 941-3553, Fax: 1 (630) 941-3551; Write: Mothers and More, P.O. Box 31, Elmhurst, IL 60126; Web site: www.mothersandmore.org.

13. *Explore! A Field Trip Through Creation*

This slick, exciting science and adventure magazine for upper elementary and middle school kids was launched in the fall of 2000 by God's World as a solid competitor to the evolutionist, environmentalist periodicals aimed at young minds. *Explore!* is lavishly illustrated with color photos. Its practical science articles offer fresh air and relief to kids caught in an environment where "save the wolves" efforts have replaced basic truths about nature as God made it. Better yet—your grandkids will love *Explore!*

To order: Phone: 1 (877) 817-4395 (toll free); Write: P.O. Box 37590, Boone, IA 50037-0590; E-mail: subscriptions @exploremagazine.com; Web site: www.exploremagazine.com

14. *World*

This newsmagazine began as a periodical for teens in Christian schools. It rapidly expanded into a Christian weekly with all the class of *Time* or *Newsweek*, but with a twist: *World* offers engaging news and commentary from a soundly biblical perspective. Recommended by top Christians and conservatives such as former Reagan education secretary William Bennett, *World* is still a wonderful resource for teens—and for their parents and grandparents.

15. *God's World News*

Available in four age-specific editions, *God's World News* is the juvenile edition of *World*. Get it as a gift if you wish your grandkids to have balanced, Bible-based exposure to the world outside their TV sets.

To order: Phone: 1 (800) 951-NEWS (951-6397) or 1 (800) 951-KIDS (951-5437); E-mail: subscribe@world mag.com; Web site: www.worldmag.com.

Other Resources

VIDEOS FOR YOUR TEEN GRANDCHILDREN

Two great videos, *No Boys Allowed* and *How to Get Your Parents to Do What You Want*, are available from Acquire the Fire Ministries. Both videos use Ron and Katie Luce, a husband-and-wife team already familiar to many youth who've watched their hard-hitting show on Christian television. These videos are not preachy, and they employ top-quality musicals, skits, comedy teen interviews, and light chat to deal with topics such as sex, anorexia, and getting along with parents.

These videos are aimed at teens of all ages, though the greatest appeal will be to the 12 to 15 crowd. Many girls age 9 to 11 will enjoy and benefit from them, too.

For Girls Only deals with sex on the moral level only, without divulging any intimate details, so there's nothing objectionable if boys—or girls not ready for the mysteries of reproduction—want to watch.

To order: Phone: 1 (800) 329-FIRE (329-3473); or Web site: www.acquirethefire.com. One free tape is given at the first call.

ADDITIONAL ORGANIZATIONS

1. *Moms/Grandmas in Touch* (MITI) is an international prayer circle that meets to pray for kids and their schools.

To contact: Phone MITI at 1 (800) 949-MOMS (949-6667) to learn of a group near you, or for help in starting one of your own. For further information see Cheri Fuller's article "Grandmas in Touch: Making a Difference," *Life Wise,* April/May 2000; or her book *When Mothers Pray,* available at your local Christian bookstore.

2. *Kids' Hope USA*

This program, begun in 1984 by International Aid, connects local churches across America with elementary schools. Workers, many of them grandparents, are placed as tutors to special-needs children. They build one-on-one relationships on a year-round basis. No proselytizing is allowed on school grounds, but plenty of opportunities arise for ministry in off-campus settings.

To contact: Phone: 1 (616) 846-7490 or 1 (800) 968-7490; Write: Kids' Hope USA, 17011 W. Hickory, Spring Lake, MI 49456.

3. *Foster Grandparents*

Foster Grandparents places retirees 60 or older in public schools as tutors for several hours daily during the school year. It is a federal Senior Corps program that works through churches and civic organizations.

To contact: Foster Grandparents, 1201 New York Ave. NW, Washington, D.C. 20525; Phone: 1 (800) 424-8867 or 1 (202) 606-5000; E-mail: webmaster@cns.gov; Web site: www.seniorcorps.org.

4. *True Love Waits*

This program of LifeWay Christian Resources (Southern Baptist) has enlisted more than one million teens in pledges to retain their virginity for marriage. TLW is part of a growing chastity trend on high school and college campuses across the nation. Since it is church-sponsored—dozens of the sponsoring churches are non-Baptist—grandparents will not ordinarily be directly involved. But if your church is interested in pursuing this program, you will want to give TLW your informed encouragement.

To contact: Phone: 1 (800) 458-2772; Web site: www.lifeway.com.

THE WEB FOR GRANDPARENTS

I'm a granddaddy who had to be dragged (drugged!—well, almost) to get me Internet-connected. And the Web? Well, it sounds like a weapon a Roman gladiator would toss before spearing his victim. And I've learned that the World Wide Web really does have some of those sinister characteristics. It can certainly grab you!

The good side of the Web is that it offers instant access to information (good *and* evil) without having to run to a university library or wait for periodicals to arrive by mail. You log on to a Web site and it's right there for you to read, or download and print out for later perusal—knitting patterns, Bible study materials, today's news, articles dealing with teen sex, or the pros and cons of Christian college students kissing before they marry. You will also find information on Christian organizations, many local churches, government statistics, and good practical stuff like how to build toys for your grandkids, and how to buy discounted airline tickets.

1. *JUNO*

JUNO offers free e-mail service or file transfer capacity for $2.95 a month to send or receive photos of those grandchildren. Right now JUNO has Internet for $2.95 a month, but that may change.

To Contact: Phone: 1 (888) 829-5866; Free software: 1 (800)TRY-JUNO (579-5866)

2. *Rated-G.com.*

This Christian Internet service features Dr. Gary Chapman as well as an excellent Q & A advice service for Christian teens.

To contact: Phone: 1 (888) 711-6381, or Web site: www. rated-G.com.

3. *Focus on the Family*

Focus does not offer an Internet service, but it has an impressive list of filtered Internet providers.

To contact: Phone: 1 (800) A-FAMILY/(232-6459); Web site: www.family.org, then type "Filtered Internet access" into the box.

4. *Lifewayonline*

These are the people who sponsor True Love Waits.

To contact: Phone: 1 (888) 454-5965; Web site: www. lifeway.com; CDs are available free in some Christian bookstores.

5. *Family University*

This site has articles on grandparenting and a myriad of other family-related topics.

To Contact: Web site: www.familyuniversity.com.

6. *Crown Ministries*

This is popular Christian radio financial counselor Larry Burkett's site. Order his books or access financial information here.

To contact: Web site: www.cfcministry.org.

7. *Crosswalk*

This Christian Web site is loaded with information of interest to Christians of all ages.

To contact: Web site: www.crosswalk.com.

8. *Academy of Lifelong Learning*

This is the University of Delaware's continuing education program for folks over 50. We recommend that you also explore the offerings of your local Christian college, community college, or your state's university system.

To contact: Phone: 1 (302) 573-4417; Write: Academy of Lifelong Learning, 2700 Pennsylvania Ave., Wilmington, DE 19806; Web site: www.udel.edu/ce/.

9. *Hobby Industry Association*

This Web site includes handcrafts you can make as gifts, for fun, or to market. Grandmothers and mothers will enjoy working together to create these crafts.

To contact: Web site: www.i-craft.com.

10. Woodworking

This is "your gateway to woodworking on the Web," the sponsors state. It has tool and pattern catalogues, and patterns for projects ranging from birdhouses to china cabinets.

To contact: Web site: www.woodworking.com.

11. *Grandsplace*

This Web site offers useful information, much of it state-specific, on legal issues for grandparents rearing grandchildren. Can you legally permit a doctor to remove eight-year-old Zeke's infected tonsils? What are your legal responsibilities if a grandchild living with you wishes to drive your car? Can you enroll Zeke in a public school, or get copies of his records from the school he attended last year? How do you apply for Medicaid for a grandchild? What are your rights as custodial grandparent if Zeke's absent parent—who's perhaps been out of his life for several years—suddenly appears and demands custody? What should you do if your ex-son-in-law has visiting rights and returns your grandchild to you, and he or she appears to have been beaten?

Grandsplace will help you find an attorney to deal with these and similar situations.

To contact: Phone: 1 (860) 763-5789; Write: Grandsplace, 154 Cottage Road, Enfield, CT 06082; Web site: www. grandsplace.com.

FOCUS ON THE FAMILY®

Welcome to the Family!

Whether you received this book as a gift, borrowed it from
a friend, or purchased it yourself, we're glad you read it! It's just
one of the many helpful, insightful, and encouraging
resources produced by Focus on the Family.

In fact, that's what Focus on the Family is all about—providing inspiration, information, and biblically based advice to people in all stages of life.

It began in 1977 with the vision of one man, Dr. James Dobson, a licensed
psychologist and author of 16 best-selling books on marriage, parenting,
and family. Alarmed by the societal, political, and economic pressures
that were threatening the existence of the American family, Dr. Dobson
founded Focus on the Family with one employee—an assistant—
and a once-a-week radio broadcast, aired on only 36 stations.

Now an international organization, Focus on the Family is dedicated
to preserving Judeo-Christian values and strengthening the family
through more than 70 different ministries, including eight separate
daily radio broadcasts; television public service announcements;
13 publications; and a steady series of books and award-winning
films and videos for people of all ages and interests.

Recognizing the needs of, as well as the sacrifices and important
contribution made by, such diverse groups as educators, physicians,
attorneys, crisis pregnancy center staff, and single parents,
Focus on the Family offers specific outreaches to uphold and
minister to these individuals, too. And it's all done for one purpose,
and one purpose only: to encourage and strengthen individuals
and families through the life-changing message of Jesus Christ.

• • •

For more information about the ministry, or if we can be of help to your
family, simply write to Focus on the Family, Colorado Springs, CO 80995
or call 1-800-A-FAMILY (1-800-232-6459). Friends in Canada may write
Focus on the Family, P.O. Box 9800, Stn. Terminal, Vancouver, B.C. V6B 4G3
or call 1-800-661-9800. Visit our Web site—www.family.org—
to learn more about Focus on the Family or to find out if
there is an associate office in your country.

We'd love to hear from you!

Great Resources to Enjoy With Your Grandchildren
From Focus on the Family®

The Secret Garden

When Mary Lennox's parents die, the pampered 10-year-old's world changes dramatically. Sent to live in her rich uncle's mansion, she doesn't like all the rules . . . or the secrets. Why are certain parts of the mansion forbidden territory? What secrets lie hidden in the garden her uncle has locked up? And most perplexing of all, who—or what—is behind that wailing Mary hears at night? Recorded in London with superb talent and film-style sound, Focus on the Family Radio Theatre's *The Secret Garden* is an enchanting audio dramatization of the classic novel listeners of all ages will enjoy. Available on two cassettes or two compact discs.

Bedtime Blessings

Strengthen the bond between you and your grandchildren by making *Bedtime Blessings* a special part of your evenings together. From best-selling author John Trent, Ph.D., and Heritage Builders, this book offers countless ways to reaffirm the love God has for your grandchildren. Designed for children ages 7 and under, it's a wonderful way to develop a habit of speaking encouraging words and blessing just before your grandchildren go to sleep. Hardcover.

Prince Caspian

Peter, Lucy, Susan, Edmund—and the magnificent lion Aslan—are back in Focus on the Family Radio Theatre's thrilling dramatization of *Prince Caspian.* A faithful adaptation of the classic *Chronicles of Narnia* novels by C.S. Lewis, this enchanting audio drama tells the tale of an evil king who threatens the life of Narnia's rightful king—the young Prince Caspian. Recorded in London with some of England's finest actors and utilizing film-style sound design and a rich musical score, *Prince Caspian* creates an imaginative world that will inspire listeners of all ages, reminding them of God's protection and faithfulness. Available on three cassettes or three compact discs.

● ● ●

Look for these special books in your Christian bookstore or request a copy by calling 1-800-A-FAMILY (1-800-232-6459). Friends in Canada may write Focus on the Family, P.O. Box 9800, Stn. Terminal, Vancouver, B.C. V6B 4G3 or call 1-800-661-9800.

Visit our Web site (www.family.org) to learn more about the ministry or find out if there is a Focus on the Family office in your country.